Ideology and Power

studies in major ideas

IDEOLOGY
AND
POWER

and events of the twentieth century

CHRISTOPHER THORNE
senior history master Charterhouse

COLLIER-MACMILLAN LTD, LONDON
THE MACMILLAN COMPANY, NEW YORK
COLLIER-MACMILLAN CANADA LTD, TORONTO

First published in 1965 *by*
Collier-Macmillan Ltd, 10 South Audley Street, London W1
Collier-Macmillan International,
a division of The Macmillan Company, New York,
New York, Toronto, Sydney, Mexico City, Manila

The Macmillan Company, New York
Collier-Macmillan Canada Ltd, Toronto

First printing
Set in Monotype Times New Roman 10 *on* 11½ *point*
Printed in Great Britain by Willmer Brothers & Haram Ltd

contents PAGE

illustrations

43809

acknowledgements

The extent to which I have relied upon the work of
others is indicated in the bibliographies. In particular,
however, I wish to acknowledge my great debt to
Professor Hans Kohn for his invaluable studies in the
history of nationalism; to Elizabeth Wiskemann for my
knowledge of 'Czechs and Germans' in the Historic
Provinces; to K. M. Panikkar in the field of Asian
nationalism, and to the late R. N. Carew Hunt's
Theory and Practice of Communism.
Many pupils have, by their reactions, helped me
improve these studies, and I particularly wish to thank
those who played a large part in presenting simplified
outlines to wider audiences. Philip Whitting and Dennis
Gunning were kind enough to read the typescript and
make many invaluable suggestions; I am, of course,
responsible for the faults that remain. My greatest debt
is to my wife, who has typed and retyped the
manuscript and encouraged throughout.

August 1964   C.G.T.

INTRODUCTION

The twentieth century is an age of political dogma, imperfectly understood, frequently anachronistic, but for these reasons uttered all the more vehemently. It is also an age of power; not merely economic power, or the power of ideas and persuasion, but simply power, the power of 'the era of violence'. These two threads may be traced separately, but they continually become intertwined. They help condition each other. Through power, the realization of a dogma can be sought; through that dogma, mass support can be obtained, the will can be strengthened, the road to power made easier.

The Russian Revolution and the Munich crisis offer outstanding material for study in these directions. Following the decay and defeat of an autocratic empire and to the accompanying clamour of a bewildered and hungry populace, a disciplined, revolutionary minority seize power and hold it. In a Europe which is divided, bitter, apathetic, one man, acclaimed by his nation, wields a power which brings fear, exposure and shame. Both events, dramatic and significant in themselves, invite the exploration of their ideological background.

I am not for a moment suggesting that the ideas can supply a sufficient explanation for the events. I suspect that the great majority of mankind are moved more by concern for their own material circumstances than by steady allegiance to any transcendent belief. In Russia, defeat, hunger and the policies of the regime were only some of the other factors involved; behind 'Munich' lie the personalities of Hitler and Chamberlain, the readiness and unreadiness of armies, and much besides.

Yet it is impossible to ignore the force of political ideology in modern times. This is in no way lessened by the fact that men and governments frequently fail to act in accordance with their professed beliefs, or by such beliefs being, in reality, the convenient sublimations of self-interest. We may not be allowing the intellect much influence when we shout 'uhuru' or describe someone as a 'bourgeois imperialist'; the strength of the idea remains unimpaired. 1917 witnessed the success of men who sincerely believed that they alone possessed the blueprint of an inevitable and perfect society and that their opponents would be 'swept away into the garbage-heap of history'. Their quarrels amongst themselves and with the other socialists can be comprehended only in the light of the

I

writings of Marx; with their victory, the wider acceptance of Marxist teachings was assured. Similarly, 1938 can be understood only in the light of long-standing problems of nationality in the Historic Provinces of Czechoslovakia, of the doctrine of national self-determination, and of the pathological nationalism of the Third Reich. To many, the remorseless events of the years before the war could be attributed to the worship of a single political concept. When a survey of that concept was published in 1939 under the auspices of the Royal Institute of International Affairs, it gave as its raison d'être: 'contemporary developments of nationalism appear to threaten the very future of civilization.'

Both these events and both their accompanying ideologies have, moreover, strong links with one another. Europe between the wars was constantly being reminded of the terrible example of 1917 and the bogey of Bolshevism. The ensuing fears helped Mussolini and Hitler into power; they provided a false but widely-accepted accusation against Czechoslovakia, and they prevented Chamberlain from considering a Russian alliance against Germany in 1938. Conversely, the Revolution itself had given a new incentive to the efforts of nationalists in Central and Eastern Europe and further afield, in Asia. It helped produce that blend of nationalism and socialism which has since been a feature of emergent States.

The effect of nationalism on Russia since 1917 has also been marked, provoking the question whether international circumstances brought this about, or whether nationalism is, in fact, a stronger force than Communism. Whether the issue has been Socialism in One Country, the Great Patriotic War, the technical achievements behind the sputnik, or the doctrinal clash with China, pride of country has been evident. So, too, has the extension of this into imperialism, overriding other nationalisms within its own State, for instance; 'the Soviet Government is a monstrously distorted and inflated offspring of Nicholas II.'[1] There are links elsewhere in the Communist bloc. The countries of Eastern Europe which welcomed the Russian liberators in 1944-5 did so the more joyously because, for many, the West still meant 'Munich'; when disillusionment followed, it was fostered by nationalism. Hungarians, Rumanians, Yugoslavs and Poles retained a distinct self-awareness, and their young intelligentsia proved capable of displaying the same independence towards their mentors as those of Asia and Africa towards the West. Over Transylvania, for instance, Rumania and Hungary showed that friction between nations would not be removed by the possession of a common political doctrine.

One obvious similarity remains. Pathological nationalism in Germany

[1]Seton-Watson: *Nationalism and Communism*, p. 160.

and Marxist proletarian dictatorship in Russia both produced totalitarian regimes. If Hitler's was the more frenzied, Stalin's was the more thorough; even Trotsky scarcely acted in such a way as to contradict his own slogan, 'My Party, right or wrong'. The historian's shorthand frequently conceals complexities, and if we were asked to define what was meant by such phrases as 'France turned to de Gaulle', or 'Britain declined the leadership of Europe', the task would not be easy. Dictators appear to save us some trouble. At the time of Munich, 'Germany decided' and 'Russia waited' seem clearly enough to refer to the will of two men. Yet there is a case for suggesting that Hitler voiced a wider, 'general will', while British decisions of the time frequently appear to stem from Chamberlain alone. To analyse power, in fact, is often no simpler than to assess ideas. Both remain fundamental to the history of this century.

These studies were written because of my own interest in their subjects, and because of what I conceived to be a need, as well as an interest, among students of twentieth-century history. The period after 1914, rich and fascinating, has for the most part received attention in the form of advanced scholarship at the one extreme, or simplified outline at the other. There are, of course, many excellent text-books on modern history. They proliferate until, like the symphonies of Haydn or battles of the Isonzo, they appear to be without number. There is also a vogue for the collection within one cover of the views of various historians on a single topic. Neither, however, gives the young specialist much 'feel' of the original material involved. The former tend to have their judgements reproduced without an awareness of the difficulties involved; they answer questions rather than ask them. The latter all too often exude a deadness which seems to spring from the application of scissors and paste rather than creative intellect; neither lends itself easily to group discussion. Individual reading must be the foundation of study for those I have in mind, but experience convinces me that perception and enjoyment can be greatly increased if there exists some material which can be used by a group as the basis for questions, discussion, and further individual work.

I have, therefore, produced studies based on the writings of Marx, Lenin and nationalist prophets, the published British and German documents for 1938, the memoirs and diaries of those involved in 'Munich' and 1917. I have also attempted to present these studies in such a way that they may be read either individually or aloud in a form or seminar. The 'Revolution' and 'Munich' provide many parts, and a narrator can be used for the introduction and commentary. 'Marxism' takes the form of a dialogue; 'Nationalism' does the same (change of speaker being indicated by extra spacing) with additional quotation requirements. I have used them in this manner with history specialists and as part of the increasingly important 'modern subjects' courses given to students of all disciplines. The use of photographs, maps, chronological tables and tape-recordings[1] can provide added interest, and make possible the presentation of simplified versions to a larger audience.

There are obvious points which need amplifying and discussing as they arise in the text: the dialectic, for instance, or the essence of a nation. 1917 and 1938 provide similar examples: Lenin's 'April Theses' 'shocked the Russian Marxists in 1917; they considered it a betrayal of scientific socialism'; 'in Baldwin and MacDonald (England) had received the leaders it deserved'; 'after 1933 it became apparent that the Locarno period was, indeed, at an end'. There are also many aspects which should form the basis of individual work, such as the preparation, with evidence, of the cases for and against appeasement in the 1930's. In the discussion sections I have indicated several such topics. Where I have thought it necessary I have given some detailed material; elsewhere I have deliberately framed the question and no more. If some of the more topical questions provoke strong disagreement, they will have served their purpose. Related topics, such as the career of Stalin, the decline of the Weimar Republic and the history of colonial struggles need no underlining.

The subjects studied lead naturally to wider historical perspectives, such as revolutions in general, their patterns and ingredients. Trotsky's *History* contains interesting comparisons of 1917 with 1642 and 1789, of Nicholas II with Charles I and Louis XVI; Professor Seton-Watson's *Nationalism and Communism* and *Pattern of Communist Revolution* provide enlightening reflections on the nature of revolutions in the present century. When we study the career of Lenin, are we forced to bring revised opinions to the debate on how far an individual may be said to alter the course of history? Here reference might be made to E. H. Carr's outstanding essay, *What is History?* How is policy formulated in a democracy? Do the comments of Sir Neville Henderson and the role of Sir Horace Wilson reflect uncomfortable truths?

An awareness of the periods under discussion may also lead to wider general reading. I am thinking, for instance, in the 1930's, of Richard Hillary and Huxley, of Lady Diana Cooper and *The Long Week-End*, of Spender, Auden, and C. Day Lewis. Interest in Russia and Com-

[1]There is, for instance, a B.B.C. record which includes the voices of the major participants at Munich and such events as Chamberlain's return to Heston and his speech on the declaration of war in 1939.

munism could lead to *Dr. Zhivago* or *Darkness at Noon*, to Brecht or Solzhenitsyn, to such films as Eisenstein's 'October', 'Ivan the Terrible' or 'The Boyars' Plot'. It should be possible to enjoy the great visual art of the director and, in addition, to appreciate how and why not only the Mensheviks but also Trotsky are being shown in a poor light; how 'Socialism in One Country' permitted the portrayal of a heroic, Stalin-like Ivan; and how the 'oprichniki', on whose strength Ivan relies, become, by implication, the vanguard of the proletariat, a sixteenth century forerunner of the Party itself. Similarly, discussion of Marx's great awareness of the 'alienation' of modern man should lead not only to contemporary Marxist works like Fischer's *Necessity of Art*, but to an 'uncommitted' writer like Camus, whom Fischer succeeds in misunderstanding.

One of two further notes of explanation may be called for. The nature of the events and the material of 1917 and of 1938 have imposed their own stylistic patterns: the confusion of the crowd and the tumult of angry debate produce a staccato impression, whilst the exchange of diplomatic documents has a more measured tread. Both events share ingredients with the other, but the overriding contrast remains. In the cases of 'Marxism' and 'Nationalism', emphasis is placed upon the background to events previously described; the studies are deliberately compressed thereafter. In the former, I have taken the liberty of surmising the attitudes of Marx and Engels to their Russian and Chinese adherents, even to the point of a little disagreement between two such devoted comrades.[1] I have also, when discussing totalitarian democracy, for instance, followed Shaw's dictum on the business of the stage, and 'made its figures more intelligible to themselves than they would be in real life.' The dialogue deliberately repeats some of the more difficult aspects of the subject. Most of it comprises direct quotation or slightly simplified paraphrase of original sources; these are so intermingled, however, that, apart from the case of one or two outstanding passages, no attempt has been made to distinguish between them.

It was tempting to base 'Nationalism' on an imaginary dialogue between, say, Hegel and Mill, or Mazzini and Acton. Unlike Marxism, however, which needs to be completely tendentious in its exposition, this is a subject requiring whatever degree of historical objectivity is attainable. Therefore the conversationalists remain unnamed. On the other hand, it has been possible in this case to distinguish throughout between quotation and comment.

Bibliographies inevitably overlap a little; where more than one edition

[1] Only here and there have I attempted to convey something of the characters of the two men; my aim lies elsewhere.

exists I have given the pagination of the cheaper, paperback one. I have tried to allow for a fairly wide range of abilities and depths of study, as well as the interests of the general reader. The question of source-references has been a difficult one: had I given them in detail, footnotes would have rivalled text, and I was anxious that this should not happen. I have, therefore, confined footnotes to other matters, and given a broad outline of sources in the bibliographies.

the Russian Revolution

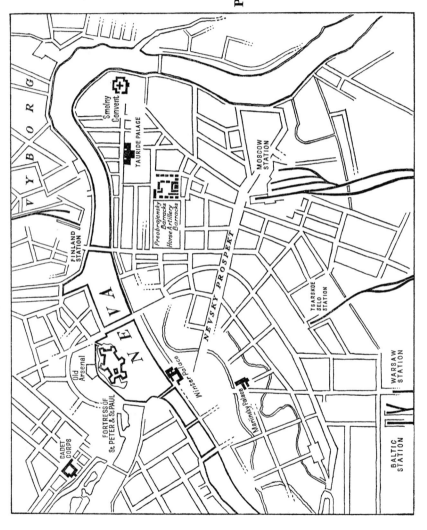

Petrograd in 1917

9

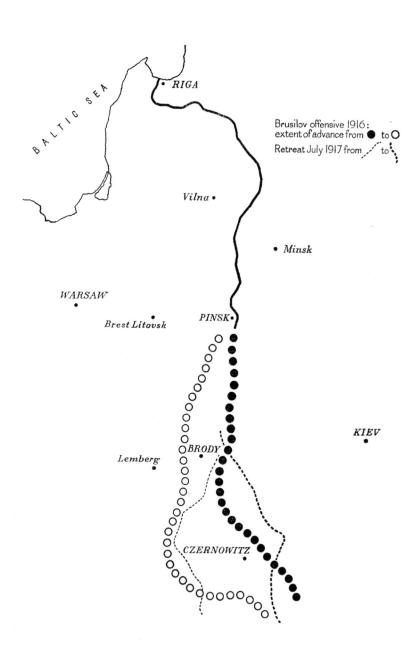

The Brusilov offensive of 1916, and the retreat of July 1917

THE RUSSIAN REVOLUTION

Russia at the end of the nineteenth century was a vast Empire of about 150 million people, Ukrainians, Latvians, Estonians, Finns, Poles, Armenians, Georgians and many others,[1] stretching from the Caspian to the Arctic, from the marshes of East Germany to the Pacific. Between Russia and Western Europe lay a great gulf in political, social and economic development.

The extent of Russia's backwardness had been emphasised by the Crimean war, and Tsar Alexander II, who succeeded to the throne in 1855, was prepared to countenance reform. His liberal intentions succumbed to reactionary influences and the weight of circumstances, however, and even though the Russian peasantry, that vast, inarticulate and illiterate mass, was freed from serfdom in 1861, the act failed to produce a tranquil realm. The opposition of the landowners was only to be expected, since their decline as a class was clearly foreshadowed; the serfs had to pay excessive prices before their ownership of small allotments of land was recognised; the Tsar's confidence in such liberal measures was weakened by a revolt in Poland in 1863. Exiled revolutionaries like Herzen and Bakunin continued to call for the establishment of an entirely new society. Russian agriculture and the economy as a whole remained backward, a situation aggravated by rapid increases in population. Agricultural under-development and rural poverty were matched by a crippling lack of industrial progress: the number of Russian industrial and communications workers—the proletariat—was only half a million in 1880 (though two and a half million by 1905). Russia was 'caught in a vicious circle: rural poverty hindered the development of industry by restricting the domestic market; lack of industry prevented the absorption of surplus agricultural population, the chief cause of poverty.'[2]

Meanwhile, Alexander II was attempting limited reform in the judicial and local government spheres, and planning a small relaxation of despotism, when he was fatally injured by a terrorist's bomb in 1881. The assassination only hindered the liberal cause, for the new Tsar, Alexander III, succeeded amid a reactionary atmosphere, determined to assert his imperial prerogative and consolidate authority at all levels.

[1] Great Russians formed only 43% of the population in 1897.
[2] *New Cambridge Modern History*, Vol. XI, p. 354.

Terrorists were suppressed, and the ineffectual nature of those liberal intellectuals who had been 'going to the people' became even more apparent. Jews were persecuted, and attempts made to enforce russification upon other national minorities.

In the economic sphere, however, significant changes were occurring in the last quarter of the century, stimulated by large sums of foreign capital—mainly French—and by long overdue government measures. State-financed railway construction made considerable progress and the expansion of industry was fostered by protective tariffs. But such improvements brought their own, new problems, and there was great social distress. Wages fluctuated around the subsistence level, living conditions in new towns and old villages were appalling, and food supplies were generally inadequate. Factory conditions were unregulated and therefore bad, strikes and trade unions were illegal. The Russian mortality rate was the highest in Europe at 35 per 1000, compared with 18 per 1000 in Britain. In 1891-92 there was catastrophic famine accompanied by cholera. There was acute land shortage and most peasants had difficulty in providing for their families and meeting their obligations to the state, a problem reflected by the ever-increasing sum owed in tax arrears.

In 1894, Alexander III was succeeded by Nicholas II, last of the Tsars, whose character and intellect could scarcely have been less suited to his task. Obstinate and shallow, dominated by his German wife, confident in the security, rightness and righteousness of his own position, Nicholas mistrusted ministers cleverer than himself and tended to surround himself with advisers of exceptionally low ability. He ensured the isolation of the monarchy from all sections of Russian society.

The growing discontent around the turn of the century manifested itself in an increasing number of strikes and disturbances. Any hopes that such demons could be exorcised by the triumphant efforts of the nation in arms were speedily dashed: the war which broke out between Russia and Japan in 1904 was as unpopular as it was unsuccessful. Its main effect was to prepare the way for open conflict between the Tsar and the revolutionaries whose origins, beliefs and growth must now be examined.

The nature of the revolutionary movement in Russia can be appreciated better if its physical environment is borne in mind. The extremes of heat and cold, the immensity of the land, seem to reduce the individual to insignificance. In such a setting, the absolutism of the government was met with extreme and idealist revolutionary creeds; half-measures, so it seemed, would be lost in the landscape. In addition, the fact that communications were difficult over such a large area encouraged separatist feelings in regions like Poland, the Ukraine and the Caucasus, among peoples like the Finns, Lithuanians and Don Cossacks.

The Poles had their own socialist party, the Jews their Social-Democratic 'Bund'. The two main revolutionary parties, however, were the Social Democrats and the Socialist Revolutionaries. The former were the principal Marxist party; their socialist revolution would be organised and carried through by the industrial workers, the proletariat. On this point they fiercely opposed the Socialist Revolutionaries, heirs of the *narodniki*, whose creed was based on agrarian socialism, with the peasants as beneficiaries and instruments of change.

The founder of the Russian Social Democratic Party was Plekhanov who, like many of the early revolutionaries, spent much of his life in exile. In the 1890's a new figure appeared: Vladimir Ulyanov Lenin. It was not long before Lenin and his young friends disagreed with older members like Plekhanov and Axelrod over the question of organisation. Lenin envisaged the party as a small, strong group of professionals, organising revolution under centralised control, as opposed to a democratically-constituted party, open to all; in 1902 he made this clear in a pamphlet, *What is to be Done*? At the party congress in 1903 the issue, together with that of co-operation with or implacable hostility towards bourgeois liberals, split the party committee into two factions, known as Bolsheviks and Mensheviks (majority-men and minority-men respectively).[1] In fact, although the Bolsheviks, Lenin and his extremist followers, called themselves the majority, they were soon in a minority, and for the next decade it was the Mensheviks who were superior in numbers and organisation. At the time of the 1905 rising Lenin had little support; all the other leading Social Democrats, including Plekhanov and Martov, were opposed to the Bolsheviks. Trotsky strove to reunite the Party, but Lenin would not consider this unless his own programme and control were assured.

The revolt of 1905 emphasised the importance of political strikes as the weapon of the Russian worker. On January 22nd, 1905, a procession of about 200,000 marched on the Winter Palace, home of the tsars in St Petersburg, in order to petition Nicholas for certain liberal reforms. Panic seized the palace guards who opened fire on the crowd, killing about 500 and wounding thousands more. The day became known as 'Bloody Sunday', and it was followed by more strikes, demonstrations and terrorist activities. The crushing defeat of the Russian navy by the Japanese stimulated further revolutionary acts: the crew of the battleship

---

[1]The Menshevik position, closer to that of 'reformist' parties in the West, was to appeal on the whole to the more skilled workers, the Bolshevik position to the unskilled. The Mensheviks rejected the idea of an alliance between proletariat and peasantry; Lenin urged that it was essential for revolutionary success.

Potemkin rebelled and nationalist risings occurred in Poland, the Caucasus, and the Baltic States. There was a general strike in St Petersburg, where Trotsky organised a workers' committee, or Soviet, forerunner of the 1917 Soviet. Rather belatedly, advice poured in from revolutionaries in exile.

Only then did there emerge a non-socialist liberal group known as the Constitutional Democratic Party, usually referred to as the Cadets; they aimed at parliamentary democracy of the British kind, and their leader was Paul Miliukov. Their weakness lay in the fact that in Russia the relatively small industrial and commercial middle class possessed nothing like the economic and political influence of their Western European counterparts.

Eventually the Tsar issued the October Manifesto, which promised full civil liberties and an elected parliament (the Duma) with limited legislative powers. It was enough to break the strike, and it satisfied the Cadets. Slowly, the government regained control of the situation. Lenin had returned to Petrograd too late, and was forced to leave for Finland to escape arrest; Trotsky, the outstanding figure of the rising, was exiled to Siberia.

The revolution of 1905 opened a new era in Russia; for the first time it was conceded that the basis of government might be broadened. Though the experiment was fitful and severely limited, and though conditions among the peasants were still harsh, this was a hopeful period, more prosperous than any before. Numbers taking part in political strikes dwindled from over half a million in 1907 to 4,000 in 1910; Lenin himself admitted that he did not expect to see the revolution during his lifetime.

The constitutional experiment itself was doomed to failure, however. Just before the first meeting of the newly-elected Duma, the Tsar dismissed his capable Prime Minister, Witte, and issued several edicts restricting the powers and scope of the new assembly. Its first session set the pattern for the next ten years. After a brief period of co-operation between the government and the Duma, the irresponsible and supreme position of the former produced deadlock, and the frustrated assembly was first ignored and then dissolved. For a while the Tsarist ministers ruled alone, until they felt that the appearance of popular approval was required; then the Duma was recalled.

Political absolutism was, however, combined with agricultural reform by the Tsar's one really able premier of these years, Stolypin. His increase in the number of peasant landowners, if continued, might have raised new barriers against revolution. But Stolypin came into conflict with Rasputin and the Tsar. Rasputin was a dissolute peasant who became a monk. Taking advantage of the royal family's religious mysticism, and

14

his own apparent powers of healing over one of their children, he influenced the Tsarina to such an extent that, through her and the Tsar himself, he became virtual ruler of Russia, to the disgust of Petrograd society. Stolypin himself was opposed on all sides, including the Duma, but remained in office as the only possible candidate until his murder in 1911. By 1912, when the fourth and last Duma was elected, the difficulties of the regime were increasing. Political strikers numbered half a million in 1912 and one million in 1914, before the outbreak of war.

Meanwhile the revolutionaries in exile fought among themselves.[1] The 1905 revolution had left the Social Democratic Party very weak, and the Mensheviks, as its largest element, urged the necessity of unity. Lenin refused all attempts at reconciliation, and by 1911 he was almost alone, his violent extremism scorned, the Bolsheviks dwindling and disorganised. In 1912, however, with remarkable audacity, he called a Bolshevik conference, and in the name of the whole Social Democratic party it adopted the Leninist programme. Such tactics left the Mensheviks confused and incapable of the firmness their numbers warranted.

Yet it needed the turmoil and hardship produced by war before the Tsarist regime could be overthrown. For a time, the outbreak of war against Germany and Austria-Hungary in 1914 filled Russia with patriotic fervour; it was the one thing which could unite the Tsar with his people. The vast army was heaved into action before it was ready, in response to the pleas of Russia's hard-pressed allies, France and Britain, in the West. Fifteen million Russians were called up in the war, of whom five and a half million were killed, captured or wounded. The army was badly equipped and poorly commanded. The effects of early mishandlings and of the crushing defeats of Tannenberg and the Masurian Lakes were soon felt, and by the summer of 1915 desperate defence had superseded expectation of victory. Indeed it was in an attempt to ensure continued Russian effort, as well as to allay suspicions of ulterior British motives behind the Dardanelles campaign, that the allies promised Russia Constantinople in a secret treaty of 1915. In December 1916, one million men were listed as deserters from the Russian Army.

The Tsarina was now completely under the influence of Rasputin and was widely credited with pro-German sentiments; the reputation of the government and the bureaucracy could scarcely have been lower. In September 1915, Nicholas left for the front to take personal command of the army.[2] At once the Tsarina and Rasputin acted: the Duma was

---

[1]This was over political rather than economic matters. For details of their theories in the latter sphere, see Carr: *The Bolshevik Revolution*, Vol. 2, Chapter 15.

[2]Dates are given according to the Western (Gregorian) calendar, that is thirteen days ahead of the Julian one used in Russia at the time.

prorogued and the few capable men in the government were replaced by Rasputin's worthless lackeys.

By October 1916 the combination of Rasputin's activities in Petrograd and further defeats at the front caused every party, left and right, to unite against the government. The great offensive under Brusilov had raised hopes by its initial success; when its ultimate failure became apparent, bitterness was all the greater. Inflation continued apace. Iron, steel, and coal production was considerably less than it had been in 1914. Interest and sinking fund on the national debt exceeded revenue; half of it was owed to foreign governments and bankers. In November the Duma met again. Miliukov, leader of the Cadets, made a direct attack on Rasputin, the Tsarina and the Premier. There was open talk of deposing Nicholas in favour of his son and by the end of November the opposition were able to force the Prime Minister's dismissal and his replacement by an opponent of Rasputin. The Tsarina's exhortations to Nicholas to act savagely became frantic. The confusion, both in Petrograd and at the front was complete. On the night of December 30th, 1916, Rasputin was murdered by a group of nobles.

Yet the effect of the murder on the government was negligible and it was soon clear that Nicholas and the Tsarina meant to carry on as before. Plots against the royal couple were widely rumoured and revolution was expected; people, however, seemed to be frozen into immobility. In January 1917 temperatures were more than forty degrees below zero, and communications were at a standstill. But three different groups in Petrograd were at least planning to take action: the Union of Nobles thought in terms of a new sovereign; the revolutionary left-wing parties developed their underground organisations; the liberals placed their hopes in the Duma itself, which was due to re-assemble on February 27th. Within the Duma, all non-socialist parties had amalgamated into a single body, the Progressive Bloc, led by men like Miliukov and Prince Lvov. By the end of January it had determined to achieve radical changes in the government.

Yet this did not mean that the moderate parties wanted revolution; the thought of it terrified them. Thus, during the first week of the Duma's existence, confusion persisted in political circles. It was a sudden surge of popular discontent that precipitated the revolution.

On March 8th the celebration of International Woman's Day merged with a number of strikes and processions demanding bread, work and peace. None of the revolutionary organisations had originally called for action, though soon they were hastening to place themselves at the head of the outburst. In Trotsky's words:

TROTSKY: '... the (March) revolution was begun from below, overcoming the resistence of its own revolutionary organisations, the initiative being taken ... by the most oppressed and downtrodden part of the proletariat. .... The overgrown bread-lines had provided the last stimulus.'

The Government, too, were slow in appreciating the significance of events, and it was on this same day that the Tsar left the Petrograd area for his distant headquarters. By the following day the numbers of strikers in Petrograd had reached 200,000; the Tsarina wrote to the Tsar:

TSARINA: 'I hope that Duma man (Kerensky) will be hung for his horrible speeches—it is necessary and it will be an example. All are thirsting and beseeching that you show your firmness.'

On March 10th a general strike began. Three hundred thousand workers demonstrated in the streets of Petrograd and, significantly, the Cossacks did not charge the crowds as ordered. Panic-striken Ministers sent desperate messages to the Tsar who replied with a simple command to Petrograd's procrastinating Military Governor to stop all disorders immediately.

The next day, Sunday, March 11th, the Tsar dissolved the Duma, whose deputies dispersed but refused to leave Petrograd. Huge crowds again swarmed across the frozen river from the Vyborg district and a good many were killed in a clash with soldiers. Widespread looting occurred, prisoners were released from the gaols and fires were started. Soldiers, ashamed of shooting at civilians, began joining the revolution, regiment by regiment. A police report of that day shows the determination of the crowds:

POLICE REPORT: 'In the course of the disorders it was observed as a general phenomenon, that the rioting mobs showed extreme defiance towards the military patrols, at whom, when asked to disperse, they threw stones and lumps of ice dug up from the street. When preliminary shots were fired into the air, the crowd not only did not disperse but answered these volleys with laughter. Only when loaded cartridges were fired into the very midst of the crowd, was it found possible to disperse the mob, the participants in which, however, would most of them hide in the yards of near-by houses, and as soon as the shooting stopped come out again into the street.'

On March 12th two events of significance occurred in the Tauride Palace: the formation of a Soviet of Workers' (later Workers' and Soldiers') Deputies, on the lines of Trotsky's 1905 Soviet, and directed by a predominantly Menshevik Executive Committee, or Ex-Com; and the formation of a Provisional Committee of the Duma, forerunner of the Provisional Government. For eight months these two groups faced each other in an uneasy and artificial position of dual power. In retrospect, it is clear that the strength of the Soviets was much the greater, though at the time it was as if their leaders could not bring themselves to realise the fact and act accordingly. Nevertheless, the failure of the confused and politically disorganised liberal middle class to establish a government before the socialists set up a rival centre of authority foreshadowed their ultimate downfall, handicapped as they were by the fact that the Duma, based on an electoral law of 1907, was completely unrepresentative of the nation. The confusion of the moment may be illustrated by a question put to Miliukov on March 12th by Sukhanov, a Menshevik member of the Ex-Com, and editor of Maxim Gorky's *New Life*:

SUKHANOV: 'What is the position of the Progressive Bloc and of the Provisional Committee of the Duma? Do you propose . . . to take state power into your own hands?'

MILIUKOV: 'In the first place, I belong to a party which is bound by the decisions of a more general group—the Progressive Bloc. Without this it cannot undertake or decide anything, since both together constitute one entity. Secondly, we, as a responsible opposition, were certainly striving for power and moving towards it, but not along the path of revolution. That way is not ours.'

The only socialist who was about to become a member of the Provisional Government was Kerensky, nominally a Socialist Revolutionary, but climbing to power as an individual, who bridged the gap between Duma and Soviet. Looking back, he claims to have been aware of the decisive nature of the moment:

KERENSKY: 'On the morning of March 12th I entered the Tauride Palace with the firm conviction that from then on, we, the representatives of the democracy, the parties of the left, should be responsible for the fate of the nation. I knew definitely that a new centre of national life must be created without a moment's delay.'

Later, Miliukov announced to a delegation from the Soviet:

MILIUKOV: 'A decision has been reached; we're taking power.'

Meanwhile, the President of the Duma, Rodzianko, had sent a telegram to the Tsar:

RODZIANKO: 'The last hour has come, when the fate of the fatherland and the dynasty is being decided.'

TSAR: 'Again that fat-bellied Rodzianko has written me a lot of nonsense, which I won't even bother to answer.'

Next day, March 13th, the streets in Petrograd were somewhat quieter; there were no loyal detachments left in the city. At last the Tsar decided to return and face the situation. He set out by train and sent a telegram to the Tsarina en route:

TSAR: 'Wonderful weather. Hope you are well and calm. Many troops sent from the front. With tender love, Niki.'

His train did not reach Petrograd, however, for the railway workers diverted it to Pskov. In Petrograd the Provisional Committee of the Duma, and the Executive Committee of the Soviet, were at last acting quickly. On March 14th the Ex-Com issued its order No. 1, which gave it a great initial advantage over the Duma Committee in the vital matter of control of the armed forces:

SOVIET: 'The army and navy are under the command of the Soviet, and the soldiers' section of the Soviet, and are to obey the orders of the Duma Committee only if they do not contradict those of the Soviet.'

By March 15th Miliukov had formed a Provisional Government. He was the effective head, as Foreign Minister, though Prince Lvov was President of the Council of Ministers. Kerensky accepted the Ministry of Justice, with some misgivings about the reactions of his fellow-socialists in the Ex-Com. Later, after Kerensky had become head of the Government, subsequently vanishing into exile, Sukhanov wrote:

SUKHANOV: 'It was a heavy load that history laid upon feeble shoulders. Kerensky had golden hands, meaning his supernatural energy, amazing capacity for work, and inexhaustible temperament. But he lacked the head for statesmanship and had no real political schooling. ... Kerensky was really persuaded that he was a Socialist and a democrat. He never suspected that by conviction, taste, and temperament he was the most consummate middle-class radical. But he believed in his providential mission ... (and) saw himself ... as a little bit of a Bonaparte.'

His histrionic tendencies were needed when he explained a delicate matter to the Soviet:

KERENSKY: 'Comrades! Do you trust me? I speak, comrades, with all my soul, from the bottom of my heart, and if it is necessary to prove this—if you don't trust me—here and now—before your eyes—I am ready to die. ... Comrades! In view of the formation of a new Government, I had to give an immediate reply, without waiting for your formal approval, when I was offered the post of Minister of Justice.'

Meanwhile, it was believed by the generals at the front that the Duma alone held power; such a situation they were prepared to accept, just as they were ready to see Nicholas abdicate. This was by now inevitable. On March 15th, in his train at Pskov, the Tsar renounced the throne in favour of his brother, the Grand Duke Michael. Miliukov and the Cadets hoped to preserve a constitutional monarchy, but popular feeling suggested that even this would not be possible. Nicholas himself made a bitter entry in his diary:

TSAR: '... I left Pskov with heavy feelings; around me treason, cowardice, deceit.'

He was shortly to be confined to his palace at Tsarskoe Selo; when exile in England seemed possible the Ex-Com insisted that the Provisional Government prevent this.[1] Meanwhile, Grand Duke Michael announced that he would accept the throne only from the Constituent Assembly, and that until such a time he too would abdicate. The second abdication document was duly signed, leaving Russia without a tsar. As Moscow and the provinces followed the lead of Petrograd, the March revolution drew to a close. Only in Petrograd had there been violence, and even there the killed and wounded amounted to less than 1,500.

Now, however, the awkward reality of dual power—Provisional Government and Soviet—had to be faced. Even before the end of March the War Minister would be informing the Chief of Staff:

GUCHKOV: 'The Government, alas, has no real power; the troops, the railroads, the post and telegraph are in the hands of the Soviet. The simple fact is that the Provisional Government exists only so long as the Soviet permits it.'

One of the few people who had a clear answer to the problem was Lenin. Still in exile in Switzerland, he wrote a series of 'Letters from Afar' to Bolsheviks in Russia:

LENIN: 'The workers and soldiers of Petrograd ... self-sacrificingly fought against the tsarist monarchy—for freedom, for land for the peasants, for peace as against the imperialist slaughter. Anglo-French imperialist capital, in order to continue and develop the slaughter ... incited and encouraged ... Miliukov, and contrived a new government, which, ready made, seized power after the proletarian struggle

---

[1]On July 16th, 1918, he and his family were shot at Ekaterinburg by order of the local Soviet.

had delivered the first blows against tsarism.... (This) government . . . could give neither peace, nor bread, nor freedom, even it if were sincere in its desire to do so.'

Lenin's attitude was supported by some Bolsheviks in Petrograd—notably Molotov. But the two party members who formulated policy through *Pravda* in the absence of the main leadership were Kamenev and the little-known Stalin. Their ideas were at this time closer to those of the Mensheviks and S.R.s who dominated the Ex-Com: to attempt to achieve reforms like the eight-hour day, but not openly to attack the Provisional Government; to co-operate with fellow socialists, and not to cease at least defensive vigilance at the front.[1] The Marxist dialectic was believed to prove the inevitability of a bourgeois-democratic society and régime at this stage, and Russia's unreadiness for proletarian revolution.

Lenin's reaction was made clear in a telegram to Petrograd on March 19th:

LENIN: 'Our tactic; absolute lack of confidence; no support to the new government; suspect Kerensky especially; arming of proletariat the sole guarantee; immediate elections to the Petrograd Duma; no rapprochement with other parties.'

Trotsky, writing later in an exile forced upon him by the triumphant Stalin, echoed Lenin's criticisms:

TROTSKY: 'Notwithstanding their opposite characters, it was no accident that Kamenev and Stalin occupied a common position at the beginning of the revolution: they supplemented each other . . . Kamenev was always . . . beneath the tasks of the revolution (and) Stalin, the empiric, was open to alien influences . . . on the side of the intellect. Thus it was that this publicist without decision, and this organiser without intellectual horizon, carried Bolshevism in March 1917 to the very boundaries of Menshevism.'

In the light of later history, an even more remarkable comment came from Sukhanov:

SUKHANOV: 'Stalin . . . produced—and not only on me—the impression of a grey blur, looming up now and then dimly and not leaving any trace. There is really nothing more to be said about him.'

Throughout these upheavals, Russia remained embroiled in the Great War, but fraternisation with the enemy and mass desertions showed that

[1] The Menshevik Left-wing internationalists were anxious for peace, but it was to be a negotiated, bourgeois-democratic peace, and not Lenin's peace resulting from European revolution.

the news of revolution had greatly weakened the army. The Allies reacted with mixed feelings. For some, like Lloyd George, there was relief that Russia was at last rid of an oppressive autocracy. But far stronger were the fears that Russia would withdraw from the war and make a separate peace, or that the Russian front would simply collapse; these fears were particularly prevalent in France. On the other hand, America was the first Western Power to recognise the Provisional Government on March 22nd, following this with considerable financial assistance. Moreover, the fall of the Tsarist régime facilitated American entry into the war, since no longer would the latter feel herself allied to a reactionary power. Miliukov reassured the Allies of Russia's determination to continue the struggle, remembering, of course, that victory would give her control of the Straits, as promised in the secret treaty of 1915.

Lenin for his part would not countenance the prolongation of the war, even in the defensive form approved by the majority of the Soviet:

LENIN: 'Our party would completely disgrace itself, would commit political suicide if it were lured by such deception . . . I would rather face a break with anyone in our party than make concessions to . . . social-patriotism . . . or to . . . social-defencism. . . .'

Lenin was still in Switzerland, where he had been since the beginning of the war. Now he negotiated with the Germans for a train to carry him and other revolutionary exiles back to Russia. The Germans, only too glad to hasten the internal collapse of Russia, agreed. Lenin feared, correctly, that he would be accused of being an agent of Germany, and attempted to forestall this by having the train 'sealed', with full diplomatic immunity, as it crossed Europe. He would arrive on April 16th. His return was contemplated with mixed feelings by the Provisional Government and the Ex-Com, and there were misgivings within the Bolshevik Party itself. Nevertheless, a lavish reception was prepared at the Finland Station in Petrograd, and the Ex-Com president composed a speech of welcome.

The man they awaited has some claim to be regarded as the greatest revolutionary leader the world has yet seen. Bruce Lockhart later thought that at first sight he could be taken for a provincial grocer; 'Yet in those steely eyes there was something that arrested my attention, something in that quizzing, half-contemptuous, half-smiling look which spoke of boundless self-confidence and conscious superiority.' Lenin dominated nearly everyone who came in contact with him. 'His words', wrote Gorky, 'always gave one the impression of the physical pressure of an irresistible truth'. It is impossible to avoid the schoolmaster simile: Lunacharsky afterwards recorded how, at a congress in 1905, a report he had to make was planned for him in advance by Lenin; the latter then read the completed manuscript and made final corrections, even on points of insignificant detail. Dan described him as the only man 'who is occupied with the Revolution 24 hours a day, who has no thoughts except the thoughts of the Revolution, and who even when he goes to sleep, dreams only of the Revolution.'

Behind this dedication and ruthlessness lay no desire for self-glorification, but a deep hatred of suffering and unhappiness. This fact was attested by many who knew him, and is captured in Lenin's remarks to Gorky as they listened together to Beethoven's 'Appassionata':

LENIN: 'I know nothing that is greater than the 'Appassionata'; I'd like to listen to it every day . . . I always think with pride—perhaps it is naïve of me—what marvellous things human beings can do! But I can't listen to music too often. It affects your nerves, makes you want to say stupid nice things and stroke the heads of people who could create such beauty while living in this vile hell. And now you mustn't stroke anyone's head—you might get your hand bitten off. You have to hit them on the head, without any mercy, although our ideal is not to use force against anyone. Hm, hm, our duty is infernally hard.'

Now, as his train approached Petrograd, Lenin was doubtful about the nature of his reception; he was reassured by supporters who boarded the train outside the city. His arrival at the Finland Station is described by Sukhanov:

SUKHANOV: 'A thunderous *Marseillaise* boomed forth on the platform, and shouts of welcome rang out. We stayed in the imperial waiting-rooms while the Bolshevik generals exchanged greetings. . . . The gloomy Chkheidze . . . (President of the Ex-Com, who was to make a speech of welcome) got up, went to the middle of the room, and prepared for the meeting . . . Lenin came, or rather ran, into the room. He wore a round cap, his face looked frozen, and there was a magnificent bouquet in his hands. Running to the middle of the room, he stopped in front of Chkheidze as though colliding with a completely unexpected obstacle. . . .'

CHKHEIDZE: 'Comrade Lenin, in the name of the Petersburg Soviet and of the whole revolution we welcome you to Russia. . . . But—we think that the principal task of the revolutionary democracy is now the defence of the revolution from any encroachments either from within or from without. We consider that what this goal requires is not disunion, but the closing of the democratic ranks. We hope you will pursue these goals together with us.'

SUKHANOV: 'Lenin plainly knew exactly how to behave. He stood there as though nothing taking place had the slightest connection with him—looking about him, examining the persons around him, and even the ceiling of the imperial waiting-room, adjusting his bouquet (rather out of tune with his whole appearance) and then, turning away from the Ex-Com delegation altogether, he made this "reply":'

LENIN: 'Dear Comrades, soldiers, sailors and workers! I am happy to greet in your persons the victorious Russian revolution, and greet you as the vanguard of the world-wide proletarian army.... The piratical imperialist war is the beginning of civil war throughout Europe.... The worldwide Socialist revolution has already dawned ... Germany is seething— ... Any day now the whole of European capitalism may crash. The Russian revolution accomplished by you has prepared the way and opened a new epoch. Long live the world-wide Socialist revolution!'[1]

SUKHANOV: 'Suddenly, before the eyes of all of us, completely swallowed up by the routine drudgery of the revolution, there was presented a bright, blinding, exotic beacon ... Lenin's voice ... was a "voice from outside". There had broken in upon us in the revolution a note that was ... novel, harsh, and somewhat deafening.'

Lenin rode from the station in triumph on top of an armoured car, picked out by searchlight. But he was arousing resentment, even among the Bolsheviks; in a two-hour outburst at the party meeting celebrating his arrival he adopted a particularly uncompromising attitude with regard to the Petrograd Soviet, the Ex-Com and the Provisional Government. Furthermore, the circumstances of his journey were very dubious: Lenin had negotiated with the Germans and his acceptance of transport provided by the enemy had not been sanctioned by the Provisional Government. Many people felt that Lenin should now keep quiet and begin to understand the realities of the situation.

Lenin, however, had no intention of keeping quiet. He defended his journey in the German train to the Ex-Com, who received him coolly and issued no formal approval of his actions. Lenin then went on to a meeting of the Social-Democratic members of the All-Russian Conference of Soviets, where he presented a summary of his views, later published as the 'April Theses':

LENIN: I. 'Not the slightest concession must be made to "revolutionary

---

[1] It is essential to remember that throughout 1917 and much of 1918, Lenin assumed that European revolution would occur and, indeed, set the pace for international socialism.

defencism", for under the new government . . . the war on Russia's part remains a predatory imperialist war. . . .

2. The peculiarity of the present situation in Russia is that it represents a transition from the first stage of the revolution . . . to its second stage which is to place power in the hands of the proletariat and the poorest strata of the peasantry. . . .

3. No support to the Provisional Government; exposure of the utter falsity of all its promises. . . .

4. Recognition of the fact that in most of the Soviets . . . our party constitutes a minority, and a small one at that. . . . While we are in the minority, we carry on the work of criticism, . . . advocating all along the necessity of transferring the entire power of state to the Soviets. . . .

5. Not a parliamentary republic . . . but a republic of Soviets. . . . Abolition of the police, the army, the bureaucracy (and the universal arming of the people).

6. Confiscation of all private lands. Nationalisation . . . and management of such lands by local Soviets of Agricultural Labourers' and Peasants' Deputies.

7. One general national bank, over which the Soviet should have control.

8. Not the "introduction" of Socialism as an *immediate* task, but the immediate placing of the Soviet . . . in *control* of social production and distribution of goods. . . .

I propose that the name of the party be changed, that it be called the Communist Party. The majority of the official Social-Democrats have betrayed Socialism. . . . Have the will to build a new party . . . and those who are oppressed will join you.'

This exposition did little to remove the friction between Lenin and the majority of his party, and it alarmed the Mensheviks even more. Abramovitch, one of their leaders, has written recently:

ABRAMOVITCH: '. . . If the sections of (Lenin's) theoretical analysis which concerned a social-economic programme for Russia held to the traditions of orthodox Marxism, an uncommonly radical and revolutionary note emerged in other parts of the document. For Lenin envisaged the Russian revolution as the prelude of a world revolution in the more advanced capitalist countries on both sides of the battle lines; and this world revolution would help Russia overcome her general backwardness and enable . . . the Bolsheviks to turn her into a socialist country. This concept shocked the Russian Marxists in 1917; they considered it a betrayal of scientific socialism, a reversion to the old, utopian, Bakuninist, maximalist-anarchist ideas, which

Russian Marxism had been combatting for three decades before the revolution. Many of Lenin's friends and pupils were embarrassed by these views. Even his wife, N. Krupskaya, was worried. She is reported to have told an old personal friend: "I am afraid it looks as if Lenin has gone crazy".'

But the very consistency of Lenin's uncompromising attitude stood him in good stead among other politicians and parties which were constantly swinging first one way and then another. He was strengthened by the outcry that greeted Miliukov's note to the Allies of May 1st:

MILIUKOV: 'The declarations of the Provisional Government permeated by the new spirit of liberated democracy . . . cannot offer the slightest cause to assume that the accomplished upheaval will result in a weakening of Russia's role in the common struggle of the Allies. Quite the contrary . . .'

Though many moderate socialists regarded the Hohenzollerns and Habsburgs as enemies who must be fought, they demanded a 'democratic peace without annexations and indemnities', and this was not what Miliukov or the Allies had in mind. The Ex-Com demanded an explanation, and furious crowds threatened violence in the streets until ordered to cease by the Soviet. Lenin's reaction to the Foreign Minister's announcement was characteristic:

LENIN: 'The cards are on the table. We have good reason to be grateful to . . . Miliukov for (his) note. . . . No class-conscious worker, no class-conscious soldier will further support the policy of "confidence" in the Provisional Government. The policy of confidence is bankrupt.'

On May 15th Miliukov resigned. The government agreed to reduce the terms of the note, but it was clear that the Cadets lacked popular support. A new government emerged—a coalition of the Cadets and the moderate socialists. The latter, though they still commanded a majority in the Soviets, were playing into Lenin's hands, for in supporting the government they seemed to destroy the independence of the Ex-Com. The Bolsheviks were left to become the focal point of opposition, aided by the Government's continued postponement of elections to a Constituent Assembly.

On May 17th, Trotsky arrived from America. Aware of the superiority of his own intellect, cutting of speech and ruthless in action, Trotsky watched himself creating history, and was not displeased by what he saw. Though not officially a Bolshevik, he soon joined forces with Lenin; they formed a remarkable revolutionary combination.

Throughout May and early June the Bolsheviks were growing stronger and their underground activities continued unabated. On June 16th, the First All-Russian Congress of Soviets was in session. Replying to a suggestion by a Menshevik Minister that no party in Russia wanted power at that time, Lenin startled and amused his audience, less than one-sixth of whom were Bolsheviks, by declaring:

LENIN: 'The citizen-Minister of Posts and Telegraphs said that there is no political party in Russia that would express willingness to take all state power into its hands. I say: "Such a party exists! . . . Our party does not refuse it. (It) is ready at any moment to take all power into its hands".'

The Soviet delegations might laugh, but when they called for an all-party demonstration in support of peace and the Coalition Government on July 1st, Bolshevik slogans were surprisingly numerous. Indeed, by the middle of the month, the Provisional Government was so unpopular that those socialists within it were isolated from their own followers. Hatred of the bourgeois ministers and total disillusionment with the war now produced the uprising known as 'The July Days' in Petrograd. Rank-and-file Bolsheviks had earlier been active in the factories of the Vyborg district; several army units and the Kronstadt sailors were demanding action. On July 17th about 6,000 sailors from Kronstadt landed on the Neva quays. Red Guards and soldiers were in the streets, further in-flamed by news of the crushing defeat of that month's Russian offensive ordered by Kerensky, now Minister of War. A group of sailors took the Fortress of St. Peter and St. Paul; others seized Chernov, an S.R. member of the Government and, but for Trotsky's frantic efforts, might have lynched him. On the platform of the Soviet, Chkheidze had a rifle thrust under his nose by an infuriated worker. The Bolshevik leadership, how-ever, failed to impose itself on the now-chaotic scene, and rain dispersed many of the crowds. Those troops remaining loyal to the moderate Soviet majority reasserted themselves and on July 19th the Kronstadt sailors, finding themselves isolated in the Peter-Paul Fortress, agreed to with-draw. Sukhanov gave the following account of the July Days, based on a conversation with a leading Bolshevik, Lunacharsky:

SUKHANOV: 'Lenin was definitely planning a coup d'état . . . (It) was to proceed in this way: the 176th Regiment, arriving from Krasnoe Selo, was to arrest the Central Ex-Com, and at about that time Lenin was to arrive on the scene of action and proclaim the new Government. But Lenin was too late. The 176th Regiment was intercepted and became disorganised. The "rising" had failed.'

27

Trotsky, however, probably correctly, denied that the Bolshevik leaders had any part in planning the rising:

TROTSKY: 'The Bolsheviks made every effort to reduce the July movement to a demonstration.'

Whatever the truth, the immediate result of the July Days was clear: there was a general desire for revenge on the disturbers of the peace. Documents were published purporting to show that Lenin was a German agent. The effect was shattering, coming as it did on top of the German routing of Kerensky's offensive. It seemed that the Bolsheviks had timed a rising to coincide with the German onslaught. Lenin had to go into hiding, Trotsky was arrested, and the Bolsheviks temporarily abandoned their cry of 'all power to the Soviets'.

Prince Lvov's coalition crumbled, but Kerensky utilised the anti-Bolshevik reaction by forming a new coalition with the Cadets, its emphasis on the right, and himself as Premier. It proved no stronger than its predecessor, and by the end of August Kerensky's position was precarious. Strikes and unemployment were growing[1]; separatist national movements became more determined. Many felt that only a strong military dictatorship could cure Russia's ills, and they looked to the new Commander in Chief, General Kornilov, both to depose Kerensky and crush the Bolsheviks. On September 3rd the Germans captured Riga; on the 7th Kornilov ordered strong units of Cossacks to march on Petrograd. On September 8th Kerensky denounced Kornilov and appealed to all socialists, Bolsheviks included, to defend the government and the revolution.[2] Agitators undermined the resolution of the approaching Cossacks, and railway workers sabotaged their route. On September 9th Kornilov's advance halted. The next few days witnessed his arrest and the collapse of his movement.

The Kornilov affair was vital for the fortunes of the Bolsheviks, obliterating as it did the stigma of treachery so recently fastened upon them. At the height of the crisis about 25,000 workers were enrolled in companies and given arms by the Government. When the latter asked for the arms back, the Bolsheviks refused. In addition, the Kornilov affair widened the splits in the Social Revolutionary party, with Right wing elements following Kerensky and the extreme Left drawing closer to the Bolsheviks. The Second Coalition collapsed, and for nearly a month no wider form of government could be established than the vacillating,

[1]Between February and July, wages increased by 53%, whilst prices of rye bread rose by 150%, of potatoes by 175%, of clothing and shoes by 170%.

[2]Kerensky and other moderates found it hard to forget that the Bolsheviks were fellow-socialists; Lenin, on the other hand, regarded the former as dangerous enemies.

personal rule of Kerensky. In retrospect it is clear that a political vacuum now existed. At the same time the Bolsheviks at last obtained a clear majority in the Petrograd and Moscow Soviets, with Trotsky, released on bail, President of the former.

Winter was closing over Russia. John Reed, an American correspondent and Bolshevik sympathiser, described Petrograd as the second revolution drew near:

REED: 'September and October are the worst months of the Russian year—especially the Petrograd year. Under dull grey skies, in the shortening days, the rain fell drenching, incessant. The mud underfoot was deep, slippery and clinging . . . worse than usual because of the complete breakdown of the Municipal administration. Bitter damp winds rushed in from the Gulf of Finland, and the chill fog rolled through the streets. At night, for motives of economy as well as fear of Zeppelins, the streetlights were few and far between; in private dwellings and apartment houses the electricity was turned on from six o'clock until midnight.... It was dark from three in the afternoon to ten in the morning. Robberies and house-breaking increased. In apartment houses the men took turns at all-night guard duty, armed with loaded rifles.... Week by week food became scarcer.... The daily allowance of bread fell from a pound and a half to . . . a quarter-pound.... For milk and bread and sugar and tobacco one had to stand in queue long hours in the chill rain.... Of course all the theatres were going every night, including Sundays.'

The Bolsheviks had also gained majorities in the Kiev and Odessa Soviets. They declared that the existing Central Executive Committee of the All-Russian Soviets no longer represented the wishes of the masses, and summoned a Congress of all Soviets to meet in Petrograd on November 2nd. Demands for peace came from the front; peasants began plundering and dividing up country estates on a wide scale.[1] Lenin pressed the Bolshevik Central Committee for immediate action:

LENIN: 'We must make the task clear to the party, place on the order of the day the armed uprising in Petrograd and Moscow . . . the conquest of power, the overthrow of the government.... History will never forgive us if we do not assume power now.'

On October 22nd he secretly returned from Finland to Petrograd. Meanwhile, Kerensky, about to form a third and even weaker Coalition, had

---

[1]The Bolsheviks and, increasingly, the Left S.R.s approved of such forcible seizures, supporting the poorer peasants. The Right S.R.s insisted upon the legal transference of land, and tended to support the *kulaks* (wealthier peasants).

summoned a Democratic Conference to open in Petrograd on September 27th. The delegates were carefully vetted in order to minimise the influence of the Bolsheviks. The Conference lasted until October 4th, achieving no more than the formation of a weak and temporary body known as the Pre-Parliament, pending the election of a Constituent Assembly. This Pre-Parliament opened on October 20th in the Mariinsky Palace in Petrograd. Trotsky, frequently interrupted by outbursts from non-Bolsheviks, left no doubt as to the implacable hostility of his Party to such proceedings:

TROTSKY: 'The propertied classes are openly steering a course for the bony hand of hunger, which is expected to strangle the revolution and the Constituent Assembly first of all. Nor is their foreign policy any less criminal, . . . this government of national treachery. Petrograd is in danger, the revolution is in danger, the nation is in danger. . . . Long live an immediate, honourable, democratic peace, all power to the Soviets, all land to the people, long live the Constituent Assembly.'

After this burst of propaganda, the Bolsheviks walked out of the conference. By this gesture, their intention of resorting to force was clear. They had established themselves, together with the Executive Committee of the All-Russian Congress of Soviets and the Petrograd Soviet, at the Smolny Institute, a former convent for the daughters of the nobility. Reed described the centre of the coming revolution:

REED: 'Smolny Institute . . . lay miles out on the edge of the city, beside the wide Neva. . . . Within were more than a hundred huge rooms . . . on their doors enamelled plaques still informing the passer-by that within was "Ladies' Class-room, Number 4" or "Teachers' Bureau"; but over these hung crudely-lettered signs, evidence of the vitality of the new order: "Central Committee of the Petrograd Soviet" . . . "Factory-Shop Committees" . . . "Central Army Committee". . . . The long vaulted corridors, lit by rare electric lights, were thronged with hurrying shapes of soldiers and workmen, some bent under the weight of huge bundles of newspapers, proclamations, printed propaganda of all sorts.'

A bourgeois newspaper assessed the situation in the last week of October:

'RUSSKAYA VOLIA:' The decisive moment approaches . . . for the Bolsheviks. Either they will give us . . . a second edition of the events of July 16th-18th or they will have to admit that . . . they have been definitely defeated.

On October 23rd a meeting of the Bolshevik Central Committee took place. Lenin yet again urged immediate rebellion and at length convinced everyone except Kamenev and Zinoviev, who felt that the Party was not yet strong enough to stage a rising. Outvoted, they replied in a letter the next day:

KAMENEV: 'We have no right to stake the whole future on the card of an armed uprising. ... The forces of the opponent are greater than they appear. ... Is the sentiment among the workers and soldiers of the capital really such that they see salvation only in street fighting, that they are impatient to go into the streets? No.'

LENIN: 'Men capable of saying that are either truth distorters or pedants. ... (They) wish to secure an advance guarantee that the Bolshevik Party has received throughout the whole country no more nor less than one half of the votes plus one. Such a guarantee history has never proffered ... (and) to advance such a demand means to mock one's audience. It was after the July days that the majority of the people began quickly to go over to the side of the Bolsheviks. ... Such a factual argument in favour of an uprising is stronger than thousands of pessimistic evasions on the part of confused and frightened politicians.'

The growing sense of urgency was apparent to Reed when he attended a meeting of the Petrograd Soviet on October 30th:

REED: 'At Smolny there were strict guards at the door and the outer gates, demanding everybody's pass. The committee rooms buzzed and hummed all day and all night, hundreds of soldiers and workmen slept on the floor, wherever they could find room. Upstairs in the great hall a thousand people crowded to the uproarious sessions of the Petrograd Soviet. ...
Stormy was the all-night meeting... of 30th October. ....The 'moderate' Socialist intellectuals, officers, members of Army Committees, the (existing Executive Committee of Soviets), were there in force. Against them rose up workmen, peasants, and common soldiers. ...'

Those who tried to convince the assembly of the need to win the war before all else were shouted down; peasants fiercely reiterated their desire for land. On the same day, Trotsky gave his view of the situation to Reed:

TROTSKY: 'The Provisional Government is absolutely powerless. The bourgeoisie is in control, but this ... is masked by a fictitious coalition. ... It is force which the bourgeoisie lacks (for) the Army is with us. The conciliators and pacifists, Socialist Revolutionaries and Mensheviks, have lost all authority—because the (class) struggle ... has become more bitter, more irreconcilable than ever. (But) the Soviets are the most perfect representatives of the people ..., based directly upon the army in the trenches, the workers in the factories, and the peasants in the fields, they are the backbone of the Revolution. There has been an attempt to create power without the Soviets—and only powerlessness has been created. . . . Our answer will be decisive. We will complete the work scarcely begun in March. . . . If we create here a Government of the Soviets, that will be a powerful factor for immediate peace in Europe; for this Government will address itself directly . . . to all peoples, over the heads of their Governments, proposing an armistice. . . . The pressure of the Russian Revolution will be in the direction of no annexations, no indemnities, the right of self-determination of peoples, and a Federated Republic of Europe.'

Trotsky was skilfully broadening support for the revolution by preparing for it in the name of the Soviets rather than the Bolsheviks alone. There is a note of considerable authority in his words. Lenin was still in hiding, and during these last days before the Bolsheviks seized power, direction came mainly from Trotsky, Chairman of the Military Revolutionary Committee of the Petrograd Soviet, the body which planned the uprising. A resolution passed by representatives of all the Petrograd regiments on October 30th announced their allegiance to this Committee:

PETROGRAD REGIMENTS: 'The Petrograd garrison no longer recognises the Provisional Government. The Petrograd Soviet is our Government. We will obey only the orders of the Petrograd Soviet through the Military Revolutionary Committee.'

On November 2nd, the Committee began making final preparations for insurrection. Regional Soviet congresses throughout the country were declaring for Soviet power. The opening of the All-Russian Congress of Soviets was postponed from November 2nd to November 7th, and the rising, so long urged by Lenin, was now timed to enable this Congress to sanction the new régime.

The fact that the Bolsheviks were planning to strike was no secret. On the 2nd Zinoviev publicly retracted his opposition to Lenin, and the party tightened its hold on the Petrograd garrison. On Sunday, November 4th, there were widespread Bolshevik demonstrations, without violence, but indicating impressive strength.

On the 5th the Government belatedly acted: Kerensky called a Cabinet meeting and an emergency was declared. The Soviet Military Revolutionary Committee was declared illegal, and an order was issued for the arrest of Trotsky and other Bolshevik leaders; Bolshevik newspapers were banned. Kerensky remained confident, claiming to possess ample force to deal with any rising; yet no attempt was made to attack the real centre of trouble, Smolny. On the same day, Trotsky addressed uncommitted elements of the garrison of the Fortress of St. Peter and St. Paul and won them over. Thus control was gained of a large arsenal from which arms were distributed in lorries and carts to the Red Guard, Bolshevik workers given basic military training, but without uniforms.

On November 6th officer-cadets smashed the type at the Bolshevik printing plant and sealed the doors; the Military Revolutionary Committee sent down friendly troops, and publication was resumed. The cruiser *Aurora* was ordered by the government to leave the Neva for sea; the Committee countermanded the order and she remained ready to support revolutionary action. The city was quiet but tense, and at the Mariinsky Palace delegates to the Pre-Parliament did not conceal their alarm. Kerensky denounced Lenin and read out one of the latter's inflammatory articles:

KERENSKY: 'We have to do not so much with the movement of such and such political party, as with the exploitation of the political ignorance and criminal instincts of a part of the population, a sort of organisation whose object is to provoke in Russia, cost what it may . . . destruction and pillage. . . . I qualify such acts . . . as acts of treason to Russia . . . and I propose immediately to proceed to an investigation and make the necessary arrests.'

Kerensky was then passed a copy of the latest Smolny order. He read it to the delegates:

MILITARY REVOLUTIONARY COMMITTEE: 'The Petrograd Soviet of Workers' and Soldiers' Deputies is menaced. We order immediately the regiments to mobilize on a war footing and to await new orders. All delay or non-execution of this order will be considered as an act of treason to the Revolution.'

KERENSKY: '(This) is an attempt to incite the rabble against the existing order, and prevent the convening of the Constituent Assembly. . . . I have come with the conviction that the Provisional Government . . . will win the unanimous support of everyone, except those who have not the courage of their convictions—to tell the truth openly. . . . (The Provisional Government declares that) all the elements of Russian society . . . which have dared raise their hand against the free will of the Russian people . . . should be . . . liquidated!'

On the night of November 6th-7th Lenin, heavily disguised, arrived to join Trotsky at Smolny. In the building there was a particularly turbulent meeting of the Petrograd Soviet:

REED: 'Delegates (were) falling down asleep on the floor and rising again to take part in the debate. Trotsky (and others were) speaking six, eight, twelve hours a day. . . . As night fell the great hall filled with soldiers and workmen, a monstrous dun mass, deep-humming in a blue haze of smoke. . . . It was after midnight when . . . Dan rose to speak, in a tense silence, which seemed to me almost menacing:'

DAN: 'The masses are sick and exhausted. They have no interest in the Revolution. If the Bolsheviks start anything, that will be the end of the Revolution. . . . You must obey the orders of the . . . (existing Executive Committee of Soviets) elected by you. "All power to the Soviets"—that means death! Robbers and thieves are waiting for the moment to loot and burn.'

Trotsky rose to speak, greeted by thunderous applause:

TROTSKY: 'The history of the last 7 months shows that the masses have left the Mensheviks. . . . Dan tells you that you have no right to make an insurrection. Insurrection is the right of all revolutionists! When the down-trodden masses revolt it is their right. . . .'

On the morning of November 7th the Bolsheviks, claiming to be defending themselves against counter-revolution, began to gain control of the city. Reed describes the early stages of insurrection:

REED: 'Towards four in the morning, I met (a Bolshevik) in the outer hall, a rifle slung from his shoulder.

"We're moving!" said he calmly, but with satisfaction. "We pinched the Assistant Minister of Justice and the Minister of Religions. They're down in the cellar now. . . . The Red Guard is out. . . ."

On the steps of Smolny, in the chill dark, we first saw the Red Guard—a huddled group of boys in workmen's clothes, carrying guns with bayonets, talking nervously together.

Far over the still roofs westward came the sound of scattered rifle fire where (officer cadets) were trying to open the bridges over the Neva, to prevent the factory workers and soldiers of the Vyborg quarter from joining the Soviet forces in the centre of the city; and the Kronstadt sailors were closing them again. . . . Behind us great Smolny, bright with lights, hummed like a gigantic hive. . . .'

During these last hours before the actual insurrection, the Bolshevik leaders had to assess the loyalties of the Cossacks and the ordinary troops. The Government was relying to a considerable extent on the former who, as owners of land and horses, had always considered themselves superior to mere peasants. But two cavalry regiments, one of them Cossacks, now resisted the orders of their commanders, and demanded that they should no longer be used as punitive troops by the civil power.

As for the Bolsheviks, they were relying primarily on the Kronstadt sailors, troops from Finland, and workers of the Red Guard, particularly those of the Vyborg district:

TROTSKY: 'As in (March) the Vyborg district focusses (the) basic forces of the revolution. . . . The district is wholly in control of the workers. If the government should raid Smolny, the Vyborg district alone could re-establish a centre and guarantee the further offensive.'

Before daybreak on November 7th the Bolsheviks seized the railway stations, the Tauride Palace, the State Bank, the power stations, food and munitions stores, bridges over the Neva, and the telephone exchanges. Smolny had been converted into an armed camp: detachments of soldiers and Red Guards were brought up to defend the headquarters of the insurrection. The most striking aspect of this process of infiltration was the ease with which it was achieved. It was in many ways quite unlike a revolution. Instead of barricades, looting and bloodshed, there was merely a strange, tense silence. Kerensky, suddenly realizing that his confidence and preparedness for the struggle were utterly unfounded, fled to the front, though the event is described in rather more colourful fashion in his memoirs:

KERENSKY: 'It is needless to say that the whole street . . . immediately recognised me. I saluted as always, a little carelessly and with an easy smile.'

TROTSKY: 'Incomparable picture! Carelessly and smiling—thus the (March) régime passed into the kingdom of shades.'

The Pre-Parliament was dispersed by soldiers and sailors. Now only the Provisional Government—minus Kerensky—remained, barricaded inside the Winter Palace, protected by a Right-wing woman's unit, officer-cadets, and Cossack machine-gunners—a garrison of 2,000 at the most. Trotsky was jubilant as, on the afternoon of the 7th, he declared to the Petrograd Soviet that the Provisional Government no longer existed:

TROTSKY: 'They told us that an insurrection would drown the revolution in torrents of blood. . . . We do not know of a single casualty. . . . The Winter Palace is not yet taken, but its fate will be settled in the course of the next few minutes. . . . The will of the Congress (of Soviets) has been anticipated by the colossal fact of an insurrection of the Petrograd workers and soldiers. It now remains only to develop our victory.'

Trotsky's estimate of the time needed to capture the Winter Palace, however, proved optimistic. Kronstadt units which were to take part had been summoned too late, and the assault was postponed. But by late afternoon a complete blockade of the Palace had been established, backed by the guns of the *Aurora* and other warships and of the Fortress of St. Peter and St. Paul. Despite this, the Ministers decided to continue their resistance, moving to an inner room of the building.

Firing on the Palace began after 9 p.m.; it was ineffective, but the armed women decided to surrender, and the Cossack machine-gunners had already left. Small parties of Red Guards penetrated the outer rooms and skirmished with the officer-cadets within; outside, the Bolshevik ring thickened. Spasmodic shelling continued and in the early hours of November 8th sailors and Red Guards infiltrated the Palace in large numbers and arrested the Cabinet Ministers. John Reed entered the building shortly afterwards:

REED: 'We walked into the Palace . . . upstairs, and wandered through room after room. . . . The old Palace servants in their blue and red and gold uniforms stood nervously about, from force of habit repeating, "You can't go in there! . . . It is forbidden—"

We penetrated at length to the chamber . . . where the Ministers had been in session. . . . The long table . . . was just as they had left it, under arrest. Before each empty seat was pen, ink and paper; the papers were scribbled over with beginnings of plans of action, rough drafts of proclamations and manifestos. Most of these were scratched out, as their futility became evident, and the rest of the sheet covered with absent-minded geometrical designs. . . .'

Simultaneous with the assault on the Winter Palace was the first session of the second All-Russian Congress of Soviets at Smolny. The existing Executive Committee were voted down, and a new, mainly Bolshevik one took its place. Suddenly, above the shouting and applause, the thud of guns was heard. Martov, his voice a hoarse croak, gave vent to the horror of the moderate socialists:

MARTOV: 'The civil war is beginning, comrades! . . . Our brothers are being shot down in the streets! At this moment . . . the question of power is being settled by means of a military plot. . . .'

REED: 'Always the methodical muffled boom of cannon through the windows, and the delegates, screaming at each other. . . . So, with the crash of artillery, in the dark, with hatred, and fear, and reckless daring, new Russia was being born.'

Army officers denounced the Congress and urged all soldiers present to leave; they were answered by men from the ranks and by Trotsky, his face 'pale and cruel':

TROTSKY: 'All these so-called Socialist compromisers, these frightened

Mensheviks, Socialist Revolutionaries, (Jewish Social Democrats), let them go! They are just so much refuse which will be swept away into the garbage-heap of history!'

The Mensheviks withdrew and held a separate meeting, quarrelling among themselves over Martov's decision to leave the Congress altogether. The session continued to run its tumultuous course, however. S.R. delegates bitterly protested against the arrest of the socialist Ministers in the Winter Palace; Trotsky accused the latter of plotting against the Soviets, and reminded his audience of the measures taken against the Bolsheviks in July. A declaration was passed, announcing the deposition of the Government and the transference of local power to the Soviets. At 5.17 a.m. Krylenko, 'staggering with fatigue', appeared with a telegram in his hand:

KRYLENKO: 'Comrades! From the Northern Front. The Twelfth Army sends greetings to the Congress of Soviets, announcing the formation of a Military Revolutionary Committee which has taken over command of the Northern Front!'

REED: 'Pandemonium, men weeping, embracing each other ... Lenin ... and the Petrograd Soviet had overthrown the Provisional Government, and thrust the coup d'état upon the Congress of Soviets. Now there was all great Russia to win—and then the world! ... Although it was six in the morning, night was yet heavy and chill. There was only a faint unearthly pallor stealing over the silent streets, dimming the watch-fires, the shadow of a terrible dawn grey-rising over Russia. ...'

On the 8th, however, the Bolsheviks were still by no means secure, in spite of assurances of support from the front. Their opponents had formed a Committee for Salvation of Country and Revolution, joined by the Menshevik and other moderate delegates who had walked out of the Congress at Smolny. The Bolsheviks antagonised many potential neutrals by the violence done at the Winter Palace. Kerensky's movements were unknown; Kornilov had escaped from captivity; rumours flew around that the two of them had mustered a force and were now marching on the city. Posters and newspapers of all other parties, and of bodies like the Municipal Duma, denounced the events of the previous 24 hours. The Committee for Salvation's appeal was typical:

COMMITTEE FOR SALVATION: 'Such violence committed against the Government of Revolutionary Russia at the moment of its greatest external danger is an indescribable crime against the fatherland. ... Civil war, begun by the Bolsheviks, threatens to deliver the country to the horrors of anarchy and counter-revolution, and cause the failure of the Constituent Assembly.... The Committee ... takes the initiative in forming a new Provisional Government (and) summons you, citizens, to refuse to recognise the power of violence. Do not obey its orders! Rise for the defence of the country and the Revolution!'

The Military Revolutionary Committee was working at fever pitch, turning out a stream of orders and appeals. Capital punishment was abolished in the army, though death was decreed for plundering; temporary Commissars were appointed to control the vital branches of administration. Many Bolsheviks remained uneasy, not knowing that Kerensky was discovering at the front how fickle were the loyalties of his troops and generals; but *Pravda* offered reassurance:

'PRAVDA': 'Workers, soldiers, peasants! In March you struck down the tyranny of the clique of nobles. Yesterday you struck down the tyranny of the bourgeois gang.'

At 8.40 that evening, the 8th, the second session of the Congress of Soviets commenced:

REED: 'A thundering wave of cheers announced the entrance of the praesidium, with Lenin—great Lenin—among them. A short, stocky figure, with a big head set down on his shoulders, bald and bulging. Little eyes, a snubbish nose, wide generous mouth, and heavy chin; clean-shaven now but already beginning to bristle with the well-known beard of his past and future. Dressed in shabby clothes, his trousers much too long for him. Unimpressive to be the idol of the mob, loved and ¡revered as perhaps few leaders in history have been. A strange popular leader—a leader purely by virtue of intellect.... Now, ... gripping the edge of the reading-stand, (he let) his little winking eyes travel over the crowd as he stood there waiting, apparently oblivious to the long-rolling ovation, which lasted several minutes. When it finished, he said simply:

LENIN: 'We shall now proceed to construct the Socialist order! ... The first thing is the adoption of practical measures to realise peace. ... We shall offer peace to the peoples of all the belligerent countries upon the basis of the Soviet terms—no annexations, no indemnities, and the right of self-determination of peoples. At the same time ... we shall publish and repudiate the secret treaties. ...'

He spoke without gestures, bending forward for emphasis. Roars of applause punctuated his words as he went on to read a proclamation to the peoples and governments of all belligerent nations:

LENIN: 'This proposal of peace will meet with resistance on the part of the imperialist governments. ... But we hope that revolution will soon break out in all the belligerent countries. . . . We want a just peace, but we are not afraid of a revolutionary war.'

REED: 'It was . . . 10.35 when Kamenev asked all in favour of the proclamation to hold up their cards. One delegate dared to raise his hand against, but the sudden outburst around him brought it swiftly down. . . . Unanimous.

Suddenly by common impulse, we found ourselves on our feet, mumbling together into the smooth lifting unison of the *Internationale*. A grizzled old soldier was sobbing like a child. . . . The immense sound rolled through the hall, burst windows and doors and soared into the quiet sky. "The war is ended! The war is ended!" said a young workman near me, his face shining.'

Sukhanov, too, was present in the public seats, now that the Mensheviks, against his will, had left the Congress. His comments epitomise the agony of those who, though opposed to the Bolsheviks, were socialists, and even Marxists.

SUKHANOV: 'The whole Praesidium, headed by Lenin, was standing up and singing, with excited, exalted faces and blazing eyes. . . . The delegates were . . . completely revivified. . . . Applause, hurrahs, caps flung up in the air. . . . But I didn't believe in the victory, the success, the "rightness", or the historic mission of a Bolshevik régime. Sitting in the back seats, I watched this celebration with a heavy heart. How I longed to join in, and merge with this mass and its leaders in a single feeling! But I couldn't. . . .'

Then Lenin read the decree on land. The Bolsheviks had dropped their own policy of nationalisation and, with astute political opportunism, adopted in its entirety the Socialist-Revolutionary programme of the distribution of all land to the peasants according to their needs:

LENIN: 'This is not the project of (the Provisional Government, which) spoke of erecting a framework and tried to realise the reforms from above. From below, on the spot, will be decided the questions of divisions of the land. . . .'

The Decree was passed with only one negative vote at 2 o'clock on the morning of November 9th. At 2.30 Kamenev read the Constitution of Power:

KAMENEV: 'Until the meeting of the Constituent Assembly, a provisional workers' and Peasants' Government is formed which shall be named the Council of People's Commissars. . . . Control over the . . .

People's Commissars, and the right to replace them, shall belong to the All-Russian Congress of Soviets. . . .'

Kamenev went on to read the list of Commissars, each name being followed by a burst of applause, especially those of Lenin (President of the Council) and Trotsky (Foreign Affairs). But then two speakers—a Menshevik Internationalist and a Left Socialist Revolutionary—spoke against an exclusively Bolshevik government and in favour of a coalition. Trotsky replied:

TROTSKY: 'These considerations on the danger of isolation of our party are not new. On the eve of insurrection our fatal defeat was also predicted. Everybody was against us. . . . How is it that we were able to overturn the Government almost without bloodshed? . . . That fact is the most striking proof that we were not isolated. In reality the Provisional Government was isolated; the democratic parties which march against us were isolated, are isolated, and for ever cut off from the proletariat! They speak of the necessity of a coalition. There is only one coalition possible—the coalition of the workers, soldiers, and poorest peasants; and it is our party's honour to have realised that coalition.'

Though he later added that all parties and groups who adopted the Bolshevik programme would be welcome in the Government, only the Left Socialist Revolutionaries accepted the offer.

At 5.15 a.m. the Congress was dissolved. But this day, the 9th, brought further ominous declarations of opposition from Kaledin, leader of the Cossacks, and from Kerensky:

KALEDIN: 'The Cossack Government declares that it considers these acts criminal and absolutely inadmissable. In consequence, the Cossacks will lend all their support to the Provisional Government . . . I take upon myself all power in that which concerns the region of the Don.'

KERENSKY: 'I, Minister President of the Provisional Government, and Supreme Commander of all the armed forces of the Russian Republic . . . order all the troops of . . . Petrograd, who . . . have answered the appeal of the (Bolshevik) traitors . . . to return to their duty without delay.'

Moreover, it was yet to be seen whether the rest of Russia would accept the lead of Petrograd. The railway and telegraph workers, opposed to one-party government, made wireless almost the only form of Bolshevik communication for a time. The Allies showed no sign of recognising the new Government. In such circumstances, Lenin justified the suppression of all newspapers inciting resistance:

LENIN: 'In such a critical time . . . it is essential that the enemy do not retain (in the press), a weapon no less dangerous than bombs or machine-guns.'

But this move failed to kill free speech. An enormous poster of the Executive Committee of the Peasants' Soviets denounced the Bolsheviks:

PEASANTS' SOVIETS: 'These Bolsheviks dare to say that they are supported by the Soviets of Peasants' Deputies, and that they are speaking on behalf of the Peasants' Deputies. . . . Let all working-class Russia know that this is a LIE AND THAT ALL THE WORKING PEASANTS . . . refute with indignation all participation of the organised peasantry in this criminal violation of the will of the working class. . . .'

The railway workers, a most important body, negotiated with the Mensheviks and S.R.s, and demanded a coalition socialist government. Their threat of strike action, and widespread proletarian support for a socialist coalition, forced the Bolsheviks to enter into discussions on the 11th November. The need was all the greater in that Kerensky was approaching Petrograd with a force of Cossacks. On the 10th, Reed had listened to the apprehensive comments of men at Smolny:

BOLSHEVIKS: 'They'll never take us alive.'
　　'Tomorrow maybe we'll get a sleep—a long one.'
　　'What chance have we? All alone. . . . A mob against trained soldiers.'

MILITARY REVOLUTIONARY COMMITTEE: 'We call on the regional Soviets and the factory committees . . . to send a large number of workmen to dig trenches, to erect barricades . . . and wire obstructions . . . to be ready to come to the aid of the army and the revolution with all your means.'

REED: '. . . (In) the dark and gloomy day, all around the grey horizon, factory whistles were blowing a hoarse, nervous sound, full of foreboding. By tens of thousands the working people poured out, men and women . . . Red Petrograd was in danger! . . . They poured through the shabby streets . . . men, women, and children, with rifles, picks, spades, rolls of wire, cartridge belts over their working clothes. . . . They rolled along torrent-like, companies of soldiers borne with them, guns, motor-trucks, wagons.'

On Sunday November 11th, fighting took place inside Petrograd between the Red Guards and officer-cadets who had seized a telephone exchange, the Telegraph Agency, and other buildings. Armoured cars fought in the streets. Reed describes the assault on one of the cadet (*yunker*) barracks:

REED: 'Another demand to surrender was met by the *yunkers* shooting down two of the Soviet delegates. . . . Now began a real bombardment. . . . The *yunkers* defended themselves desperately; shouting waves of Red Guards . . . crumpled under the withering blast. . . . Frenzied by defeat and their heaps of dead, the Soviet troops opened a tornado of steel and flame against the battered building. . . . At half-past two the *yunkers* hoisted a white flag; they would surrender if they were guaranteed protection. This was promised. With a rush and a shout thousands of soldiers and Red Guards poured through windows, doors and holes in the wall. Before it could be stopped, five *yunkers* were beaten and stabbed to death. The rest, about two hundred, were taken to Peter-Paul. . . . On the way a mob set upon the party, killing eight more *yunkers* . . . more than a hundred Red Guards and soldiers had fallen.'

The Bolsheviks regained control of Petrograd. Then, on the night of November 12th-13th, Kerensky's small force, its morale already undermined, was defeated at Tsarskoe Selo. The news came in a telegram from Trotsky to the Petrograd Soviet:

TROTSKY: '(This night) will go down in history. The attempt of Kerensky to move counter-revolutionary troops against the capital of the Revolution has been decisively repulsed. . . . The grand idea of the domination of the worker and peasant democracy closed the ranks of the army and hardened its will. . . . Before us are struggles, obstacles and sacrifices. But the road is clear and victory is certain. . . . Long live revolutionary, popular, Socialist Russia!'

News came in of bitter fighting in Moscow, where officer-cadets and White Guards held the Kremlin against Soviet attacks. Sailors of the Black Sea and Baltic Fleets declared their allegiance to the new régime; from Finland to Siberia, the country argued, struggled, waited. On November 14th, Kerensky, deserted by the Cossacks, fled; any remaining sympathy left him.

Lenin now felt strong enough to defy the railwaymen. Overcoming resistance within his own party, he insisted that the inter-party negotiations must be abandoned. At the same time, he urged on the proletariat:

LENIN: 'Comrades! Take all local power into your own hands. Take and guard . . . the grain, factories, implements, products and transport—all these are from now on wholly yours; they are public property.'

The exaltation created by such pronouncements is captured for us by

Reed as he careered back from Tsarskoe Selo to Petrograd in a truck filled with Red Guards:

REED: 'Across the horizon spread the glittering lights of the capital, immeasurably more splendid by night than by day, like a dike of jewels on the barren plain. The old workman who drove held the wheel in one hand, while with the other he swept the far-gleaming capital in an exultant gesture.

"Mine!" he cried, his face all alight. "All mine now! My Petrograd!"'

The new Government also issued a Declaration of the Rights of the Peoples of Russia:

'The Council of People's Commissars has resolved to adopt, as the basis of its activity on the problem of nationalities in Russia, the following principles:

1. The equality and sovereignty of the peoples of Russia.

2. The right to free self-determination of peoples, even to the point of separating and forming independent states.

3. The abolition of each and every privilege or limitation based on nationality or religion.

4. The free development of national minorities ... inhabiting Russian territory.'

But such bold declarations of principle could not alone overcome the problem of getting the country's economy moving again after the strikes and insurrection. Many officials concerned with services and administration refused to co-operate with the Bolsheviks. Hence, on November 22nd the following proclamation was issued:

MILITARY REVOLUTIONARY COMMITTEE: '... The higher functionaries of the Government institutions, banks, railroads, post and telegraph are on strike and impeding the work of the Government in supplying the Front with provisions. ... Each hour of delay may cost the life of thousands of soldiers. The counter-revolutionary functionaries are most dishonest criminals ...

THE MILITARY REVOLUTIONARY COMMITTEE GIVES THESE CRIMINALS A LAST WARNING. In the event of the least resistance ... on their part the harshness of the measures which will be adopted against them will correspond to the seriousness of their crime.'

Swift measures were also necessary if the war itself was to be ended. Lenin sent an order to General Dukhonin to open armistice negotiations, and urged all soldiers and sailors to fraternise with the enemy. Dukhonin, Supreme Commander at the front, refused to comply with the order. He

43

was dismissed. On December 2nd the Moghilev garrison seized the city and arrested Dukhonin, who was beaten to death by a howling mob.

Before this, however, a further obstacle had confronted the Bolsheviks. On November 25th, elections to the long-awaited Constituent Assembly had begun; the need for such a body had been the one common cry of all parties, Bolsheviks included. Now the results of the poll were a major setback to the latter. 41.7 million votes were polled; only 9.8 million or 24%, went to the Bolsheviks. Their only consolation was majorities in those vital army units nearest to the capital and Moscow. The Social Revolutionaries were clear at the head of the poll with 58% of the votes. At once, the Bolsheviks changed their slogan to 'Down with the Constituent Assembly', and Lenin postponed its opening from early December to an unspecified date in January. But by December 11th, many deputies had arrived in Petrograd and an unofficial meeting was held. Though the Bolsheviks posted guards around the Tauride Palace, the deputies forced their way in and passed a resolution that the Assembly, whatever the obstacles, should open on January 18th. Mass meetings and demonstrations supported their stand. The Bolshevik answer was to seize hostile printing presses and increase the intensity of police searches and arrests. On December 14th Lenin declared:

LENIN: 'We are asked to call the Constituent Assembly as originally conceived. No, thank you! It was conceived against the people, and we carried out the rising to make certain that it will not be used against the people.'

The Bolsheviks were divided amongst themselves over the line to be taken, however, and on the 18th January the Assembly met, after a crowd demonstrating in its favour had been fired on by Bolshevik guards. The Cadets had been outlawed, and several Right S.R.s arrested; the remaining deputies were jeered by the guards as they entered the Tauride Palace and were kept waiting for four hours by the Bolshevik delegation. The latter then seized the platform, and Sverdlov made the opening speech, requesting the Assembly to ratify a declaration recognising that all power lay with the Soviets. When the S.R. majority elected Chernov president and proceeded with business, the Bolsheviks howled down the speakers; after their declaration had been rejected they withdrew from the Assembly, followed an hour later by the Left S.R.s. Shortly before 5 a.m., a Bolshevik sailor announced that the meeting must end 'because the guard is tired.' The lights were turned off, and the delegates were escorted from the building. That day an Ex-Com resolution dissolved the Assembly; guards ensured that it never met again.

LENIN: 'Comrades! Collision between the Soviet Government and the

Constituent Assembly has been prepared by the entire history of the . . . Revolution. The transition from a capitalistic to a socialistic structure of society must necessarily be accompanied by a long and stubborn struggle. . . . The Constituent Assembly, which failed to recognise the power of the people, is now dispersed by the will of the Soviet power. . . . The Soviet Republic will triumph, no matter what happens!'

Later in the month, the third All-Russian Congress of Soviets adopted a Declaration of Rights of the Toiling and Exploited People. It announced that:

'The Russian Socialist Soviet Republic is created on the basis of a voluntary union of the peoples of Russia in the form of a federation of the Soviet republics of these peoples.'

In July, a constitution[1] which embodied these principles followed. Bolshevik power seemed assured.

Overwhelming difficulties would have to be faced, however. It had been decided to leap ahead, politically and economically, in a country whose resources and experience in both spheres were severely limited. German troops were imposing a savage peace-treaty; civil war, encouraged by the West, was about to plunge the country into greater chaos and famine. In answer to revolts and political assassinations, the ideals which had permitted the officer cadets captured at the Winter Palace to go free would recede; the *Cheka* would spread its probing fingers throughout the State, its successor, the G.P.U., throughout the Party as well. The real meaning of federalism; the power of local Soviets against the centre; the place of other socialist parties in the State; the possibility of socializing peasant-owned land; the control of industry from the centre, or by workers' committees, with their anarcho-syndicalist tendencies; the machinery of distribution and exchange between town and country; the role of trade unions; inflation; these and many other questions would have to be resolved. Power had been won; now it had to be used.

FURTHER DISCUSSION

1. What were the underlying causes of the revolution? Can one accept the recent statement of the Menshevik Abramovitch that 'If there was a single cause for the Russian Revolution of 1917, it was undoubtedly the First World War. The war's defeats and inevitable demoralization were the primary source of all the disruptive changes in Russian society . . . economy, and . . . politics which contributed to the upheavals of

---

[1]By the Constitution of 1923, the R.S.F.S.R. was merged into the U.S.S.R.

February and October 1917.' ?[1] This would seem a strange interpretation for a member of a Marxist party, and is questionable history. Was it not rather that 'The fundamental cause of the Russian Revolution . . . was the incompatibility of the Tsarist state with the demands of modern civilisation. War accelerated the development of revolutionary crises, but their deep-lying causes could not be wished away in times of peace.' ?[2]

Abramovitch's statement rests on the belief that 'Russia on the eve of the war was well advanced on the path of evolution towards a modern democratic state. . . . It seems clear . . . that, had peace been maintained in Europe for another decade or two, a peaceful evolution in Russia towards modernisation, democratisation, and rapid economic growth would have taken place.' Again, can this be accepted?

2. What reasons were given by those involved in the revolution for the success of the Bolsheviks? Why did the more moderate parties fail? In the opinion of Miliukov:

> 'The Bolsheviks acted without a programme on July 16th-18th. If they had triumphed they would not have known what to do with their victory. But . . . the experiment . . . showed them what elements they had to deal with, how to organise these elements and, lastly, what resistance the government, the Soviet, and the military units could offer. . . . The Bolsheviks saw how easily power could be seized. . . . (On the other hand) it can be said that the winners took their rapid victory too lightly, and by no means appreciated the importance of those factors whose effect had caused them several unpleasant hours. The momentary fear passed, and everything seemed to have settled back into the old channels. Life, with its problems of the moment, again hid from them the depths which for several moments had yawned before them. The main problems of the revolution remained unsolved, even though they had now been posed in full.'[3]

Kerensky, too, blamed the blindness of other parties and individuals, including Miliukov:

> 'Our tragedy lay in the fact that at the time of this unprecedented (March) social upheaval, its essential nature was not understood, not felt, either by the leaders of the middle class in the Duma, or by those of the proletariat in the newly-formed Soviet. . . . The Bolshevik Party in 1917 was a party of the political rabble (and) Lenin was a past master at inventing social slogans which stirred up the most anti-social instincts. . . . There were no "class" proletarian reasons for a civil war, because the proletariat itself, the peasantry, and the radical middle class were already in power. . . . The

---

[1] *The Soviet Revolution*, p. 1.

[2] Hill: *Lenin and the Russian Revolution* p. 11.

[3] *History of the Second Russian Revolution*; from passages translated in McNeal, ed: *The Russian Revolution* (quoted by permission of the publisher; Holt, Rinehart and Winston, Inc.).

Bolshevik rising in November was strictly an internecine act within Russian democracy.... The triangular contest continued as before: the Provisional Government, the Allies and the Kornilov faction, the Germans and Lenin.... (After the Kornilov affair) Russia had returned in a flash to the mentality of the first few weeks of the revolution.... The uphill struggle for the reconstruction of the State and the affirmation of liberty was wasted.... But even the terrible warning of the Kornilov affair failed to sober the Russian liberals and the Allies... (They argued), let the Bolsheviks oust the Provisional Government; it will not take us above three weeks to settle them!'[1]

But the personality and role of Kerensky himself were perhaps not well suited to the tasks of the time. Chernov, Minister of Agriculture in the Second Coalition, and a centre Socialist Revolutionary leader, had this to say:

'One striking feature of 1917 was the unprecedented growth of the S.R. party.... This very strength of the party was the source of its weakness. The motley, many-headed street poured resistlessly into its ranks.... People who yesterday had absolutely no conception of the party today vied in calling themselves S.R.s and in deciding questions of party life.... The S.R.s were sharply divided on whether they should make the war "their own" or regard it as "alien" to socialists.... The fact that Kerensky was enrolled as an S.R., caused frightful complications for the party. Their responsibility for him was intimate.... Yet his policy contradicted the entire S.R. platform.... There was... the danger of a party split, the founding of a "national S.R. party" and desertion of the party ranks by many men with big means. A split just before the elections to the constituent assembly might compromise all the party's successes.'[2]

Other parties had their troubles: bourgeois awareness and fear of the masses had undermined the Menshevik programme of genuine co-operation in that direction; the Menshevik's own refusal after 1905 to follow Lenin in envisaging a proletarian/peasant alliance prevented it in another. Splits followed. Tseretelli stood at the head of the Right wing, with Plekhanov, alone, even further to the Right; Chkheidze led a Centre group, and Martov the Left-wing Menshevik internationalists. 'The Menshevik party (were led) away from Martov... into... the camp of the bourgeoisie. Only a small group remained with Martov. It was a catastrophe.... The Bolsheviks... were among the masses, at the factory benches, every day without a pause.... For the masses they had become their own people because they were always there.... They had become the sole hope. Our logical proletarian class ideology was useless,

---

[1]Taken from *The Crucifixion of Liberty*, chapters XIII–XVIII.
[2]*The Great Russian Revolution*, pp. 392-8.

and offensive. . . . The disappointed, weary and hungry masses swept over our heads . . . to the devastating fury of Bolshevism.' (Sukhanov). Sukhanov's own paralysis is reflected throughout his book; what he writes about his leader, Martov—perhaps the one great figure who might have successfully challenged the Bolsheviks—could apply to himself:

> 'Martov is an incomparable thinker and a remarkable analyst because of his exceptional intellect. But this intellect dominates the whole personality to such an extent that . . . Martov owes (to it) not only . . . his highly cultivated thinking apparatus but also his *weakness in action.* . . . To a considerable extent it is precisely Martov's breadth of view that ties his hands in intellectual combat and condemns him to the role of critic, of perpetual "Opposition". . . . The centres of restraint are too strong to allow him the . . . revolutionary feats that no longer demand the reason, but only the will.'[1]

Another Menshevik leader, Dan, also attacks Kerensky. On November 6th he and two Right S.R. leaders pressed Kerensky for action to forestall the Bolsheviks. They proposed the announcing of peace negotiations, the transfer of land to local peasants' committees, and the advancing of the date of the Constituent Assembly. According to Dan, Kerensky replied 'irritably with a philippic.' (The incident is also described by Sukhanov).

Although action was here being urged, the Mensheviks and S.R.s convey at times an impression of fatalism. They had no drastic answer that would end the hopeless position of dual soviet/government power; they allowed the Cadets to continue to postpone elections for a Constituent Assembly. Abramovitch writes:

> 'The S.R.s and Mensheviks were aware that the rising tide of political and social discontent was carrying the Bolshevik Party toward victory. But, unable to end the war and refusing to undertake radical social reforms before the Constituent Assembly had been elected and convened, the two democratic socialist parties could merely attempt to mark time as long as possible. They tried to postpone the date of the Second All-Russian Congress of Soviets, but the pressure from the Bolsheviks was too strong. And so the Congress was convened by the old Executive Committee, though the democratic parties were fully aware that disaster lay ahead.'[2]

Needless to say, Bolshevik interpretations were rather different:

> 'The proletariat and peasantry voted for the Mensheviks and Social Revolutionaries not as compromisers, but as opponents of the tsar, the capitalists and the landowners. But in voting for them they created a partition-wall between themselves and their own aims. They could not now

[1]Sukhanov: *The Russian Revolution*, p. 355.
[2]op cit p. 77.

move forward at all without bumping into this wall erected by themselves, and knocking it over.'[1]

3. A further reason for the Bolshevik success was the absence in Russia of a strong middle class and of a tradition of parliamentary government. There was a long history of organised, secret revolutionary movements. 'In order to control a rebellious and evasive peasantry all over the vast Russian spaces, an absolute, highly centralized and bureaucratic government had come into existence. The autocracy conditioned the movements which stood out against it. Opposition was necessarily revolutionary. This was so whether it took the form of the wild peasant revolt of Pugachev or of the Guard's palace revolutions, which in the eighteenth century made and unmade tsars, until the aristocratic conspiracy of the Decembrists in 1825 brought old and new together—the last Guard's revolt . . . and the first revolutionary movement influenced by the liberal ideas of the West. As control by the police inside Russia tightened, so the opposition movements became increasingly conspiratorial.'[2]

Thus, an extreme creed such as Marxism found, in some ways, more ready acceptance in Russia's conditions than in the more industrialized West, where capitalism had built up wide and powerful vested interests. The fact that Slavophils continued to glorify Russian feudalism provoked many intellectuals into accepting the scornful denunciations of Marx, though they themselves desired only parliamentary liberalism. 'Nearly everyone became a Marxist', remarked Lenin in 1902.

4. Clearly the behaviour of the Provisional Government contributed to the Bolshevik triumph, not only in their failure with regard to increasing misery and resentment against the war, but in their feebleness when faced with a coup. Kerensky, despite his memoirs to the contrary, seems to have remained unduly confident. True, a committee of three was set up to deal with the approaching uprising, but its chairman, Colonel Polkovnikov, 'hated the Provisional Government and particularly Kerensky more than he did the Bolsheviks. He not only failed to take any precautions, but also systematically gave Kerensky false information, assuring him that all was well and the defence prepared. In acting thus, Colonel Polkovnikov reflected a general attitude among the rightist officers which was shared by some civilians. These people saw Kerensky and the Provisional Government, and not the Bolsheviks, as their chief foes; the latter, they thought, would only last a couple of weeks. . . . The same opinions prevailed in anti-Bolshevik units of the Petrograd garrison, notably among the Cossacks. All these troops were convinced of the ultimate victory of the Right.'[3]

[1]Trotsky: *The Russian Revolution*, pp. 191-2.
[2]Hill, op cit p. 61.
[3]Abramovitch, op cit p. 90.

Miliukov and Sukhanov were convinced that Polkovnikov's one briefly successful action—the closing down of Bolshevik newspapers early on November 6th—could have been repeated elsewhere, perhaps even at Smolny itself. (Polkovnikov did, in fact, suggest an attack on Smolny, but by the time he did so there was no coherent force for the purpose.) On the other hand, it should be remembered that the Pre-Parliament could arrive at no clear decision regarding policy, and that Bolshevik propaganda proved capable of undermining even the Cossacks who later marched on Petrograd under Kerensky.

5. It remains doubtful, however, just how much support there was for the Bolsheviks among the Petrograd workers before the rising. Whereas, not surprisingly, participants like Trotsky and Reed and historians like Christopher Hill claim that it was widespread, Abramovitch, again not surprisingly, holds the contrary view. Part of his evidence lies in the reports made to the Central Committee of the Bolshevik Party at the end of October.[1] Abramovitch quotes at length from the meeting of the 29th October, and it is clear that many who advocated armed uprising were nevertheless gloomy about the prospect of support from trade unions, the army, and some city districts. In the Moskovsky district, for instance, though the mood was 'reckless', the people would 'rise only if called by the Soviets, not by the party.'[2] The widespread support for socialist inter-party negotiations after the uprising would seem to confirm the same emphasis.[3] So, too, would Lenin's caution immediately after the uprising, promising on November 8th that 'As a democratic government we cannot ignore the will of the people even if we disagree with it. . . . And even if the peasants continue to follow the Socialist Revolutionaries, even if they give that party the majority in the Constituent Assembly, we will say: so be it.'[4]

6. Abramovitch concludes, therefore, that 'the "proletarian revolution" was accomplished while the working masses of the capital stood by passively. The struggle . . . was won by war-weary peasant lads in soldiers' or sailors' uniforms.' (He will add, later, that the most intelligent of these 'lads', the Kronstadt sailors, would become disillusioned to the point of revolt by 1921.) One must treat such a conclusion with care. Schapiro, for instance, describes the Red Guard (which he numbers at 20,000) as 'the real armed might behind the Bolshevik coup d'état.'[5] It is

[1] The minutes of the committee meeting of October 28th, for instance, may be read in Bunyan and Fisher (eds): *Documents of the Bolshevik Revolution* pp. 69-74.

[2] See Abramovitch, op cit pp. 79-82.

[3] The tone adopted by a delegation from the Putilov works when they interrupted these negotiations is instructive; see Bunyan and Fisher, op cit p. 167.

[4] Quoted in Abramovitch, op cit p. 103.

[5] *The Communist Party of the Soviet Union* pp. 173-4.

clear, however, that the party itself was not very large, membership being less than 30,000 in February 1917. Sverdlov estimated it at 200,000 in August, and it probably grew further by November.[1] But 'as late as 1920 the Mensheviks secured the election of 45 delegates in the Moscow soviet, over 225 in Kharkov and substantial delegations in some two dozen other soviets. In many, if not all, of the trade unions, Mensheviks and their supporters far outnumbered the handful of unpopular communists, who dominated the trade union organs.... Zinoviev, always prone to exaggerate, estimated in 1921 the total anti-communist following in the trade unions variously at 90 and 99%. Even Trotsky admitted that anti-communists were "very numerous".'[2] And yet, of course, there remains the fact that the Party commanded sufficient support to win the civil war, even if much of that support was created by the borrowed S.R. land programme and by the political ineptitude of the White forces.

7. Miliukov and others stressed the coherence of Bolshevik aims as their main asset. Yet the divisions within the party over immediate aims and methods presented Lenin with one of his greatest problems. The periods and subjects of some of these divisions may be noted:

(i) *Before Lenin returned to Russia.* The Bolsheviks in exile indulged in frequent quarrels, two of which were of significance for the future. Lenin argued, mainly against Bukharin, that the state apparatus would have to continue after the revolution, as the basis of the dictatorship of the proletariat; and Bukharin, Rosa Luxemburg and others attacked Lenin's belief in the right of each Russian nation to self-determination as undermining the world solidarity of the proletariat.[3] Lenin also engaged in polemics with party members in Russia; his opposition to the idea that dialectical materialism pointed to limited co-operation with the bourgeoisie has been described in the text.[4]

(ii) *On Lenin's return in April.* The text has given the broad outlines of this.

(iii) *Before the final uprising.* Lenin had great difficulty in getting the Bolsheviks to leave the Pre-Parliament. His view that the time had come for armed uprising was approved only after a stormy meeting of the Central Committee on October 23rd. Kamenev and Zinoviev not only voted against the motion, but broadcast the plan and their opposition to it in the press. In addition, 'Nine full members of the Central Committee of 22 were ... not present, and of those at least three, Nogin, Rykov and Miliutin, would certainly have opposed the resolution. A full meeting would thus have revealed an opposition

[1]See ibid pp. 170-1. [2]Ibid p. 193.
[3]See ibid pp. 147-8. [4]Ibid pp. 162-3.

approximating to a quarter of the members.'[1] Trotsky's chapter: 'Lenin Summons to Insurrection' should be read for more details of this period.

(iv) *After the uprising*. There were two great issues here. The first was the desirability or otherwise of entering into a coalition with the other socialist parties. Lenin agreed to inter-party discussions only to gain time and only until Kerensky's advance on Petrograd had been defeated. The Bolshevik differences were then fully exposed.[2] On November 17th Nogin, Rykov, Miliutin, Teodorovitch and Shliapnikov resigned from the Council of Peoples' Commissars, stating their reasons:

'We are in favour of a Socialist Government composed of all the parties in the Soviets. We consider that only the creation of such a Government can possibly guarantee the results of the heroic struggle of the working class and the revolutionary army. Outside of that, there remains only one way: the constitution of a purely Bolshevik Government by means of political terrorism. This last is the road taken by the Council of People's Commissars. We cannot and will not follow it. We see that this leads directly to the elimination from political life of many proletarian organisations, to the establishment of an irresponsible régime, and to the destruction of the Revolution and the country.'[3] At the same time Kamenev, Rykov, Miliutin, Zinoviev and Nogin resigned from the Central Committee of the Bolshevik Party, giving similar reasons.

The second major issue was that of peace or war, arising when the harsh nature of the German demands at the Brest-Litovsk negotiations (December 1917-March 1918) became apparent. Should a revolutionary war be waged against Germany? Lenin refused to countenance such an exhausting prospect, however humiliating the alternative might be. A majority of the Petrograd Committee and the entire Moscow Regional Bureau thought otherwise, and when the final vote in the Central Committee was taken on February 23rd, it was only after Lenin had threatened to resign that a decision for peace was secured, by seven votes to four, with four abstentions. 'The decision to submit to terms of peace which condoned annexation of territory by the Central Powers shook the party to its foundations. More was at issue than a mere question of expediency. ... For the advocates of revolutionary war the acceptance of the

[1]Ibid p. 169.
[2]The arguments that took place on November 14th can be read in Bunyan and Fisher, op cit pp. 192-6.
[3]Quoted, for instance, in Reed: *Ten Days that Shook the World* p. 228.

terms . . . seemed a betrayal of their duty as revolutionaries.'[1] It was over this issue, incidentally, that the Left Socialist Revolutionaries abandoned their coalition with the Bolsheviks.[2]

8. Further Bolshevik splits had their roots in the suspicion that Lenin had betrayed the ethics of the revolution by taking German money. The official Party line has always been, of course, to deny that this was ever so. The documents from the archives of the German Foreign Ministry, however, together with other evidence, make it extremly likely that Germany did subsidise the Bolsheviks. On the other hand the Germans did this only to remove Russia from the war, and there is no evidence that the former sought to dictate policy or tactics to the Bolsheviks.[3]

9. It is clear that the remarkable leadership of Lenin and Trotsky was the decisive factor in holding the Bolsheviks together and driving them on to the seizure of power. Such leadership was made possible by the fact that Lenin came to accept Trotsky's doctrine of Permanent Revolution (i.e. no necessity for a long stage of bourgeois-democratic rule) and Trotsky's acceptance of Lenin's concept of the party as a revolutionary élite. There can be little doubt that Lenin was a sincere Marxist, but his general approach was, perhaps, reflected in the title of his last work (January 1923): *On s'engage, et puis—on voit*. And as Carmichael points out, 'What Lenin had done in effect was to transform the traditional Marxist formula that in the last analysis economics determine politics into the Leninist view that political power may succeed in determining economics.'[4]

10. How valid were the reasons given by the Bolsheviks for dissolving the Constituent Assembly? Their main argument (echoed by Hill in his *Lenin and the Russian Revolution*) was that the S.R. electoral list had been deceptive, since it took no account of the split between Left and Right elements within the party. The majority of Right faction over Left (370 to 40) in the Assembly did not represent the wishes of peasant masses who had voted for the S.R.s; the coalition of the Left with the Bolsheviks did. To allow the Assembly to continue would have been to revive the situation of dual power, therefore.

It is true that the act of dissolution met with little protest. It was officially admitted, however, that there had been 21 deaths when the crowd was dispersed on the 18th; Maxim Gorky and Rosa Luxemburg

[1]Schapiro, op cit p. 184.

[2]The final split between Left S.R.s and Bolsheviks occurred later, when the latter began to centralize agriculture under War Communism.

[3]The documents involved are to be found in *Germany and the Revolution in Russia, 1915-1918*, ed. Zeman; Schapiro comments upon them, op cit pp. 175-7; the matter is also dealt with by Alan Moorehead in his *Russian Revolution*.

[4]Introduction to Sukhanov: *The Russian Revolution* p. xxx.

were among those who bitterly protested at the time, the latter posing Trotsky a pertinent question: if the Assembly had not reflected the real feelings of the people, why were not new elections held immediately afterwards to rectify matters?[1] It should also be remembered that the Left S.R.s were soon to leave the coalition and that real power lay not with the Soviets but with the Bolshevik Party. Trotsky's views on the relationship between revolution and what he terms 'the judicial fetishism of the popular will' can be found in his chapter on 'Who led the February Insurrection?' They echo Robespierre and Saint-Just.

11. What effect did the policy of the Allies have upon the course of the Revolution? Is it true that that policy was largely selfish? Lloyd George, in his *War Memoirs*,[2] condemns the 'selfish obtuseness' of the military directors of Britain and France who, he claims, starved Russia of vital arms which they could well have spared. It is certainly true that Tannenberg and 1917 have frequently obscured the help given the Allies by the Russian war effort. Concern for the state of Russia in 1917 was expressed by the Allies only through a policy described by Sir Bruce Lockhart as being 'to cajole or bully Russia into continuing the war.' The visit of an Allied delegation in January 1917 was abortive, largely because of the atmosphere of impending catastrophe. One may speculate whether things would have been different had the Dardanelles campaign succeeded[3] or whether Russian opinion would have been heartened by, say, a successful Stockholm conference in 1917 as a step towards a negotiated peace.[4] But the feeling of isolation experienced by Russian politicians at the time is clear:

'The vicious circle which the Socialist parties were unable to break all those months was not of their own creation. It was a product of the early defeat of Tsarist Russia in the war and the insurmountable contradiction between the necessity of radically rebuilding the country under war conditions, and the impossibility of ending the war without betraying democracy and Socialism. In fairness to the Russian leaders, who were tyros in war and statecraft, one must note that not one of the leaders of the West understood the tragedy of the Russian revolution. Not one could suggest a means of reconciling the conflict between natural Russian patriotism and the need to save Russian democracy by making the concessions that had to be made, in the face of rising extremist utopianism and an irresistable urge for peace at any price. Neither President Wilson, nor his Secretary of State, nor his ambassador in Petrograd, knew anything about the tremendous difficulties of Russia at that period. As is made clear by George Kennan's *Russia*

[1] See. Abramovitch, op cit pp. 124-8.
[2] Vol. I, chap. XIV.
[3] Cf. Churchill: *The World Crisis* chapter xxxix.
[4] Cf. Abramovitch, op cit p. 51 passim.

Leaves the War, Lloyd George, Clemenceau, and the other European statesmen took it for granted that the Russians would manage somehow.'[1]

12. There are further topics arising out of this one, some of which may be mentioned briefly: what was the effect of intervention by the Western powers in the ensuing Russian civil war? What was the immediate impact of the Revolution on the European political scene? (Lenin, for instance, had always had great hopes of swift proletarian revolution in Europe; for a time, events in Germany, in German Austria and in Hungary, seemed to justify his expectations. But ultimately, were such outbreaks helped or hindered by what had happened in Russia?) Finally, what have been the effects of the 1917 Revolution on the ensuing history of this century?

FURTHER READING

I have used the documents collected in

Bunyan and Fisher (eds.): *The Bolshevik Revolution, 1917-18*, together with

Lenin: *Collected Works*, Vols. XX and XXI

and the records of several eye-witnesses and participants:

Trotsky: *The History of the Russian Revolution* (Victor Gollancz Ltd.)

Sukhanov: *The Russian Revolution 1917: a Personal Record* (Oxford University Press)

Chernov: *The Great Russian Revolution* (Yale University Press)

Kerensky: *The Crucifixion of Liberty*

Abramovitch: *The Soviet Revolution* (George Allen & Unwin Ltd.)

Reed: *Ten Days that Shook the World* (Lawrence & Wishart Ltd.)

My great debt to the last-named work will be clear from the text.

Brief introductions to the subject can be found in

Moorehead: *The Russian Revolution*

New Cambridge Modern History, Vols. XI and XII

More detailed studies include

Chamberlain: *The Russian Revolution*

Carr: *The Bolshevik Revolution*

Schapiro: *The Communist Party of the Soviet Union* (Eyre & Spottiswoode Ltd.)

Kennan: *Russia Leaves the War*

Biographies include

Hill: *Lenin and the Russian Revolution* (English Universities Press Ltd.)

Deutscher: *Trotsky* (*The Prophet Armed* is the volume dealing with this period)

Wilson: *To the Finland Station*, has excellent chapters on Lenin up to April 1917.

[1]Ibid pp. 70-71. Cf. Kerensky, op cit, Chapter XVII.

*Acknowledgement is made to the publisher for permission to quote from this book.

Examples of the wider repercussions of the Revolution will be found in:

Ryder: *The German Revolution*, 1918-19 (Historical Association pamphlet)

Zeman: *The Break-up of the Habsburg Empire*

Seton-Watson: *The Pattern of Communist Revolution: An Historical Analysis*

The last-named is probably the most important further reading which one can recommend.

Works of fiction that are of value in creating an understanding of the pre-revolutionary background are plentiful; perhaps Chekhov should receive special mention. Novels covering the revolutionary period include:

Sholokov: *And Quiet Flows the Don*

Pasternak: *Dr. Zhivago.*

the Marxist exhortation

The cover of the first edition of the
Manifesto of the Communist Party

THE MARXIST EXHORTATION

MARX : Our conversation can be assumed to be taking place some time in the latter half of the 19th century. Later on, however, we shall have to assume rather extraordinary powers of foresight as we consider events and trends that have taken place after our death.

I was born in 1818 at Trier in the Rhineland. I am a Jew, and there had been a long tradition of rabbis in the family, although my father was actually a lawyer. When I was six the family became Christian, but religion, the opium of the people, meant nothing to me. I studied law at Bonn University, and then at Berlin. There, of course, I came under the tremendous influence of Hegelian philosophy, though as we shall see, I rejected much of it in the end.

In 1842 I joined the staff of a newspaper, the *Rheinische Zeitung* in Cologne, and became editor very soon. Unfortunately, in the following year the Prussian government took exception to my vehement radicalism and the paper was suppressed. Having married, I went to Paris and there met Proudhon, Bakunin, and the poet Heine amongst others. And it was in Paris that I met you, Friedrich. What had you been doing before then ?

ENGELS : Well, I was born in 1820 in Barmen, not far from Cologne. My father was a wealthy cotton spinner, a typical capitalist, in fact. He was a staunch Calvinist and I found the atmosphere at home stifling. I led a rather gay youth, actually, and after doing my military service went to Berlin University in 1841 and there read much the same as you did. In the following year I went to England where my father had business interests. I was deeply influenced by what I saw there, particularly in Manchester. It was there that I got a first-hand knowledge of the condition of the working class under capitalism; I was much in sympathy with the Chartist movement, and gave it a certain amount of help. It was about then—1844 I should think—that you must have read that article I wrote for a paper on the doctrines of British liberal economists. We then started a correspondence, and I visited you on my way through Paris. On this occasion, unlike that brief meeting we had had earlier in Cologne when you were decidedly rude to me, we saw eye to eye, having developed much the same ideas independently. Our collaboration proved invaluable to both of us.

MARX : Indeed. I owed far more than people realise to your practical help, experience and co-operation. In 1845 I was expelled from Paris at

59

the request of the Prussians. You followed me to Brussels and there we joined a number of socialist bodies, to which we set forth our views. Above all, we fostered the growth of the 'Communist League', for which we completed the *Communist Manifesto* early in 1848.

ENGELS: But we ought briefly to mention what we owed to other thinkers before we go any further.

MARX: I have never denied that, whilst my complete philosophical structure is original and revolutionary, many elements within it were brought home to me by reading the works of others.

Hegel, for instance, was the man who revealed the logical process of the dialectic to our generation. He stated that progress results from the clash of opposites, from the fusion which is created by such antagonisms. The dialectical process is this one of thesis, antithesis, synthesis. The thesis affirms a proposition; the antithesis denies it; the synthesis embraces what is true in both.

ENGELS: Hegel revolutionised German philosophy in the first half of the nineteenth century. But we cannot follow him when he talks of the unfolding of history in terms of 'the Ideal', of thought as the only driving force in history. It is not ideas that count, but matter.

MARX: Of course it is. Feuerbach was quite correct here. Works like his *Theses on Hegelian Philosophy* and his *Essence of Christianity* proved that the ideal is nothing else than the material world reflected by the human mind and translated into forms of thought. As you yourself once wrote, 'Nothing exists outside nature and man, and the higher beings our religious phantasies have created are only the fantastic reflection of our own essence.' Hegel, in other words, had got things completely the wrong way round.

ENGELS: Yes, but it needed Saint-Simon to perceive that the determining factor in history is economic relationship.

MARX: True, and he it was who, at the beginning of this century, saw that the ownership of the economic resources of the community was the distinguishing trait of the dominant minority, was the very trait which made that minority class dominant. We owe much to Saint-Simon's demonstration that history is composed of continuous conflict between economic classes, between dominant minority and dependent majority. As he says, the essence of a class is its antagonism to any other.

ENGELS: It is interesting to note that the very word 'class'—as opposed to 'ranks' or 'orders'—was first used in a country like England only in the late eighteenth and early nineteenth centuries, and was one of the products of the so-called industrial revolution.

MARX: Saint-Simon's work was, of course, vital when it came to interpreting the dialectic. We could now see that the dialectic works through class conflict and not the conflict of States. The fundamental units in the historic process are classes and not, as Hegel held, nations.

And Saint-Simon, like Hegel, believed in the progress of history, though they differed as to the goal. There can be no doubting the inevitability of the move towards socialism. Hegel's dialectic, properly applied, becomes our instrument of proof. We reject Saint-Simon, of course, when he urges the continuance of private property, when he dreams of a community run by altruistic bourgeois technocrats. And though we must also mention Louis Blanc, who, in his book *Organisation du Travail* (1839), insists that the State must be used to set up a new social order, we deplore his lack of revolutionary fire.

ENGELS: Yes, and by the State you must understand we do not mean the bourgeois State-machine, which must be obliterated. The new order will be established by the vanguard of the proletariat, as stated by Babeuf. Auguste Blanqui uses the phrase 'dictatorship of the proletariat'; this will force people to be free.

MARX: Robespierre, Babeuf, Buonarroti, they all emphasised the need for an enlightened body of law-givers, enforcing virtue in the best interests of the people. To quote Buonarroti: 'It is of less consequence, even as regards (and for the sake of) the real popular sovereignty itself, to busy ourselves in collecting the votes of a nation, than to make the supreme authority fall ... into hands that are wisely and vigorously Revolutionary.'

The law-givers, the vanguard of the proletariat, in other words our Communist Party, reinforcing history by teaching revolution, will enforce freedom.

ENGELS: This, of course, is the principle later historians will call 'totalitarian democracy'. As you know, totalitarian democracy evolved, as did liberal democracy, from eighteenth century patterns of thought. The split between the two types of democracy, totalitarian and liberal, occurred during and after the French Revolution. What happened was that the liberal or bourgeois exponents of eighteenth century revolutionary thought became scared by the logical conclusions to be drawn from that thought. They could not see that, if they were to obtain a perfect society, imperfect elements must be transformed or liquidated. It is surely obvious that all those who refuse to aid the realization of our programme for a society in which all men are free and virtuous, all those who hinder its coming, are automatically wicked and selfish and must be combatted. Our programme is democratic in that we are working for a perfect society for everybody; it is totalitarian in that it is a programme for every part of people's lives. Above all, totalitarian methods must be used to bring about the creation of a genuinely free society. Robespierre realised this in the political sphere of course, but Babeuf saw the need for it in economic matters as well.

MARX: The eighteenth century liberals wanted to convince, rather than exterminate their opponents; they also refused to see their democratic programme extended to the economic sphere. It seems obvious that a society with all its contradictions resolved is incompatible with the unchecked reign of man's acquisitive, aggressive spirit in the economic field. The inequalities of private property, the laissez-faire economic principles of the liberals, are incompatible with a perfect society.

ENGELS: And when the bourgeois democrats heard the people's cry for the abolition of property, they soon realised the full implications of true democracy, and reverted to liberal democracy which, far from abolishing the class struggle, is merely a ruse to keep the capitalist class in power and to misrepresent the people in parliament.

MARX: The only cure for the ills of the people is force, the midwife of progress. But how many realise this? Look at our contemporary, Proudhon. He, like me, demands the economic reorganisation of society, for he sees as I do that the State is nothing but the force of dispossession, levelling the majority to create an unobstructed view for the dominant minority class. But look at him! He repudiates direct political action and clings to the basis of existing society, belief in private property.

ENGELS: Fourier is no better. He, like Proudhon, demonstrates the evils of unchecked competition, and of the growth of capitalist monopolies; and, remember, he points out the error of Saint-Simon in working for a government of bankers, industrialists, and technicians. Yet his proposed solution of *phalansteries*, or self-sufficient communities, is just the type of idealistic utopianism we have to eliminate.

MARX: And Owen likewise. And Feuerbach. The latter sees that the idea of heaven is concocted to drug the sufferings of the people without actually removing the causes of the sufferings. Even so, what does he do to remove those causes? The only attitude he respects is the theoretical one; the significance of revolutionary action is quite lost on him. All philosophers have ever done is to offer interpretations of the world; the point, however, is to change it.

ENGELS: The contradictions of the material world which cause suffering, lie, as Saint-Simon teaches, in the economic structure of the community.

MARX: But it was the English classical economists who furnished us with the mechanics of the exploitation of one class by another. For instance, the labour theory of value, outlined by Adam Smith and formulated by Ricardo, is the basis of the theory of surplus value. Adam Smith declared: 'The value which workers add to their materials resolves itself into two parts of which one pays their wages and the other is profit for the employer'. The second of these parts we call 'surplus value', and the money it brings in, which should go to the worker by right, is stolen from him by the employer.

ENGELS: And when we go on to discuss the future course of the capitalist world, we must remember that it has already been forecast to some extent by the early nineteenth century Swiss economist, Sismondi. He has pointed out that whereas all previous class struggles occurred as the result of a scarcity of goods, the introduction of new, mechanical means of production which would swamp the globe with excessive production would themselves, unless checked, create a depressed class of unprecedented proportions. The law of increasing misery we have formulated is based directly on Sismondi's scientific theory of the inevitability of the regular recurrence of economic crises, leading to revolution. And then the solution which Morelly sought, the solution in which misery is absent, will be grasped. Morelly explained this in his *Code de la Nature* as long ago as 1755. The possessors of the key to progress have the absolute right to forward its realization by every means to hand. Bourgeois and humanistic principles of morality are irrelevant, as he showed.

MARX: To think that our all-embracing scheme interprets to the full the whole sweep of history!

ENGELS: So many have thought that, Hegel for one. But we, by correcting and blending their thought, have arrived at the one true conclusion. In possession of this, destiny is ours.

MARX: It's time to recall how Europe took a step nearer this destiny in the years around 1848, and the effect these events had on us. Above all, 1848 was the year in which we flung our revolutionary challenge to the world in *The Communist Manifesto*.

ENGELS: Indeed. You remember it was commissioned in 1847, by the London centre of the Communist League.

MARX: Yes. This was a body whose growth we had fostered, based as it was on other societies like the German Workers' Educational Association. The trouble was that not all members were genuine revolutionaries.

ENGELS: Still, it was most important that the Communist-League programme should follow the right lines. And we certainly scared the Belgian government with it; for its publication we were exiled from Brussels, our home for the last three years.

MARX: Then we went to Paris. We might well have gone anyway; revolution broke out there the day after our expulsion from Brussels.

ENGELS: Ah, but our real place was in our homeland on the Rhine. You had to dissuade me from going there with the German Legion, an army recruited from exiled German revolutionaries which marched to the help of the German peoples.

MARX: I could see, of course, that there was no sign of revolt among the politically unconscious German masses. It was obvious to me that this escapade of untrained intellectuals was a waste of revolutionary energy. And, inevitably, it was defeated by the Prussian army.

ENGELS: Instead we went to Cologne to see what could be done by propaganda to further the political awakening of the German proletariat. There we formed a newspaper, *Neue Rheinische Zeitung*, and you, Karl, were its editor. Even now your inflammatory writings stick in my mind; you were the only revolutionary in Germany with a clear political and economic plan of action, or with a reasoned and scientific theory to back it up.

MARX: Remember that at this time I advocated a proletarian alliance with the liberal bourgeousie, since, for the moment, the interests of this bourgeoisie coincided with the interests of the rising proletariat. Their common enemy, dynastic absolutism, had to be defeated. And the only way to bring this about was to send delegates to the Frankfurt Assembly, was by direct political participation. I was bitterly opposed to the blindness of those rabble-rousers who, by their desire to keep the proletariat 'unsullied', endangered and isolated the masses.

ENGELS: But it was in vain this time. The masses remained blind to their true interests. The parliamentary cretinism of the Frankfurt assembly, the machinations of the liberal bourgeoisie, had deluded the workers and lulled them into a state of beast-like apathy. Their sheer stupidity proved a worse obstacle to revolution than did capitalism.

MARX: It was a different tale in France. There the Parisian proletariat was miserably betrayed by bourgeois liberal cowards and saboteurs, and by the peasants, who are essentially a lower stratum of the middle class (and thus, by definition, opposed to the proletariat). The Revolution was betrayed, as I have stated in my pamphlet *The Class Struggles in France*. Herein I have clearly demonstrated that in the fighting of the June days, revolutionary socialism revealed itself in its savage and menacing aspect. It was the naked struggle of one class against another, and blood was not spared. In this clash, the proletarian class was consciously contending against liberals as well as legitimists. And in this clash, the Parisian workers embodied the hope and despair of the oppressed everywhere.

ENGELS: Tragically they were vanquished; but as the dialectic teaches, out of seeming reversal comes progress. And clashes that spontaneously arise out of the conditions of bourgeois society must be fought to the end.

MARX: The German bourgeois attempt at revolution failed too. The Prussian government attempted to suppress the Frankfurt Assembly. When we supported the Assembly's declaration that all government taxes were illegal, they suppressed our paper too and put me on trial. I gave the court a lecture on the state of Germany, for which the jury thanked me when announcing my acquittal. But by 1849 the only home I could find was in London.

ENGELS: 1848 was not only the year of revolution, it was the year of the revolutionary challenge, our *Manifesto*. Here we stated our beliefs: how the history of all previous society is the history of class struggle; how class antagonism has been simplified into two great classes directly facing each other—bourgeoisie and proletariat; how the bourgeoisie has now won for itself in the modern, representative State exclusive political sway; and how, by tearing away the motley feudal ties that bound man to his natural superiors, and by leaving only one real relation between them—the cash-nexus, naked self-interest has manipulated its power to secure naked, shameless, direct, brutal exploitation.

MARX: But this state of affairs must on no account be regarded as final, as the *Manifesto* showed. The frequent economic crises due to over-production are a symptom of capitalism's inability to control its own resources. And how does the bourgeoisie get over these crises? On the one hand, by the enforced destruction of a mass of productive forces; on the other, by the conquests of new markets, and by the more thorough exploitation of old ones. That is to say, they pave the way for more extensive and more destructive crises and diminish the means whereby crises are prevented. This illustrates the truth that the productive forces at the disposal of society no longer tend to further the development of the conditions of bourgeois property. On the contrary, they have become too powerful for these conditions by which they are fettered, and as soon as they overcome their fetters they bring disorder into the whole of bourgeois society. For many a decade past the history of industry and commerce is but the history of the revolt of modern productive forces against modern conditions of production, i.e. against the property relations that are the conditions for the existence and rule of the bourgeoisie.

ENGELS: Not only has the bourgeoisie forged the weapons that bring death to itself in these gigantic new productive forces; it has also called into existence the men who are to wield those weapons: the modern working class. The bourgeoisie have succeeded in destroying the power of all rival classes, the aristocrats and the small artisans. But the proletariat it cannot destroy, for it is necessary to its own existence. And in the very act of exploiting it, the bourgeoisie inevitably discipline and organize their executioner. With the development of industry, the proletariat increase in number and become concentrated in greater masses. Their power spreads throughout the world, for the bourgeois compel all nations to become bourgeois themselves, with their attendant proletarian masses.

MARX: As you say, the international of capitalism breeds inevitably, as its own necessary complement, the international of the working class, the one really revolutionary class. The immediate measures that class will execute once in power, at least in more advanced countries, are also stated in the *Manifesto*:

1. Abolition of property in land and application of all rents of land to public purposes.

2. A heavy progressive or graduated income tax.

3. Abolition of all right of inheritance.

4. Confiscation of the property of all emigrants and rebels.

5. Centralisation of credit in the hands of the state, by means of a national bank with state capital and an exclusive monopoly.

6. Centralisation of the means of communication and transport in the hands of the state.

7. Extension of factories and instruments of production owned by the state; the bringing into cultivation of waste lands and the improvement of the soil generally in accordance with a common plan.

8. Equal obligation of all to work. Establishment of industrial armies, especially for agriculture.

9. Combination of agriculture with manufacturing industries; gradual abolition of the distinction between town and country, by a more equitable distribution of the population over the country.

10. Free education for all children in public schools. Abolition of

children's factory labour in its present form. Combination of education with industrial production, etc.

This is the programme of elementary reform of the Communist Party, who have no interests separate and apart from those of the proletariat as a whole. Communists do not oppose other working-class parties, though they point out and emphasise to workers of separate nations their supranational class interests.

ENGELS: The theory of Communists may be summed up in a single sentence: abolition of private property. The enemies of socialism declare that this will destroy liberty and subvert the foundations of religion, morality and culture. This is admitted. The abolition of bourgeois freedom, bourgeois culture and bourgeois individuality is undoubtedly aimed at. In existing society, private property is already done away with for nine-tenths of the population, and bourgeois freedom means no more than the freedom to exploit. That culture, the loss of which is lamented, is, for the enormous majority, a mere training to act as a machine. The foundation of the present bourgeois family is based on capital, on private gain, and talk of the 'rights of the individual' refers only to the bourgeois owner of property.

MARX: As we state: Communism deprives no man of the power to appropriate the products of society; all that it does is to deprive him of the power to subjugate the labour of others by means of such appropriation.

ENGELS: These aims belong to our party alone. We openly declare that our purposes can only be achieved by the forcible overthrow of the whole existing social order. Let the ruling class tremble at the prospect of a Communist revolution. Proletarians have nothing to lose but their chains. They have a world to win.

MARX: The events of 1848-9 were clearly a blow to hopes of immediate revolutionary success. However, we had to learn the lessons of these years, to learn that there was no hope in future of any alliance with the liberal bourgeois, to abandon any traces of messianism or utopianism, to set out a new, clear blueprint for revolution, to teach the masses awareness of their destiny and task. The *Manifesto* was a start. In the following years we produced the full exposition of our theory.

ENGELS: I think our theory could be conveniently split into three basic elements.[1] First, there is the dialectical philosophy developed from Hegel, which we turned into dialectical and historical materialism. Then, secondly, the economics of it; the labour theory of value and its necessary

[1] I am following here the division adopted and developed at greater length by R.N. Carew Hunt in his *Theory and Practice of Communism.*

conclusion, the theory of surplus value. The third and final basic element of our ideas concerns the nature of the State and the inevitability of revolution.

MARX: But let us remind readers to be careful with regard to your first point—the dialectic. Do not give Hegel too much credit; he made a great many mistakes. We accept the basis of the dialectic; that is that the world is made up of contradictions, and that they lie at the root of everything, and that only out of the clash of opposites can any true progress come. But Hegel wraps the dialectic in mystification. You have to turn it the right way up, so to speak, before its rational kernel becomes apparent. Only then will you realise the way in which history progresses through the clash of opposites. Any thesis will raise up against itself an antithesis; out of their confrontation will emerge a synthesis, containing what is best and most progressive from both. The antithesis—the negation—has itself been negated, and the same will happen to the synthesis.

ENGELS: And, of course, we are one step nearer the ultimate truth, or, if you prefer, the ideal society. But this is only achieved by what you might call the 'unity of opposites'. Just as a road to the West is also a road to the East, just as North and South poles exist in one magnet, so bourgeois and proletariat both exist, 'in unity', in one capitalist society. Capital presupposes wage-labour; wage-labour presupposes capital. They condition each other; each brings the other into existence.

MARX: In this rational form, the dialectic is bound to be a scandal and an abomination to the bourgeoisie because it not only supplies a positive understanding of the existing state of things, it at the same time furnishes an understanding of the negation of that state of things, and enables us to recognise that that state of things will inevitably break up. The dialectic regards every historically-developed social form as transient. Nothing overawes the dialectic. It is in its very nature critical and revolutionary.

ENGELS: Add to this the fact that dialectical change is a change not only of quantity but of quality. If you heat water, its temperature rises as a matter of quantity; but there comes a point when it turns into steam—a change of quality. Similarly, the inherent weaknesses of capitalism, and attacks on it from without, will prepare the way for the dialectical leap into socialism—a change of quality, a revolution.

MARX: Let us repeat what is perhaps the most important dialectical development from our point of view, the dialectics behind our society today. Feudalism, because of inherent weakness—the inability to accommodate a merchant class as much as anything—broke down, and this thesis was negated by its inevitable consequence, capitalism.

Capitalism (the antithesis) is similarly breaking down; it is incapable of reconciling the oppressors and the oppressed, the bourgeoisie and the proletariat. Following the collapse of the antithesis it is negated by the synthesis—in this case socialism. Every stage in the dialectic takes what is good from the stage before; socialism will inherit from capitalism its advanced technology and at the same time reject exploitation and the class struggle. Ours is an optimistic philosophy; man is bound to progress.

ENGELS: The trouble is that people fail to realize the universality of the dialectic. It is a grave error not to *think* dialectically. Formal logic is based on the assumption that things are static; that this is untrue has been conclusively and scientifically proved by Darwin in the realm of biology, for instance. Dialectical thought acknowledges that everything is in a state of becoming something else; it faces the facts, and is thus clearly superior to formal logic, which tries to pin down words to static definitions. Thus, the dialectic contains the germ of a more comprehensive view of the world.

MARX: Moreover, the dialectic is, like the rest of our theory, scientific. We have thrown overboard the utopian dreams of other writers, we have abandoned that wishy-washy idealism which has misted the vision of earlier thinkers. Our theories are based on scientific facts. Take that example of the scientific nature of the dialectic which you used in your book, *Anti-Dühring*, of the grain of barley which germinates and dies, and from which arises a plant which is the negation of the grain. The plant grows, and produces a stalk at the end of which are further grains of barley. As soon as these are ripened the stalk dies and is in turn negated, and as a result of this negation of the negation the original grain of barley is multiplied tenfold.

ENGELS: Now I think this brings us to our ideas about materialism and knowledge. I always think that that passage of yours from the introduction to *Capital* is a good starting point.

MARX: I'll read it. 'My own dialectic method is not only different from the Hegelian, but is its direct opposite. For Hegel . . . the thinking process is the (creator) of the real world, and the real world is only the outward manifestation of "the Idea". With me (as I said earlier) the ideal is nothing else than the material world reflected by the human mind and translated into terms of thought.'

I would add, however, that both Hegel and I look always for the expression of the universal in the particular. Neither of us, for instance, would consider the political history of a country apart from its art, philosophy, poetry, and so on, since all express a particular stage of dialectical development.

ENGELS: Nevertheless, there is this great gulf between Hegel and ourselves. For us, the final cause of all social changes and political revolutions is to be sought not in men's brains, not in man's better insight into eternal truth and justice, but in changes in the modes of production and exchange. It is to be sought, not in philosophy, but in the economics of each particular epoch.

MARX: And furthermore, we believe, unlike the idealist philosopher, that a real knowledge of the world is obtainable. It may be true that sensations from the material world do not alone provide knowledge; but they are a stimulus in that direction, and as we act on that stimulus knowledge becomes complete.

ENGELS: Just as a cat pounces on a mouse as soon as it sees it. Perception and action are one and the same process.

MARX: This activist theory of knowledge is the essence of our revolutionary creed; it's no good explaining the world unless you act to change it. Theory and action cannot be divorced from each other; they are one. Consequently we shall have to make very great efforts to ensure that those who practise socialism get their ideology correct. Theory and practice are one.

ENGELS: This, of course, is bound to lead to some pretty rigorous witch-hunting in future Marxist parties! But this is as it should be, since our dialectical materialism is the only scientific explanation of reality.

MARX: And so, having established the validity of dialectical materialism, we then started applying it. The first application is to history. As I began my *Critique of Political Economy*, the first question to ask is what principle governs all human relations?

The answer is, not surprisingly, that one end all men pursue, namely the production of those things which support life, and then the exchange of things produced. This is the basis of all history, all society, and its change the basis of all change. Not only the relation of one nation to another, but also the whole internal structure of the nation itself depends on the stage of development reached by its production. The degree to which the productive forces of a nation are developed is most clearly shown by the extent of the division of labour.

ENGELS: So we examined the whole business of production, and saw that there were two major factors concerned. The first, man and his skills, tools and material, we called productive forces. The second, that relation between man and man whereby productive forces are exploited, we called productive relations.

And what did we perceive? Simply that as productive forces (the relations between man and things) change, so they in turn change productive relations (the relations between man and man). This may sound difficult, so you'd better illustrate.

MARX: I will, since this is the key to comprehending all societies that there have ever been, or ever will be. In a primitive society, all men co-operate and pool their productive forces; in their productive relations they are equals. That society will be run basically as a democracy. But very soon certain members of society are able to gain control of the productive forces—perhaps they buy up all the land. As a result the productive relations alter, and the majority finds itself subservient to those who control the productive *forces*. They have to work as slave, serf, or wage labourer.

This split of society into two basic, hostile camps or classes occurred very early in the history of man, and has existed ever since under various guises. This is what provoked me to open the first section of the *Communist Manifesto* with the statement that 'The history of all hitherto existing societies is the history of the class struggle.'

ENGELS: And the next point to make clear is that our materialist conception of history rests on the proposition that the production and the exchange of things produced is the economic substructure of a society that determines the legal, political, religious and ethical superstructure. As you once wrote, 'It is not the consciousness of men that determines their being, but . . . their social being that determines their consciousness.'

The characteristics of the superstructure will always be found to reflect the interests of the dominant class. Morality, law, justice, freedom, are not everlasting truths; they change and are interpreted in different ways by different societies, and this interpretation is made by the ruling class. For each new class which puts itself in the place of the one ruling before it is compelled, simply in order to achieve its aims, to represent its interest as the common interest of all members of society. In other words, it employs an ideal formula to give its ideas the form of universality and to represent them as the only rational and universally valid ones. I should add that for us such words as 'freedom', 'truth', 'right', and 'wrong' are to be interpreted in an entirely different manner to the accepted one. There is no abstract, lasting 'right', or 'wrong', only the criterion of whether things do or do not accord with the laws of the unfolding historical process. And 'freedom' means knowledge of these laws, knowledge of the laws of necessity.

MARX: Precisely. Now if productive forces should be changed so will the whole of society. Let us take an example. From the serfs of the Middle Ages there developed the burghers who dominated early towns—

clearly forerunners of the bourgeoisie. But when great new markets were opened up, the feudal industrial system, based on closed guilds, no longer sufficed. The middle class seized new opportunities, division of labour was extended further and further, and eventually steam and machinery revolutionised the whole process. The place of small, middle-class concerns was taken by great 'captains of industry', the modern bourgeois, men whose despicable existence is the product of a series of revolutions in the modes of production and exchange. And, of course, in the political field they have won complete control of the State for their own ends.

ENGELS: Just as Darwin discovered the law of evolution in organic nature, so we discovered the law of evolution in human history. This is why you wanted to dedicate *Capital* to Darwin, though he refused permission. We discovered the simple fact, hitherto concealed by an overgrowth of ideology, that mankind must first of all eat and drink, have shelter and clothing, before it can develop politics, religion, science, art etc. Therefore the production of the immediate material means of subsistence, and the degree of economic development attained by a people during a given epoch form the foundation from which State institutions, the legal conceptions, the art and the religious ideas of the people concerned have been evolved, and in the light of which these things must be explained, instead of vice versa as has hitherto been the case.

MARX: And so we come to the final element in this stage of our theory, that is the class struggle. Anyone looking at present-day Europe can see quite clearly the great contradiction inherent in capitalism, the antagonism between the bourgeoisie and the proletariat, the oppressors and the oppressed. The distinctive feature of our era is this simplification of hitherto complex class structures. And it is the clash of classes, not the clash of nations, which is the force behind the dialectic of history. A man's loyalty is to his class, not his nation, because as we have seen a nation is only the personification of the interests of the ruling class.

The inexorable dialectic of history has decreed that the class struggle will resolve itself in the comparatively near future. The workers, driven to perform more and more monotonous tasks, will find that, as the repulsiveness of the work increases, their wages decrease. The majority of society will exist in a state of alienation. Their work is not a part of their nature, and there is no sense of fulfilment to be found in it; it is not the satisfaction of a need, but only the means of satisfying other needs; it is work for another, not oneself; in this state of alienation, all spontaneity dies.

But the growing gulf between oppressors and oppressed will end in a revolutionary cataclysm. The result must eventually be the rise of the only social class not yet to have achieved power, the proletariat. Initially it will set up a dictatorship of the proletariat, and eventually, as there is no class to come after it, the classless society will have arrived.

ENGELS: But you must remember that our theory is not fully proved until we look at the more detailed economics which finally vindicate what you have said. The first thing that one must examine is value. Here we agree with the capitalist economists of our day. As Ricardo said, 'The value of a commodity depends on the relative quantity of labour necessary to its production.' Little further need be said about that; the value of one commodity is to the value of any other as the labour-time necessary for the production of the one is to that necessary for the production of the other. On the other hand, such a commodity has got to have some use, there has to be demand for it. A useless piece of workmanship has as much value as air; one has no utility, and the other has had no labour expended on it. We recognise that there is such a factor as supply and demand, but it remains dependent on the underlying labour value.

Labour power is itself a commodity, of course, which the labourer sells to the capitalist. And its value will be the amount necessary for its production and reproduction, in other words the amount necessary for the subsistence of the labourer. Wages will generally settle at this minimum level. Even if wages are raised sometimes, the mass of society is so exploited that, under capitalism, society is unable to consume what it produces, and crises of overproduction inevitably recur.

MARX: And to show how capitalism always exploits, we must move on to the next point, the theory of surplus value. Again we are not being revolutionary in what we say. Let me repeat that Adam Smith, the father of English and indeed all modern capitalist economics, pointed out that 'The value which the workers add to their materials resolves itself into two parts of which one pays their wages, and the other is the profit of their employer.'

ENGELS: Yes, but you make us sound a little too much like bourgeois capitalists. We pointed out that there are two kinds of capital: variable capital, which can be equated with labour power; and constant capital, which is the various means of production—raw materials, machinery etc.—used up in the process of turning out the goods. Above all, labour alone has the ability to produce more than it requires for its subsistence; we have seen that the worker receives only enough to maintain him, but he works longer than this criterion alone makes necessary. If a man works 12 hours a day, in, say, six of them he has done enough work to endow a sufficient number of goods with the requisite amount of value to give him a livelihood. And what does he do in the remaining six hours of the day? He continues to work. Those six—or whatever it may be—hours work that the labourer does create surplus value; and what happens to it? It goes into the pockets of the capitalist. Thus the workers are fraudulently robbed of what is rightly theirs.

MARX: The exploitation of the workers is the sole means of obtaining a profit. Variable capital—labour—alone produces a profit. Constant capital—machinery etc.—is no more than the result of labour already expended on it. Since labour is the sole source of value, it is surely entitled to the value it creates. The rate of surplus value is an exact expression of the degree of exploitation of labour-power by capital.

ENGELS: From the theory of surplus value, three things can be deduced. First, competition forces the capitalist to accumulate constant capital, that is to install more and more labour-saving machinery. He is thus reducing the proportion of variable to constant capital. We have seen how only variable capital is profitable, and so it is clear that the *rate* of profit will decline. Actual profits may go on increasing, but not as fast as the capital that has to be invested. This is what occurred in Europe in the 1870's and 1880's, the period known as 'The Great Depression'. Trade expanded, but the rate of profits declined.

MARX: And then there is the fact that one capitalist kills many. Competition gets stiffer and stiffer, and the eventual result is the swallowing up of small firms by larger, of bigger and bigger take-over bids, and eventually the emergence of monopolies and cartels. While productive power increases in geometric, the extension of markets proceeds at best in an arithmetic ratio. The cycle of stagnation, prosperity, overproduction and crisis grinds on. The lower strata of the middle-class—small tradespeople and so on—sink gradually into the proletariat, though they (and the peasants) frantically resist the process, and are frequently not genuinely revolutionary. Nevertheless, they increase the mass of available 'slave labour'.

ENGELS: And consequently the misery of the workers will increase. As competition puts more and more pressure on the capitalists, so will they have to pass it on to the workers, by lessening wages but lengthening hours, or by installing more and more machinery, thus creating greater unemployment. Large scale unemployment enables the employer to dictate his terms, and wages will take another step downwards.

Actually I think, Karl, that you sum all this up rather well in that passage in *Capital* on the historical tendencies of capitalist accumulation.

MARX: 'Along with the constantly diminishing number of the

magnates of capital, who usurp and monopolise all advantages of this process of transformation, grows the mass of misery, oppression, slavery, degradation, exploitation; but with this, too, grows the revolt of the working class, a class always increasing in numbers, and disciplined, united, organised by the very mechanism of the process of capitalist production itself. The monopoly of capital becomes a fetter upon the mode of production, which has sprung up and flourished along with, and under it. Centralization of the means of production and socialization of labour at last reach a point where they become incompatible with their capitalist (environment). This (environment) is burst asunder. The knell of capitalist private property sounds. The expropriators are expropriated.'

ENGELS: What a message of hope; what a call to action for the underprivileged masses! Now, I don't think we've made sufficient mention of what we think about the State. In the past, philosopher upon philosopher has tried to make out that the State is a desirable phenomenon, and that it exists for the benefit of its members. Whatever men may have wished it to be, we are concerned only with what it has been and is. The State only arises when society is cleft into irreconcilable antagonisms which it is powerless to heal; it is simply the product of the class struggle. Today it is the executive committee of the bourgeoisie.

But when the classless society is established, the State will then naturally wither away, since the sole object of the State is coercion, the coercion of the subordinate class by the superior. Of course, we acknowledge that in the classless society such services as the post office will remain. What all socialists understand by the disappearance of the State is that public functions would lose their political character and be transformed into the simple administrative functions of watching over real, social interests. If you like, the government of persons is replaced by the administration of things.

MARX: Anthropologists have shown that primitive society was communal and that there existed no State. The State is manifestly a part of the superstructure of society: it is the outcome of the productive forces, and does no more than reflect the existing economic state of the country, which it protects with its army, police, legal system etc.

ENGELS: The bourgeois talk of a democratic State. This is complete hypocrisy. How can an instrument designed to suppress the lower part of society be democratic? True democracy would be classless and need no State. The bourgeois liberals lay great stress on their so-called political democracy; but political democracy is mocked by the prevailing economic tyranny. As we have demonstrated, economics are the basis of all society, and if we are not economically equal or free, to talk of political freedom or equality is mere verbiage, a dangerous delusion which will ensnare many. What real freedom has a labourer who lives in a slum and has to feed his wife and children on eight shillings a week?

MARX: Indeed, when the proletariat come to power they must smash the existing State-machine; it is riddled with bourgeois ideology. A completely fresh start must be made; it would be folly to try and adapt bourgeois democracy. On the other hand, it may be necessary for the proletariat to ally with the bourgeoisie against feudalism, so that the capitalist stage of development which is dialectically vital can be dispensed with as soon as possible. Thus, the proletariat allied with the middle class in England in 1832 in order to hasten the inevitable socialist revolution. Afterwards, some aspects of the Chartist movement were a premature and abortive attempt to achieve this later stage. They failed because the middle class had got what it wanted, and, as we might have expected, was not prepared to assist its late brother-in-arms, the working class. Also, only Ernest Jones of the Chartist leaders really understood our doctrine.

ENGELS: Oddly enough, in the late nineteenth century the English Parliament has been the most revolutionary body in the world, incurable bourgeois though they are!

MARX: Possibly, but remember that however capitalism is overthrown, Communism will not follow at once. The prerequisite for Communism is the abolition of all classes. Immediately after the revolution there will still be left the rump of the bourgeoisie, and perhaps an aristocracy. These must be eliminated. To do this there will necessarily be a short period of the dictatorship of the proletariat in which many of the forms of the odious State may have to be employed. But the main difference will be that the coercion will be of the minority by the majority, and not vice versa, as has hitherto been the case.

ENGELS: Then the State will wither away, and a true Communist society will emerge. The subordination of the majority by a minority, the degrading status of physical toil, the severe limitations upon the development of the individual will disappear. Society will proudly inscribe on its banners, 'From each according to his ability, to each according to his needs.'

MARX: So much for our theories. Now I think it would be of value briefly to have a look at the development of socialism from the middle of the nineteenth century to the middle of the twentieth century.

ENGELS: Well, I suppose the First International is as good a place to begin as any. The International started as a result of a visit by a group of French workers to the International Exhibition being held here in London in 1862. (You had been forced to make your home in London since 1849, of course.) The next year, the British workers were again hosts to a similar French delegation during a meeting to organise support for the Polish revolutionaries, and in 1864 there was a meeting in London of English and French workers and Germans, Poles, Swiss and Italians. They decided to form an 'International Federation of Working Men'. You were the key member of the executive committee.

MARX: Our object was to 'destroy the prevailing economic system.' The first constitution was drawn up by some follower of Mazzini, but it was more suited to a secret society than an international working men's federation, and my constitution was accepted by the second conference which was held in Geneva the following year. In fact annual conferences were held in Belgium or Switzerland, but since I had fairly good control over the General Council here in London, I paid little attention to them. Although a lot of laudable resolutions were passed, the attitudes of the various national delegates made any effective action unlikely.

ENGELS: The French delegates were still profoundly influenced by the ideas of Proudhon, of which we spoke earlier. They were completely opposed to any form of compulsion, and held that the State should be replaced by free, decentralized, self-governing communities, the sort of thing that caught the imagination of many of the Russian exiles. Their views got them into all sorts of odd positions, like refusing to demand a maximum working day because it was a coercive measure. They were not, however, anarchists of the violent brand, like Bakunin.[1]

MARX: Bakunin caused us trouble if ever anyone did. I first met him in Paris as long ago as 1844. He was a clever man, and it was always a wonder to me that he did not put this ability to better use than stirring up petty insurrections in Bologna, or producing followers who would throw bombs into the French Chamber of Deputies or at the Tsar. We both agreed that the State must be destroyed, and he agreed with my social diagnosis. But for him, tyranny was the greatest evil, and he was totally opposed to any form of authority. His refusal to accept any kind of plan or organisation in revolution as in everything else exasperated me.

ENGELS: Perhaps this was due to the German in you; it was noticeable that nearly all Bakunin's support came from the Latin countries or Switzerland, where he set up his League of Peace and Freedom. . . .

[1]See Joll: *The Anarchists.*

77

MARX: The Geneva Windbag.

ENGELS: Yes, I remember that's what you called it. And it was two years later, in 1869 at the Basle Conference, that it looked as if Bakunin was trying to take over the International and lead it along his lunatic, anarchist paths. At the next conference at The Hague, we succeeded in getting him excluded. Even so, his influence was dangerously strong, and I think we were right in deliberately destroying the First International by transferring it to America, rather than letting it get into his hands. The International was dissolved in 1876, you remember.

MARX: But you are forgetting the effect the Paris Commune of 1871 had on the International. I had at first opposed the insurrection, since I rather wanted a German victory over France, and it would have been a snub for Proudhon and Bakunin's anarchists. But when I saw the heroism and potential of the French proletariat, I changed my mind, and two days after the Commune fell wrote my essay, *Civil War in France*. In it I maintained that the Commune had a strong connection with the International. Many of the bourgeois-ridden, so-called socialists from England and Germany took fright and had nothing more to do with the organisation. It was thus irreparably weakened, even without Bakunin's interference.

ENGELS: Your writings in support of the bloodshed of the Commune won you notoriety throughout Europe, of course. You were called, amongst other things, the 'Red Terrorist Doctor', I remember.

MARX: Little I cared. After the First International dissolved, I had no desire to found another. It had fulfilled its purpose, and I was convinced that the time for a new international working-men's association had not yet arrived. Indeed, for this reason I regard all workers' congresses, particularly socialist congresses, in so far as they are not related to the immediate conditions in this or that particular nation, as not merely useless but harmful. They will always fade away in stale, generalized banalities.

ENGELS: I, too, was of the same opinion at first. But I hoped that, after your writings had had some years to spread, a new International would be truly Communist.

MARX: But it was not. I know my basic principles—class struggle, international unity, proletarian action and socialization of the means of production—were adopted by the Second International, but these were interpreted in all manner of ways.

ENGELS: You are right, but the great need of the time was to win the masses for socialism. If we had insisted upon a strictly Marxist basis we would have excluded most of the large-scale workers' organisations of the time.

MARX: Yes, but this was a handicap from the start. The Second International was formed in 1889, six years after my death.

ENGELS: Yes. As I say, it was an attempt to overcome the split that had been apparent for some years within socialist movements. By this I mean the split between those who remained loyal to your teachings of the class-war and the revolt of the proletariat, and those others who agreed to work for reform within the bourgeois-capitalist parliamentary framework of government. That year, 1889, two congresses met in Paris, one of Marxist revolutionaries, the other of the reformist parties. They fused under the joint chairmanship of Liebknecht and Vaillant, and the Second International held congresses every two or three years, eight altogether in fact.

MARX: The anarchists were excluded, of course, though a blend of anarchism and syndicalism was all too popular in the years to come.

ENGELS: But the reformist social democrats proved an equal menace. These reformists are extremely dangerous to revolutionary Marxism; by the sops they gain in the way of reform they sap the revolutionary energy and enthusiasm of the masses.

MARX: Tragically, with the existence of a wide franchise in most West European countries by 1900, this type of parliamentary socialism was encouraged. This less-doctrinaire socialism is a betrayal of revolutionary Communism and of working-class interests; there can be no compromise with the capitalist State-machine, though apparent collaboration to further the cause of genuine revolution is another matter.

ENGELS: This problem came to a head when Millerand, the French socialist, accepted ministerial office in the Waldeck-Rousseau Government in 1897. It was not until 1904, at the Amsterdam congress, that reformism and ministerialism were explicitly condemned. The motion stated that the class struggle forbids the entry of a socialist into a bourgeois government. Lenin condemned Millerand's acceptance of office as 'an excellent example of practical Bernsteinism.'

MARX: Bernstein! He had the audacity to attempt to revise my teachings. He 'discovered' that the workers were obtaining better conditions and not worse, as he said I had prophesied; that the capitalist system was getting stronger and not weaker as I, he said, had prophesied. I had, in fact, stressed that there might well be times when wages and so on would improve. His comments were thus totally unscientific, a fact he more or less admitted by pathetically seeking a 'moral' basis for socialism. Sentimental, compromising nonsense!

ENGELS: Unfortunately, his kind were all too successful in Western Europe. Universal suffrage and factory acts made it seem possible to combine socialist loyalties with national ones, and this at a time when capitalist imperialism was extending its sphere of enslavement.

MARX: The co-operation of socialists with the capitalist State ensnared them in loyalty to that State. Thus, the Italian revisionist leaders supported their government in its colonialist war against Turkey over Tripolitania and Cyrenaica in 1911-12. Tragically, in these clashes between nationalism and support of a capitalist State and internationalism and support of a proletarian revolution, the interests of national loyalty were usually triumphant.

ENGELS: The German revisionists, in the tradition of our one-time ally Lassalle, voted for military expenditure on the grounds that 'the German nation is not to be pressed to the wall by any other nation.' Such betrayals reached their nadir in 1914 when nearly all European socialist parties voted for war credits. Loyalty to a nation overrode class-loyalty. This was in spite of the instructions issued by the International in 1907, when the Stuttgart Congress ordered social democrats in time of war to utilize the ensuing economic and political crisis in order to hasten the destruction of the reign of capitalism.

MARX: But in fact you must admit the International had done little to settle the dilemma of socialism versus nationalism, or indeed to frame any coherent principles upon which the social-democratic parties in so many different States could be relied upon to take action in an emergency.

ENGELS: Sadly, I would agree; the Second International, for all its words, was neither revolutionary nor effective. The only party to retain genuine, revolutionary enthusiasm during the war was the Social-Democratic Party of Russia, or that part of it comprising the Bolsheviks. This division between international, proletarian interests and national, citizen-type interests appears everywhere. I always urged that when the Hohenzollern power in Germany was eventually overthrown, the German workers, backed by the French, should carry the revolutionary war against the Russian tsar, that enemy of all workers. But the French workers would do nothing to support the German proletariat, in accordance with their patriotic and anti-German sentiments.

MARX: And so wherever a large measure of social amelioration had been undertaken by the nation State, socialism forgot its overriding international loyalties. In France, Belgium, Denmark, Sweden and Britain—even in Russia later on—socialists entered war-time coalitions.

ENGELS: Things changed, of course, as the war dragged on, and more began to join the anti-war group. The International split in 1915, the betrayers of the cause lingering on in Holland, the true, anti-war socialists setting up their own machinery at Zimmerwald in Switzerland. This body included Lenin.

MARX: The Third International, or Comintern was set up in Moscow in 1919, and became entirely Russian-controlled.

ENGELS: But our work had already borne fruit. Amazingly, your writings had a greater reception in Russia than in industrialized Europe. You were more enthusiastic than I about our new disciples, and at the end of your life were wrestling with the problem of envisaging a revolution in so backward a country. In 1917 it came, with Lenin at its head.

MARX: It is Lenin who has provided the Communist Party with the strategy and tactics of revolution. And those who accuse him of distorting my teachings fail to understand how he applied my basic principles. For instance, though I had written that proletarian revolution was only possible after a bourgeois-democratic revolution, this was only in the context of industrialised Europe. To say that the Russian proletariat was insufficiently developed (as the Mensheviks did, using this as an excuse to postpone revolution) is to miss the point entirely. And after all, the October Revolution had been preceded by the emergence of a bourgeois government in place of the Tsarist one, as one would expect, dialectically. Also, it's often forgotten that the industrialisation of the country was already under way.

ENGELS: True, and Lenin did apply your fundamental principle, the complete destruction of the existing social and economic order and the realization of proletarian dictatorship and a planned economy. Lenin developed the technical details of the dictatorship of the proletariat, and realized them in practice. He saw that in fact it meant, for Russia at that time, the bourgeois State without the bourgeoisie. The complete withering away of the State could take place only at a much later stage.

MARX: Differences, even unjust differences, of wages and wealth would persist. By 1919 he had developed the idea of proletarian democracy, or the one-party system, which is the practical realisation of the theory of the dictatorship of the proletariat.

ENGELS: There are those who think that a one-party system and democracy are incompatible. They fail to see that opposing political parties are merely the reflection of the clash between different economic classes, and that once their cause is removed they need no longer exist. In a classless society there can only be one party, by definition.

MARX: And this party administers the State. Here Lenin has provided Communism with the theory of the administration of a post-revolutionary country. At first he tried to govern through the Soviets, organised bodies of workers who would control the factories or districts to which they were responsible.[1] He thought that administrative functions could be performed by any rank-and-file worker who could read and write. This was not so, of course, and by 1920 he was forced to admit that 'for the work of organizing the State, we need people who have State and business experience, and there is nowhere we can turn to for such people except the old class.' This made full control by the Party all the more necessary, as did the pressures of a civil war which was not won until the end of 1920. The economic policy of the time, with its stress upon centralization and a 'natural' instead of a 'market' economy, became known as 'War Communism'.[2]

ENGELS: But civil war also brought famine and misery. Lenin, Kamenev and others opposed Trotsky's demand for iron discipline, though the latter appeared to be vindicated when the Kronstadt sailors revolted in 1921; the garrison was harshly suppressed. Lenin insisted that the peasants must not be antagonised, however, and that for a time a mixed economy, with a private-enterprise sector, must be tolerated. This was the New Economic Policy, inaugurated in place of War Communism in 1921. After Lenin's death its main exponents were Bukharin and Rykov; they echoed their leader in the belief that the superiority of the socialized sector would enable it to absorb the private one by a gradual process, without violence.

MARX: The Left, as they were called, disagreed. For Preobrazhensky and Trotsky, it was a betrayal of my teachings to allow the economic substructure to be compromised in this way and to jeopardise the development of heavy industry for the sake of the prosperity of peasant proprietors. Kamenev and Zinoviev later subscribed to this view when Stalin began to manoeuvre them out of power.

ENGELS: Stalin was now rising as swiftly as Trotsky was falling. Lenin had realised what was happening before he died in 1924. He criticized

---

[1]For more details of this period, see Carr: *The Bolshevik Revolution* Chapter XVI (vol. 2).

[2]For details, see Carr op cit, Chapter XVII(vol. 2).

Stalin for his harsh treatment of the Georgians,[1] and left a testament which warned the Party against the ruthless centralization of power in the hands of the Secretariat, which Stalin controlled. The trouble was that Lenin had himself created a dedicated and obedient Party, and it was too late to reverse the process merely because men who did not possess his own idealism were succeeding him. With the support of Kamenev and Zinoviev, Stalin survived, stronger than ever.

MARX: Trotsky was handicapped by his evident sense of superiority; his career suggested to many that he might seek to emulate Bonaparte, and his insistence on permanent international revolution was too adventurous for a weary country. Even when briefed by Lenin to do so, he would not stoop to attack Stalin with vigour, and later repudiated one accurate account of Lenin's testament. His own creed, 'My Party, right or wrong', helped bring him down. Accused of denying the possibility of building 'Socialism in One Country', of underestimating the peasants, and of the heresy of 'permanent revolution', he was demoted and, early in 1928, exiled.

ENGELS: The accusations were ridiculous, of course, since they ignored the fact that Lenin's own actions and ideas had given support to all three policies in 1917 or later. The aim was simply to remove Trotsky, and the fact that Kamenev and Zinoviev joined him in opposition in 1926 only hastened their own downfall.

The sequel was ironic. Stalin was now strong enough to dispose of the Right, Bukharin, Rykov and Tomsky in particular. This was necessary since, with the inauguration of the Five Year Plan of 1928-29, N.E.P. was abandoned; the industrial, State-controlled plans of the disgraced Left were adopted in its place.[2] Doubtless, a major consideration behind this decision was the opportunity it afforded Stalin to rid himself of all possible rivals and to increase his own power.

MARX: You're too hard on Stalin. The independence of the peasants could not be tolerated for ever, and only by exploiting them could the proletariat be fed and sufficient capital be accumulated for the development of heavy industry. I would agree, however, that the collectivisation of agriculture—over half all peasant households in five months—was far

---

[1]Lenin saw nationalism as a necessary ally in the revolutionary struggle; indeed, in the case of White Russia, a sense of nationality was almost thrust upon the region by Moscow. Once the stage of bourgeois revolution had passed, however, the principle of self-determination naturally became, in Stalin's words, 'subordinated to the principles of socialism.'

[2]Lenin, of course, had come to expect great things of industrialization, and, in particular, electrification.

too swift. The ensuing slaughter of livestock was disastrous for the economy as a whole, and justified Lenin's earlier warnings on the subject.

ENGELS: Don't stop there. You must also recall the famine of 1932-3 which the Government allowed to ravage the villages, even to the point of cannibalism. Stalin himself later admitted that during collectivisation, 'the great bulk' of ten million peasants were wiped out by various means. Yet during the same period he declared that equality of wages was to cease, as it failed to provide sufficient incentive. The result was that by 1937 the gulf between the highest and lowest paid was greater in the Soviet Union than in the United States.

This was not all. Using the murder of Kirov—which Stalin quite possibly instigated himself—as an excuse, a series of purge trials between 1936 and 1938 decimated the Party. The victims, who were forced to confess to crimes which were highly improbable, to say the least, included all the members of Lenin's Politbureau (except Stalin and the exiled Trotsky), the chief of the General Staff, the supreme commanders of all major military districts, most ambassadors in Europe and Asia, and the two chiefs of political police who had supplied the 'evidence' for the trials. In addition, thousands of lesser Party members were involved. Seldom can the megalomania of one man have caused such bloodshed.

MARX: I must interrupt your invective with some common sense, Friedrich. You were always prone to displays of undue emotion. First, with regard to wages, I expressly wrote in my *Critique of the Gotha Programme* that in the early stages of Communism, unequal productive capacity and therefore unequal rewards must be recognised. Secondly, you should remember that Russia was friendless at this time; the defence of socialism and the defence of the people's State went hand in hand. Thirdly, the supremacy of the Party's dictates over the will of the individual member was not a new demand with Stalin; it was a logical product of our doctrines. The forced confessions you talk of were often made in a sincere and correct belief in this fact. Trotsky has already been quoted in this context. Piatakov, who was later shot, had freely insisted in 1928 that such subservience was essential.[1]

ENGELS: I find these explanations at odds with our original compassion for suffering humanity, and I am little happier about the history of the Comintern. Lenin was optimistic in 1917 regarding the likelihood of proletarian successes in other countries. This was partly due to his brilliant analysis of capitalist imperialism.

[1]See Shapiro: *The Communist Party of the Soviet Union* pp. 380-1. *Darkness at Noon* is also invaluable.

Lenin saw imperialism as the direct continuation of the fundamental properties of capitalism in general, as an aspect of monopoly capitalism, characterised by huge combines and cartels. This is the final stage of the capitalist system, succeeding the primary stage of industrial or flourishing capitalism, as characterised by free competition. Increasingly, a small group of rich, powerful nations exploit smaller and weaker ones, opening up new continents in the process; here are new, helpless markets, new sources of cheap raw materials. But at the same time, millions of recruits—in Africa, Asia and South America, for instance—are added to the international revolutionary proletariat. Finally, as the acquisition of new markets enables the exploiting country to make rapid progress at the expense of others, there occurs a great scramble and rivalry for markets, and the end of any stability among capitalist countries.

MARX: Capitalism proved to have strong powers of survival after the Great War, however. Lenin therefore made it clear in 1920 that foreign Communist parties were to take their orders from Moscow, and to support trade unions and moderate socialist parties in their own countries 'as the rope supports the hanged man.' Is it this you are unhappy about?

ENGELS: No. I would support any policy designed to bring down capitalism; but the Comintern became, under Stalin, no more than an instrument for the protection of Russia. True international, proletarian interests were ignored. The bewildering variations in policy were proof of this, together with such instances as the alliance with Chiang Kai-shek, even when he was massacring Communist workers in 1927, and the refusal to allow German Communists to cooperate with Social Democrats in defence of the Weimar Republic against Hitler. When war came to Russia in 1941 it became known, fittingly, it seems to me, as 'The Great Patriotic War'.

MARX: The success of the Soviet Union and the success of international socialism were one to Stalin, and a large step was taken in both directions at the end of the war. Between 1945 and 1948, Communist régimes were established throughout Eastern Europe. This was achieved through the domination and eventual supersession of 'People's Front', 'Fatherland Front' and similar governing coalitions. In Hungary, the coalition was, for a time, a genuine one; in Czechoslovakia, complete success had to wait until 1948. The strength of the Red Army was decisive, however. Only in Greece did a Communist revolt fail, though Yugoslavia soon adopted an independent position. A broad belt of territory was established in which the safety of Russia and the achievement of widespread social reform could be combined. The Warsaw Pact and Comecon were to epitomise this fact.

ENGELS: These territories were forced to contribute to the material reconstruction of Russia, however, and Comecon required of them an economic specialization which was to the latter's advantage rather than theirs. Stalin had not changed.

Within Russia, the war had brought untold suffering; when further material sacrifices were demanded afterwards, tension grew. Stalin's own industrialisation had created a growing white-collar class who would not forever tolerate a police State and extreme austerity. When he died, in March 1953, the new leadership was forced to allow a degree of liberalisation, and the period known as 'the thaw' began.

Though there were setbacks, evidence of the trend was clear: a new, questioning spirit among the young, new incentives for men of ability rather than sycophants, more spontaneous literature. There was also a new emphasis upon agriculture; failure in this field Stalin had admitted to Churchill to have been more disastrous than the Second World War. The cult of Stalin himself began to wane, and the amount of consumer goods increased.

MARX: Such a course had its dangers. It was not a coincidence that there were riots in East Germany in June 1953. Relations between Moscow and Belgrade were improved in 1955, and Stalin's 'cult of personality' was denounced in 1956; the result, however, was revolt. In Poland, power was handed to more moderate leaders, and violence was avoided. In Hungary, however, the Stalinist premier summoned the Red Army, and bitter fighting took place.

ENGELS: The grievances of the masses and the discontent of the intelligentsia were as instrumental as Soviet 'liberalism' in creating an explosive situation. The proletariat were crushed in Hungary by Russian troops who were repeating the events of 1849. Restlessness in Eastern Europe continues, however, and it is interesting to note that this is especially so in Rumania, another non-Slav member of the bloc. East Germany, Bulgaria and Albania, all of whom have territorial grievances against their Communist neighbours, add difficulties of their own. The last-named has joined China in attacking Russia and her policies.

MARX: Relations between China and Russia have frequently been strained since my death, of course: one thinks of disputes over Manchuria, Mongolia, and Turkestan, as well as the unfortunate affair of the Kuomintang. Nevertheless, the Chinese Communist triumph of 1949 was a great victory for our teachings.

ENGELS: But the claim of Mao Tse-tung to the status of a major Marxist prophet, and of China to the leadership of the underdeveloped nations of the world have prevented true Communist solidarity. The Chinese reject Khrushchev's[1] policy of 'peaceful co-existence' and his timidity over local wars; at one time they announced that they countenanced losing 300,000,000 lives in a nuclear conflict, and they were understandably angry when Russia failed to provide support over Formosa and the offshore islands in 1958. They have nothing like the Russian standard of living to lose by war, though in their communes they claim to possess a swifter route than the Russian to the achievement of a truly Communist society.

The fact that Russia is prepared to aid a non-Communist country like India is a further Chinese grievance; the attack of October-November 1962 was delivered possibly with the intention of forcing Moscow to make a final and uncomfortable decision on this issue. When the Indian Communist Party pledged its support to its State in the face of this attack, the situation of 1914 was tragically, but understandably, repeated.

MARX: You are overlooking several important facts. If the Chinese appear uncompromising in their statements, it is because it would be quite alien to their nature and philosophy to do otherwise. In practice, however, you will notice that they are prepared to exercise caution over Hongkong, the offshore islands, and even Vietnam and Laos, just as Russia did over Cuba. Ultimately, this was true of the Korean war also. You are also premature in describing these countries as Communist when they are still in an intermediate stage. Even in Russia, the Communist Party numbers only about 10 million out of a population of about 220 million. Note the name, 'Union of Soviet *Socialist* Republics'. The peasant basis of the Chinese régime, a position we scarcely envisaged, is bound to create added complications.

Above all, you are falling into grave error by looking at detail alone. What we discovered, and what inspires all Communists, is the key to history, the key that has told us of the inevitable victory of the proletariat and the unavoidable transition to socialism, leading eventually—perhaps via paths we could never have imagined—to the classless society and the establishment of true Communism the whole world over. This is what we discovered, and it was a discovery of a magnitude never surpassed; the key to the past, the present, and the future.

FURTHER DISCUSSION

1. Is the Marxist dialectic a satisfactory basis on which to build historical materialism? Is Marx's selection of material 'opposites' arbitrary; can two classes or systems be said to be scientifically 'opposite'

---

[1]This was written before his fall from power.

as magnetic poles are? Within the dialectic process, why should the best go forward to the next stage, and why, if the dialectic is a universal and eternal law, should it stop with the achievement of Communism? Edmund Wilson's definition may be a useful starting-point for discussion: 'The Dialectic, then, is a religious myth, disencumbered of divine personality and tied up with the history of mankind.'[1]

2. Marxist doctrines fall into that category of philosophy which Professor Popper defines as 'historicism', 'an approach to the social sciences which assumes that *historical prediction* is their principal aim, and which assumes that this aim is attainable by discovering the "rhythms" or the "patterns", the "laws" or the "trends", that underlie the evolution of history.'[2] It is upon such a basis that Marxism is claimed to be a science, a claim many think weakened by what Popper calls its 'unholy alliance' with utopianism, or Talmon 'the Messianic urge that sent Marx upon his quest.' In the opinion of Popper, 'the central mistake of historicism (is that) its '*laws of development*' *turn out to be absolute trends;* trends which, like laws, do not depend on initial conditions and which carry us irresistibly in a certain direction into the future. They are the basis of unconditional *prophesies*, as opposed to conditional scientific *predictions*. . . . That trends occur cannot be doubted. . . . There is, for example, a trend towards an 'accumulation of means of production' (as Marx puts it). But we should hardly expect it to persist in a population which is rapidly decreasing; and such a decrease may in turn depend on extra-economic conditions, for example, on chance inventions, or conceivably on the direct physiological (perhaps biochemical) impact of an industrial environment. . . . The poverty of historicism, we might say, is a poverty of imagination. The historicist continuously upbraids those who cannot imagine a change in their little worlds; yet it seems that the historicist is himself deficient in imagination, for he cannot imagine a change in the conditions of change.'[3]

In addition, Professor Popper claims to show that, '*for strictly logical reasons, it is impossible for us to predict the future course of history.*' He summarizes his argument in five statements:

'1. The course of human history is strongly influenced by the growth of human knowledge. (The truth of this premise must be admitted even by those who see in our ideas, including our scientific ideas, merely the by-products of *material* developments of some kind or other.)

2. We cannot predict, by rational or scientific methods, the future growth of our scientific knowledge.' (The logical proof of this statement,

[1]*To the Finland Station* Fontana edition p. 196.
[2]*The Poverty of Historicism* Routledge paperback edition p. 3.
[3]Ibid pp. 128-30.

which the author develops at length elsewhere 'consists in showing that *no scientific predictor*—whether a human scientist or a calculating machine—*can possibly predict, by scientific methods, its own future results.*')

'3. *We cannot, therefore, predict the future course of human history.*

4. This means that we must reject the possibility of a *theoretical history*; that is to say, of a historical social science that would correspond to *theoretical physics*. There can be no scientific theory of historical development serving as a basis for historical prediction.

5. The fundamental aim of historicist methods is therefore misconceived; and historicism collapses.' (Though not, one should note, social prediction of a conditional kind.)[1]

But in rejecting 'historicism', is there a danger of undue intellectual timidity? It could be argued that it is only by bold attempts to draw parallels, to look for patterns, and to apply them to the contemporary scene that our understanding of both past and present can be enriched.

3. Do movements of the extreme Right and extreme Left that have a belief in 'historicism' and totalitarianism in common stand in closer relation to each other than to an empirical centre? The twentieth century provides obvious material, but wider fields could be investigated: for example, the first half of the nineteenth. In this context, Professor Talmon concludes that 'it was the seeming insouciance about the ultimate things and the pragmatic temper which repelled the Messianic Left (as well as the Right) in bourgeois liberals most. The latter appeared smug and selfish to seekers after the Absolute.'[2] If such relations are discernible, is it possible and is it useful to attempt to discover the psychology behind them? An appeal for the recognition of the importance of this subject and tentative conclusions so far drawn can be found in H. J. Eysenck, *The Psychology of Politics*.

4. How decisive has been the economic factor in history? Is there not some relation whereby ideas and emotions (apparently, for Marx, part of the superstructure) form an integral part of technological, scientific, and therefore economic development (the substructure)? Professor Rostow, in putting forward as an alternative to the views of Marx, an analysis of economic growth (its stages being the traditional society; the transitional society; take-off; the drive to maturity; and high mass-consumption) concludes that

'The most fundamental difference between the two analyses lies in the view taken of human motivation. Marx's system is . . . a set of logical deductions from the notion of profit maximisation. . . . In our system, man is a more complex unit, seeking also power, leisure, adventure, continuity of ex-

[1]Ibid pp. v-vi.
[2]*Political Messianism: The Romantic Phase* p. 511.

perience and security; concerned with his family, the familiar values of his culture, and with other homely attachments; and capable, too, of being moved by a sense of connection with human beings everywhere. His net behaviour is seen . . . as an act of balancing alternative and often conflicting objectives perceived to be open to him. This more complex notion does not lead to a series of rigid, inevitable stages of history. It leads to patterns of choice.

The stages of growth analysis would reject Marx's assumption that a society's decisions are simply a function of who owns property. What Marx regards as capitalist societies at no stage ever made all their major decisions simply in terms of the free market mechanism and private advantage. . . . Nothing in Marx's analysis can explain why the landed interests in the end accepted the 1832 Reform Bill, or why the capitalists accepted progressive income tax and the welfare state; for it is fundamental to Marxism that it is over property that men fight and die.'[1]

Other objections seem to arise. Despite Tolstoy, do not outstanding individuals as well as economic forces shape history? Is there such a thing as chance which does the same, or are we to find in, say, Lloyd George's poisoned oyster and monkey bite[2] the convenient enlargement of minor factors to obscure other, uncomfortable ones? Does the very influence of Marxism undermine one of its own propositions? Professor Berlin writes:

'(The work of Marx) set out to refute the proposition that ideas govern the course of history, but the very extent of its own influence on human affairs has weakened the force of its thesis. For in altering the hitherto prevailing view of the relation of the individual to his environment and to his fellows, it has palpably altered that relation itself; and in consequence remains the most powerful among the intellectual forces which are today permanently transforming the ways in which men think and act.'[3]

It is easy, however, to over-simplify the attitude of Marx and Engels to economics, particularly if their later writings are overlooked. There is a useful discussion of this in Wilson, op cit pp. 181-191; here he quotes from a letter of Engels in old age:

'Marx and I are partly responsible for the fact that at times our disciples have laid more weight upon the economic factor than belongs to it. We were compelled to emphasise its central character in opposition to our opponents

---

[1] *The Stages of Economic Growth;* from the abridged version in *The Economist,* August 15th and 22nd, 1959, p. 529; original, pp. 149-151.

[2] The oyster caused the death of a Liberal Chief Whip who, according to Lloyd George, could have prevented misunderstandings arising between Asquith and himself. The bite killed King Alexander of Greece and thereby helped bring about the Chanak crisis; Lloyd George liked to think this was the cause and not the occasion of his fall.

[3] *Karl Marx* p. 274.

who denied it, and there wasn't always time, place and occasion to do justice to the other factors in the reciprocal interactions of the historic process.'

In *Capital*, Marx can be found writing:

'This does not prevent an economic basis . . . from manifesting infinite variations and graduations, owing to the effect of innumerable external circumstances, climatic and geographical influences, racial influences, historical influences from the outside etc. These variations can only be discovered by analysing these empirically given circumstances.'

Marx was even at times moved to deny that he was a Marxist. On the other hand, it is reasonable to ask how far such qualifications may be allowed to offset the strong element of dogmatic analysis and prediction in his work.

5. More specific points in the economic analyses of Marx and Lenin are also open to question. Can wars, for instance, be explained in economic terms only? Many besides Marx and Lenin would say that fundamentally they can, in more recent times at least. Foch approved von der Goltz's remark that 'Modern wars have become the nation's way of doing business'; when Keynes reviewed the First World War, he wrote: 'The politics of power are inevitable, and there is nothing very new to learn about this war or the end it was fought for; England had destroyed, as in each preceding century, a trade rival'; Woodrow Wilson asked in 1919 if there was anyone 'who does not know that the seed of war in the modern world is industrial and commercial rivalry?'[1] Was this true of the First World War? And of the Second? Or should we agree, with Rostow, that 'a simple analysis of war in terms of economic advantage breaks down in the face of an analysis of how different types of conflict actually came about'?

Can one accept the labour theory of value? How do you equate ten minutes of a surgeon's time with ten minutes of a gardener's? Are 'value' and 'surplus value' anything more, in Marx's system, than abstractions? Does the rate of profit in fact decline when the employer increases machinery ('constant capital') at the expense of labour ('variable capital')? And even if it did, would it be due to the amount of labour employed? If labour alone does not create value, is there any simple answer—demand, the skill and capital involved—to the question of what does?[2]

Again, has the improved condition of the masses under the 'capitalist'

[1] The three quotations are taken from Fuller: *The Conduct of War*, 1789-1961 pp. 124 and 144.
[2] See, for instance, Popper: *The Open Society and Its Enemies* Vol. 2, pp. 169-189.

system since the mid nineteenth century, with the social-welfare state, and non-Malthusian checks on birth-rate, rendered Marx's socio-economic foundations anachronistic? ('I defy you', wrote Cobbett, 'to agitate a fellow with a full stomach.') Rostow offers the following comments:

'When compound interest took hold, progress was shared, and the struggle between classes was softened; and when maturity was reached they did not face a cataclysmic impasse; they faced a new set of choices—between the welfare state, high mass consumption, and assertiveness on the world scene; whereas in Marx's theory compound interest appears in the perverse form of mounting profits, capable only of being distributed in high capitalist living, unusable capacity, and war. . . .

As to unemployment, down to 1914 the amplitude of cycles in unemployment did not increase. In the case of the unique depression of the 1930's . . . this was due to west European failure to create a setting for a prompt move into high mass consumption, and to the American failure to create through public policy an initial renewed setting of full employment, permitting the leading sectors . . . to roll forward and beyond 1929. . . .

As to diminishing returns . . . the scale and pace of scientific enterprise makes it unlikely that we shall lack things to do productively if people prefer a productive activity to leisure. . . . Finally, as to mature capitalism's alleged dependence on colonies: whilst colonialism is virtually dead, western capitalism is enjoying an extraordinary surge of growth. If anything, the capitalist societies' troubles now derive from their reluctance to concern themselves enough with the underdeveloped world. . . . Communism's hope now lies not in crises brought on by a struggle to unload exports, but in the capitalist world's excessive absorbtion with domestic markets.'[1]

6. What is 'class' and how can it be defined? By occupation, or income, or education? The question becomes particularly difficult in recent times; should we now distinguish, as psychologists sometimes do, between an objective definition of 'status' and a subjective definition of 'class'?[2] For the history of communist theory and régimes, there is particularly the problem of the 'petty-bourgeois' and peasants. Were and are the latter basically conservative, as Marx and Engels suspected and the 1848 revolutions seemed to confirm?[3] Or does the course of the revolution in China prove too big an exception to the rule?[4]

A further fundamental question arises when considering the role of the proletariat during the period of its 'dictatorship'. Can we accept Marx's assumption that this newly-dominant class will not abuse its position as

[1] Op cit pp. 529-30; original pp. 154-6.
[2] See Eysenck: *The Psychology of Politics* pp. 14-16.
[3] This is an over-simplified statement, of course. An excellent and more detailed analysis of Marx's views will be found as Note C of Carr, op cit vol. 2.
[4] See Ping-chia Kuo: *China, New Age and New Outlook* p. 140 passim.

others have done; may there not be created what de Tocqueville (in another context) called 'the tyranny of the majority,' and Bagehot, 'the rule of mere numbers'? Or is the major objection to Marx's analysis[1] the fact that, as material prosperity spreads, class divisions and proletarian self-consciousness quickly become blurred?[2]

7. Have the rulers of the Soviet Union since 1917 based their practice on a genuine belief in a clear and all-embracing economic and political creed? Or have they, at the other extreme, paid only lip-service to that creed as a useful instrument in realising their real aim—the achievement and maintenance of power? Does the truth lie somewhere between these positions? Only a careful study of the history of the Communist Party of the Soviet Union can provide the basis for an answer; meanwhile three existing views may usefully be considered:

First, that of R. N. Carew Hunt:

'Communism is . . . a "Weltanschauung" based upon a closely articulated body of doctrine—philosophic, political and social—which claims alone to provide the scientific explanation of the world. It has to be studied as a whole, and it is impermissible to abstract from it certain elements which may happen to interest us and to ignore the others. It is impossible to understand communist activity without a knowledge of the system upon which it rests. Every communist who holds any important position has been well instructed in it so that he knows just where he stands, and has an answer to everything.[3]

'. . . we must not underestimate the influence of Marx's ideas on Lenin, and fall into the error that he simply made use of them to cloak his power complex. In fact, he firmly believed in Marx, and above all in the most fundamental of the Marxist principles that "if a workers' movement is not revolutionary it is nothing." Only . . . Marx never explained how his revolutionary objectives would be actualized, and seems to have supposed that this was a matter for which the revolution itself would provide the solution. That Lenin, faced with practical problems of administration which had never entered into Marx's orbit, should have found himself obliged to adapt the classic theory accordingly was natural enough.'[4]

Next, Edward Crankshaw:

'Often in the past I have been criticised for refusing to put the official Marxist-Leninist ideology into the forefront of Soviet society and life. I

---

[1]Such as it is; a clear definition of class fails to emerge from *Capital*. The word 'bourgeois' is used sometimes with reference to the whole middle class, sometimes to capitalists in particular. Examples of what Marx has to say on the subject will be found in Bottomore and Rubel, p. 186 passim.
[2]See, for instance, Popper, ibid pp. 138-148.
[3]*The Theory and Practice of Communism* Penguin edition p. 30.
[4]Ibid p. 171.

should take more notice of this ideology if anyone could tell me what it is—other than an impressive doctrinal rag-bag full of bits and pieces of ideas and feelings (above all feelings), some of them constructive and good, others plain bad, others simply silly. There are bits and pieces of Marx's teachings about economics, of Hegel's dialectic, of Pavlov and his conditioned reflexes, of Lenin's ideas about capitalist imperialism and, more immediately, how to get power and keep it. . . . Stalin made interesting contributions, some of which were in flat contradiction to anything thought of by Lenin: e.g. his rejection of egalitarianism and his casuistical definitions of self-determination among nations and the nature of just and unjust wars. Khrushchev makes a new contribution every week. . . .

I am not in the least suggesting that Soviet official thinking is totally devoid of ideological bias and direction; it is not. But I have yet to see it demonstrated that Marxist-Leninism in the Soviet Union today means anything more than a general conviction that the State comes before the individual, that unbridled free enterprise based on the exploitation of multitudes by private and irresponsible individuals is a bad thing . . ., that the Western peoples . . . are heading for economic catastrophe, that the Soviet system . . . will prove stronger, and that it is the duty and the glory of the Soviet Union to hasten with all means in its power the collapse of the Western system and the consolidation of her own.'[1]

Finally, the American economist, Walt Whitman Rostow:

'What has emerged (in Russia since 1917) is a system of state organisation based not on economic but on political determinism. It is not the ownership of the means of production that decides everything; it is the control of the army, police, and means of communication. Lenin and his successors have inverted Marx, and set Hegel on his feet. They have operated on the perception that, in a confused society, a well-disciplined minority can seize power, hold it with an economy of force if they maintain their unity, and make the economy grow along lines which enlarge the élite's power.

Ironically, in the communist countries one can now find a fair approximation to Marx's inaccurate description of the capitalist economy. Wages are held as near the iron minimum as the need for incentives permits. Profits are ploughed back into investment and military outlays. And the system would be imperilled if the vast capacity that results were turned to the raising of real wages.'[2]

8. Several problems follow on from this. How great has been the influence of Russian nationalism (and imperialism) since 1917? Contrast with subsequent events, for instance, the Declaration of the Rights of the Peoples of Russia, though the Bolshevik interpretation of self-determination must also be borne in mind; or read of the disillusionment of a

[1] *Khrushchev's Russia* (1959) pp. 140-141.
[2] Op cit p. 530; original pp. 160-1.

leading Yugoslav Communist (as he was then) in Djilas: *Conversations With Stalin.*

Does the role of the Party, as developed by Lenin and Stalin, render the establishment of genuine Communism impossible? How is it possible to reconcile the technical and managerial élite of Russia today with the communist ideal? The 1961 programme of the party expects the USSR to reach the 'threshold' of communism by 1980: will the state then 'wither away' in any real sense?

9. Does the real appeal of Communism lie in its being 'a body of ideas which has filled the vacuum created by the breakdown of organised religion as a result of the increasing secularisation of thought during the last three centuries?'[1] This may be particularly so in Russia, revealed for instance, by the elaborate ceremony—with Stalin ensuring his own place as chief mourner and disciple—following the death of Lenin in 1924. 'The ceremony was calculated to stir the mind of a primitive semi-oriental people into a mood of exaltation for the new Leninist cult. So was the Mausoleum in the Red Square, in which Lenin's embalmed body was deposited, in spite of his widow's protest and the indignation of many Bolshevik intellectuals. To myriads of peasants, whose religious instincts were repressed under the revolution, the Mausoleum soon became a place of pilgrimage, the queer Mecca of an atheistic creed, which needed a prophet and saints, a holy sepulchre and icons. Just as original Christianity, as it was spreading into pagan countries, absorbed elements of pagan beliefs and rites and blended them with its own ideas, so now Marxism, the product of western European thought, was absorbing elements of the Byzantine tradition, so deeply ingrained in Russia, and of the Greek Orthodox style. The process was inevitable.'[2]

Is this analysis reinforced by the fact that, despite his own denials, it was moral commitment that underlay Marx's work, and gave it its force? Is it reinforced by the spiritual satisfaction Engels seemed to find in Marx? Or by the fact that 'as long as (Marx) keeps talking as if the proletariat were the chosen instrument of a Dialectic, as if its victory were pre-determined, he does assume an extra-human power'?[3] How much does the religious element owe to the Jewish 'moral genius' of Marx?[4]

10. Some of the more obvious questions relating to the present scene may be briefly stated. Are Sino-Russian differences likely to lead to a total breach in the foreseeable future, and what are the chances of peaceful co-existence now China has become a nuclear power? What are the

[1]Carew Hunt, op cit pp. 28-9.
[2]Deutscher: *Stalin*, O.U.P. paperback edition p. 269.
[3]Wilson, op cit p. 198.
[4]Ibid pp. 308-311.

roots of the Sino-Soviet conflict? Do they lie in the realm of differing ideological interpretations, or in that of Great-Power rivalry? Is the conflict forcing Russia to grant more autonomy to the countries of Eastern Europe? What signs of relaxation are there in these countries, and why do they appear in some more than in others? Is Russia likely to become less aggressive as she becomes more prosperous, with a wider distribution of consumer-durables? What are the implications for Comecon and for the political future of the Russian bloc of Rumanian intransigence? What is the position of the writer, musician and artist inside Russia, and what arguments are put forward in support of that position? What is the likelihood of Communism spreading in South East Asia, South America and Africa? Is it to be seen as what Professor Rostow calls 'a disease of the transition period,' in other words an attractive power structure for those wishing to push a society and its economy from a traditional to a modern form? If this is so, how should it be combatted?

11. Finally, what of value remains in the work of Marx for those who reject his 'historicism', his totalitarianism and his Communism? Those who are tempted to answer, 'nothing', might begin by reading Popper, *The Open Society and its Enemies*, Vol. 2, pp. 193-211 and Freedman, *Marx on Economics* pp. xviii-xx.

FURTHER READING

Few are likely to derive a great deal of profit from struggling through *Capital* or the works of Lenin, though chapters XXIII and XXIV of the former may be excepted from this remark. (Trotsky's *History of the Russian Revolution* and Engel's *Condition of the Working Class in England in* 1844 are also a different matter.) Instead, excellent selections of Communist writings will be found in

Utley & Maclure (eds.): *Documents of Modern Political Thought*
Freedman (ed.): *Marx on Economics*
Bottomore & Rubel (eds.): *Marx: Selected Writings in Sociology and Social Philosophy*

There are several valuable secondary introductions to the subject:

Berlin: *Karl Marx*
Carew Hunt: *The Theory and Practice of Communism (Geoffrey Bles Ltd.)
Wilson: *To the Finland Station*
Lindsay: *Karl Marx's 'Capital'*

are all of convenient size, whilst for more detailed background there is

Cole: *A History of Socialist Thought*

The eighteenth and early nineteenth century background of totalitarianism and messianism is traced in

Talmon: *The Origins of Totalitarian Democracy*
        Political Messianism: The Romantic Phase

*Acknowledgement is made to the publisher for permission to quote from this book.

Books on the Russian aspect of Communism include

Hill: *Lenin and The Russian Revolution* (a short work by a Marxist)

Deutscher: **Stalin: a Political Biography* (Oxford University Press)
Trotsky (Three Vols.)

Schapiro: **The Communist Party of the Soviet Union* (Eyre & Spottiswood Ltd.)

Carr: *A History of Soviet Russia*

Crankshaw: **Khrushchev's Russia* (Penguin Books Ltd.)
The New Cold War: Moscow v. Pekin

The Eastern European scene under Communism is discussed in essays by

Seton-Watson: *Nationalism and Communism*

Most valuable is the same author's

The Pattern of Communist Revolution: an Historical Analysis

As an introduction to Communism in China, there are

Ping-chia Kuo: *China: New Age and New Outlook*

Fitzgerald: *The Chinese View of their Place in the World*

For those interested in the contacts Marx and Engels made in England:

Saville: *Ernest Jones, Chartist*

contains a considerable amount of correspondence concerning Jones and the exiles, and

Briggs & Saville (eds.): *Essays in Labour History*

contains a chapter on the English aspects of the First International. Criticism of aspects of Marxism can be found in

Berlin: *Historical Inevitability*

Popper: **The Poverty of Historicism* (Routledge & Kegan Paul Ltd.)
The Open Society and its Enemies, Vol. 2

Rostow: **The Stages of Economic Growth* (Cambridge University Press)

The approach of Berlin and Popper is in turn questioned in

Carr: *What is History?*

A stimulating and more liberal Marxist approach to the arts will be found in

Fischer: *The Necessity of Art*

*Acknowledgement is made to the publisher for permission to quote from this book.

the Munich crisis

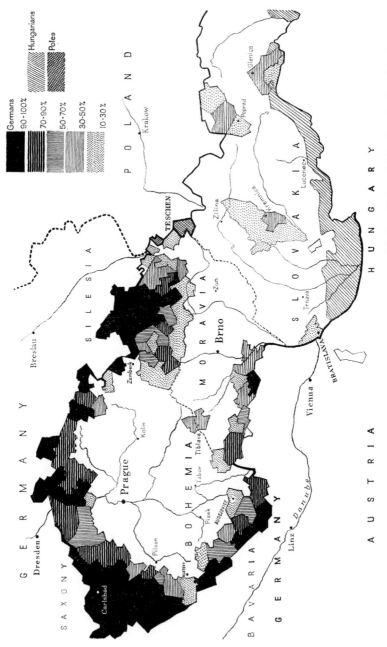

Nationalities within Czechoslovakia in 1936

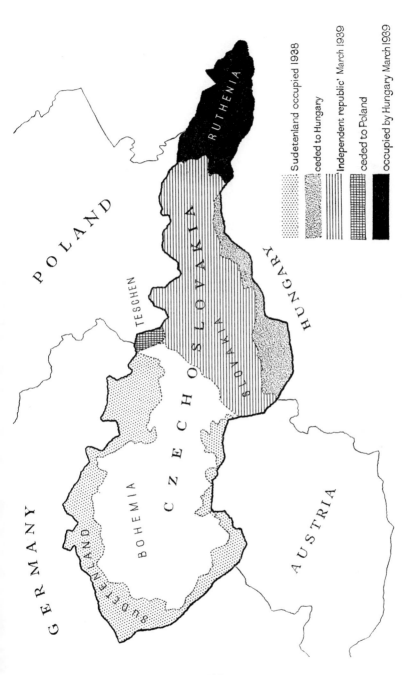

Areas taken from Czechoslovakia in 1938–9: the white portion became a German 'protectorate' in March 1939

Sudetenland occupied 1938

ceded to Hungary

Independent republic' March 1939

ceded to Poland

occupied by Hungary March 1939

THE MUNICH CRISIS

Czechoslovakia was created in 1919 and dismembered in 1938. The defeat of Germany, the break-up of Austria and the preoccupations of Russia provided one form of vacuum for the first of these events; the policies and state of Britain and France provided another for the second. The internal weaknesses of Czechoslovakia were present throughout. The heart of the new State was the Czech population of $7\frac{1}{4}$ million; the remainder, 2 million Slovaks, $\frac{3}{4}$ million Magyars, $\frac{1}{2}$ million Ruthenes, 90,000 Poles and, above all, $3\frac{1}{4}$ million Germans, were hardly devoted to the existing order. Their attitudes varied, but potentially they were explosive national minorities, ready to witness the disintegration of Czechoslovakia.

The strength of the State was particularly dependent on the German Sudetenland, with its industry and the defensive barrier of its mountains which thrust deep into Germany itself. In addition, Czechoslovakia had sought to ensure her safety against Hungary by an alliance with Rumania and Yugoslavia, and against Germany and Poland by a French treaty of 1925 and a Russian one of 1935. This array of pacts was less impressive than it appeared, however. Rumania and Yugoslavia tended to regard Germany as a useful balance against Russia and Italy respectively, and the assistance of Russia was contingent upon the prior action of France. Though Russia had entered the League of Nations in 1934, she remained an enigma, the home of the spectre of international Bolshevism. Poland and Rumania were unlikely to risk the passage of her troops which the defence of Czechoslovakia would necessitate.

France remained the main hope, and the France of Poincaré or Barthou might have justified this position. Now, however, the Fascist Leagues and the Popular Front had rent the country. The Stavisky affair was merely the most dramatic evidence of internal chaos, the machinations of Laval its projection into foreign affairs. The feeling of betrayal at the hands of Britain after 1918 had been deepened by the shock of the Anglo-German Naval Agreement of 1935. The Maginot Line reflected mental as well as military disillusionment.

Britain, too, could offer little comfort. In Baldwin and MacDonald the country had received the leaders it deserved, from Simon and Hoare the foreign policy it desired. The feeling that at Versailles Germany had been unjustly treated was increased by the writings of Keynes and Nicolson, and the Saar plebiscite seemed to underline the reasonableness of the demands of Germans in other parts of Europe. The formation of a National Government reduced opposition to insignificance and fastened upon it the stigma of faction; the Fulham by-election and the Peace Ballot, together with such straws as the 'King and Country' debate, underlined the determination to disarm. When arms expenditure for 1936-7 nearly doubled that of 1931, the indignation of the Labour Party in particular was great. Their hopes lay with the League, though where its strength was to come from was not clear.

Having been for some time the strongest member of the Government, Chamberlain became Prime Minister in 1937. Appeasement as an attitude and a policy already existed. Against the horrors of war were set uneasiness over Versailles and the clear grievances of the dictators. On the one hand was the certainty, spelled out by Baldwin, that the bomber would make further conflicts far more terrible than the last; on the other, the eighteen-year-old settlement that could not peacefully or with justice be defended. Nor can appeasement be understood without recalling the work of Chamberlain as Minister of Health, and his thoughts as he gazed from the vantage-point of a bomber-pilot upon the packed acres of a defenceless London.

Appeasement became a crusade, and to its critics it showed not only deafness but harshness. As Eden wrote in his diary in January 1938, 'Neville believes that he is a man with a mission to come to terms with the dictators'; with Chamberlain, as with Nicholas II and President Wilson, the sense that God was at his shoulder exaggerated the manifestations of an already rigid mentality. Appeasement rejected the wishes of the people at the same time as expressing them. In September 1938, Sir Neville Henderson[1] assured his German listeners that Britain should 'not be rated as a democracy but as an aristocracy. This aristocratic class was at present on the defensive against the broad masses of the popular front', but 'the English, being a virile Germanic race, preferred to be led by hunting and shooting men and not their opposites.'

Sir Horace Wilson would have agreed. Officially Chief Industrial Adviser to the government, he had been seconded to serve Baldwin and was retained in that position by Chamberlain. His power has been described by Lord Woolton as 'unequalled by any member of the Cabinet except the Prime Minister.' In February 1938 a report from the German Embassy in London informed Berlin that Wilson possessed 'a predominant influence . . . as the Prime Minister's closest adviser. It is well known that (he) is decidedly pro-German, but he keeps himself completely

[1]One characteristic he shared with Chamberlain was his realisation of the fact that he had been 'specially selected by Providence' for his post.

in the background.' For Chamberlain, Wilson and their circle, the only beneficiary from a conflict between the two pillars of Western civilization would be the anarchy of Bolshevism.

It was a view apparently shared by Hitler. The Weimar Republic had been undermined by hatred of Versailles and reparations, by business-men and intellectuals, by the political intrigues of soldiers and the un-dignified ruin of the lower middle class. It had lived unloved and it died unmourned. In 1933 Germany welcomed a leader who had clearly stated his intention of living by force and of winning space for the Teutonic master-race at the expense of the lesser breeds of Eastern Europe. *Mein Kampf* is turgid reading, however, and a complete translation appeared in England only in 1939; at the time of Munich, Chamberlain was in wide company in not having inspected even an abridged version.

After 1933 it had become apparent that the Locarno period was indeed at an end. Even before Abyssinia and the Spanish Civil War confused the West and exposed the emptiness of collective security, Germany had left the League and the Disarmament Conference, and had announced conscription and the existence of a military air-force the size of Britain's. In 1936 Hitler reoccupied the Rhineland. The French might have resisted, but it was clear that no support would be forthcoming from Britain; to be able to occupy one's own 'back garden' seventeen years after Versailles seemed a most reasonable demand. In the same year, the Anti-Comintern Pact and Rome-Berlin Axis were signed.

Chamberlain lost no time in pursuing both dictators. By-passing the Foreign Office and brushing aside the proffered assistance of Roosevelt, he wooed Mussolini with an ardour that produced the resignation of Eden in February 1938 and an Anglo-Italian Agreement two months later. At the same time an almost embarrassed Fuehrer was pressed to think in terms of colonial expansion: Tanganyika and South West Africa might prove difficult, but Henderson assured him that Belgian and Portugese territory could be made available. In November 1937 Halifax had also assured Hitler that Britain realised the unsatisfactory nature of Germany's position regarding her eastern and south eastern neighbours, and expressed the hope of four-power talks to help settle the matter.

Hitler had his own plans. On the 5th of that month he had addressed his military commanders and Foreign Minister in the presence of Colonel Hossbach. No time-table for action was presented, though Hitler ex-pressed his determination to solve the problem of space for Germany 'at the latest by 1943-45.' The Czech and Austrian questions must be settled, and though 'German policy had to reckon with two hate-inspired antagonists, Britain and France,' he 'believed that almost certainly Britain, and probably France as well, had already tacitly written off the

Czechs.' Civil strife within France or a war between France and Italy might provide the opportunity for action.

Hitler aimed to destroy Czechoslovakia entirely; he was not concerned with the Sudetenland alone, and was not moved by any belief in self-determination. Few in the West realised this until March 1939. Hitler was ready for war if necessary: 'Germany's problem could only be solved by means of force and this was never without attendant risk.' In response to the tension he now created, others added those acts of nervous initiative which hastened the required crises. Schuschnigg was the first, and the Anschluss of March 1938 bewildered by its speed. The Western powers protested at the method, but it was difficult to resist the result in the face of a 99.7% vote of approval by the Austrians themselves. The strategic results seemed obvious: Czechoslovakia's mountain barriers were partly outflanked. Though Goering assured the Czechs that the Anschluss was no more than 'a family affair', the event roused most Sudeten Germans to a frenzy. Already the Hungarian Minister in Berlin was pressing for talks on war-aims against the Czechs; the jackals were closing in.

The danger was apparent. Beneš still hoped to steer between his own and German extremists and settle the Sudeten question, but he would not be allowed to do so. Henlein, leader of the Sudeten German party, had been in receipt of Nazi funds since 1935. To many, he appeared most reasonable, and he was to make a good impression on a visit to London in May. His policy was otherwise. In March he visited Hitler, who approved of his tactics: 'We must always demand so much that we can never be satisfied.' On April 24th, at Karlsbad, he demanded autonomy for the Sudetenland, reparation for past injustices at Czech hands, and freedom to adhere to the 'ideology of Germans'. If granted, these claims would commence the disintegration of the State. It was clear that France, in the light of the treaty of 1925, must become involved. Early in April 1938, Paul-Boncour, the French Foreign Minister, spoke plainly to the German Ambassador:

PAUL-BONCOUR: '... I consider it my duty to point out that France has given a solemn promise to the Prague Government that, in the event of a German attack on Czechoslovakia, France will come to the latter's help with all the forces at her disposal. This would mean European war.'

At the same time he was urging Britain to declare publicly that if France defended Czechoslovakia against Germany, she too would act. If Germany were allowed to drive further East, he 'could not see where such a process would stop.' Time was not on their side, and to ask Germany to state her terms would be to create 'a terribly dangerous precedent.'

The British Government viewed such sentiments with alarm. Chamberlain had already, in March, decided what his attitude must be:

CHAMBERLAIN: 'You have only to look at the map to see that nothing that France or we could do could possibly save Czechoslovakia from being overrun by the Germans, if they wanted to do it. The Austrian frontier is practically open; the great Skoda munition works are within easy bombing distance of the German aerodromes, the railways all pass through German territory, Russia is 100 miles away. Therefore we could not help Czechoslovakia—she would simply be a pretext for going to war with Germany. That we could not think of unless we had a reasonable prospect of being able to beat her to her knees in a reasonable time, and of that I see no sign. I have therefore abandoned any idea of giving guarantees to Czechoslovakia, or the French in connection with their obligations to that country.'

The same feeling of helplessness was expressed by the British Minister in Prague; Germany could strangle her victim by economic pressure alone, and 'it seemed necessary to assume that no scruples would deter (her) from pursuing (her) aims by fair means or foul.' The Ambassador in Berlin delivered a similar warning on March 24th:

HENDERSON: 'Experience has taught Hitler that only by jungle law can he achieve his objectives, and I hope that by now experience will have taught the rest of Europe that jungle law can only be restrained by measures equivalent to it.'

It was an unusual statement, in the light of his subsequent utterances. On April 1st he suggested that Beneš should 'save his face by yielding to Anglo-French advice,' and it is clear that at this stage it was Britain that was resisting French desires for a stronger front. Even the fall of Blum's Popular Front Government, which pleased Chamberlain, did not alter this situation, as Daladier made plain at the Anglo-French talks in London on April 28th and 29th[1]:

DALADIER: 'Herr Henlein's real object is the destruction of the Czechoslovak State. . . . It is not really at Prague that it is necessary to bring pressure to bear. . . . Today we are faced with the question of Czechoslovakia. Tomorrow we may be faced with that of Rumania . . . (and) if and when Germany has secured the petrol and wheat resources of Rumania, she will then turn against the Western Powers. . . . We are at present still able to place obstacles in her path, but if we fail to do so now, we shall then, in my view, make a European war inevitable

[1]There is good reason to believe, however, that Daladier was secretly anxious for pressure to be put on the Czechs.

107

in the near future, and I am afraid that we would certainly not win such a war. . . .'

This was not the language Chamberlain wanted to hear. He assured the French that 'We would not, in our representations at Prague, press Dr. Beneš to accept terms which, in effect, meant the destruction of his country.' He 'doubted very much whether Herr Hitler really desired to destroy the Czechoslovak State. . . . He doubted whether at the present moment he wished to bring about the "Anschluss" of the Sudeten districts with Germany. . . .'[1] Even if we fought Germany and won, added Halifax, one would question whether 'it would in fact be possible to re-establish the Czechoslovak State on its present basis.' These sentiments were repeated by Chamberlain a few days later in an 'off the record' talk to American and Canadian newspaper representatives.

Daladier gave in, and Britain was left to put pressure on the Czechs. On May 4th, Henderson was instructed to ask the German Government if it could 'indicate the lines of a settlement which in their view would be satisfactory to the Sudeten Deutsch'; Britain would then 'consider how far they could recommend acceptance by the Czechoslovak Government.' Five days later, Henderson's First Secretary expressed matters more clearly to an official of the German Foreign Ministry:

KIRKPATRICK: 'If the German Government will advise the British Government confidentially what solution . . . they are striving after, I believe that I can assure you that the British Government will bring such pressure to bear in Prague that the Czechoslovak Government will be compelled to accede to the German wishes.'

The Ambassador himself assured Ribbentrop that he was 'preaching to one already converted' when he asserted that the existing Czech State could not be sustained.

Meanwhile, the Czech Army worked furiously to erect new defences on the old Austrian border. Beneš admitted in private that a 'State composed of different nationalities' would have to supersede a 'national State'; his ideas included a new Language Law, a Nationality Statute, and the prevention of 'pin-pricks' previously inflicted by minor Czech officials. 'Self-administration' could be granted the Germans, though not full autonomy, and negotiations with the Sudeten German Party were eventually arranged. When the British Minister in Prague expressed hopes of final settlement to his German colleague, however, the latter 'smiled at the word final, saying that nothing was ever final . . .'; in May, Henlein

---

[1]He added, however, that it 'made his blood boil to see Germany getting away with it time after time and increasing her domination over free peoples.'

informed the Czech Government that negotiations could not, after all, take place until the constitutional rights of the Sudeten Germans were guaranteed.

On May 21st, French fears appeared to be justified. The British Minister in Prague telegraphed:

NEWTON: 'Czechoslovak General Staff believes movement of German troops in the direction of Czechoslovak frontier to be general. . . . There is a feeling . . . that Czechoslovakia cannot tolerate German provocation much longer. . . . The town . . . is full of rumours of mobilisation and cars are certainly being requisitioned.'

The French reacted immediately:

BONNET: 'France will respect her treaty undertakings and provide the utmost help to Czechoslovakia if she is the victim of aggression.'

On the 22nd, Henderson was ordered to convey a personal message to Ribbentrop from the British Foreign Secretary:

HALIFAX: 'If resort is had to forcible measures, it is quite impossible for me or for him to foretell the results that may follow, and I would beg him not to count upon this country being able to stand aside if from any precipitate action there should start European conflagration.'

The statements appeared more formidable than was really the case, however. A further message left the Foreign Office that day:

HALIFAX: 'If . . . the French Government were to assume that His Majesty's Government would at once take joint military action with them to preserve Czechoslovakia against German aggression, it is only fair to warn them that our statements do not warrant any such assumption.'

Bonnet, for his part, had already warned the Czechs not to mobilise any further. He told the British Ambassador that 'if Czechoslovakia were really unreasonable the French Government might well declare that France considered herself released from her bond.' (According to Caillaux, Daladier later told him that, even had the Germans attacked, he would never have signed the decree of mobilisation.) Halifax was delighted with Bonnet's remark, and spent the next six weeks urging him to repeat it to the Czechs; when, after much wriggling, Bonnet was forced to reveal that he had not done so, he received a polite, but heavy rebuke.

The 'May scare' was unfounded in that German troops had not, in fact, moved. The common assumption was, however, that Hitler had been forced to back down. Chamberlain wrote privately that the incident showed 'how utterly untrustworthy and dishonest the German government is'; Western newspapers crowed. Hitler was enraged, and never forgave the Czechs for this humiliation. 'Operation Green', the plan for attacking Czechoslovakia, had been discussed by Hitler and Keitel on April 21st; on May 30th, a further directive was issued:

HITLER: 'It is my unalterable intention to smash Czechoslovakia by military action in the near future. It is the business of the political leadership to await or bring about the suitable moment from a political and military point of view.'

At the same time, work on Germany's Western Wall was to be speeded to the utmost. There were moments after this, it is true, when a less frenzied tone was used, though this usually seems to have been the work of others. On June 18th, for instance, a draft directive was prepared by the General Staff for Hitler's signature:

HITLER: 'I shall . . . only decide to take action against Czechoslovakia if, as in the case of the occupation of the demilitarized zone and the entry into Austria, I am firmly convinced that France will not march and therefore Britain will not intervene either.'

It should be remembered that the General Staff were anxious to avoid war; Ribbentrop, for his part, was relating in August that Hitler was 'firmly resolved to settle the Czech affair by force of arms.'[1] On the 23rd August, Hitler remarked to a Hungarian Minister: 'He who wants to sit at the table must at least help in the kitchen.'

Meanwhile, tension in Czechoslovakia was rising. The manning of frontier defences in May had led to bitter Sudeten protests. Children of both nationalities were being encouraged to display their chauvinism—the singing of 'ribald songs about Herr Hitler' giving rise to protest, for instance. A venomous press campaign in Poland concerning the Teschen area showed that Hungary was not alone in wishing Germany well. The feeling of helplessness that was being created is epitomised by one of Newton's despatches from Prague: 'If we try first one thing, then another, some solution may emerge.'

The efforts of Newton and of Halifax himself were being sabotaged by the Ambassador in Berlin. Halifax had made it clear to Henderson that his policy was to warn the Czechs what Britain might *not* do, but at the same time indicate to Germany what she might *have* to do. Henderson sent frequent assurances to London of the manful way in which he was obeying these instructions. On June 1st, he told the German State

[1]He added a remark that is the quintessence of Ribbentrop: he expected that he would be at the Fuehrer's side at the head of the leading armoured division.

Secretary, Weizsäcker, that Britain and France had warned the Czechs that they would not stand by her if she were unreasonable. At a party given by the Military Attaché early in August, the Ambassador talked to the Head of German Army Intelligence, and 'repeatedly emphasised . . . that Great Britain would not think of risking even one sailor or airman for Czechoslovakia. . . .' The Fuehrer was informed.

Henderson's personal convictions deserve careful consideration, however. One was that the Sudeten Germans has a strong moral case. On June 30th, he wrote that the May scare had 'obscured in British eyes the essential and fundamental issue'; this was that a group 'nearly as numerous as the population of Norway' were claiming autonomy on the principle of self-determination, a principle upon which the British Empire rested. Henderson further believed, correctly, that the German Army did not yet consider itself ready for war, and that Austria had not yet been digested. Before such conditions changed, the Czech problem must be finally settled. 'It might help sometimes to give credit on the chance of encouraging the German to believe that he is a good boy. He is not, but he is more likely to be if occasionally you treat him as if he were.'[1] 'I do not see how Beneš can have it both ways. He cannot hope to keep 3 million Germans permanently and unwillingly in a position of inferiority to 7 million Czechs, except by force. . . . Either therefore he must treat them as equals . . . or he must make up his mind to lose them.' 'For the moment a quiet life for the Sudeten would, I believe, satisfy Hitler.'

Discussions between Henlein and Hodža, the Prime Minister, had begun on May 23rd. On June 8th the Sudeten German Party put its demands in writing; they included a separate National Diet, total autonomy, and compensation for past damages suffered at Czech hands. Hodža's own proposals were fiercely contested within the Cabinet[2] and rejected there in July. Bodies such as the Officers' Association denounced concession. Newton later provided an excellent summary of the state of the country between March and September:

NEWTON : 'Since (the Anschluss) the Czech public has been subjected to a continued series of shocks, for, having basked for years in the sunshine of the Beneš optimism, it had failed to appreciate, in its heart if not in its head, how the rise of Hitler Germany had completely transformed the position of this country and destroyed the dream of gradually assimilating the Sudeten Germans into the Czech mould. The Government . . . having created the "Czech myth" and fed the

---

[1]Henderson wrote in 1940 that the world would not 'have failed to acclaim Hitler as a great German if he had known when and where to stop; even, for instance, after Munich and the Nuremberg decrees for the Jews.'

[2]The Government was made up of six separate parties.

public on it for so many years, ... were unable, or unwilling, to undertake the complete *volte-face* which the new state of affairs demanded. ... Since then the country has been living in a state of permanent crisis. ... While the pressure from the Reich and the attitude of the Sudeten Germans have naturally angered the Czech public ... the pressure from the friendly Powers has tended to bewilder it. ... The resentment is, however, not directed only against Great Britain ... it falls also upon the leaders of the country who are thought to be responsible for having landed it in its present undignified and dangerous position.'

Inevitably, negotiations made no substantial progress, though Britain, and to a lesser extent France, were putting what Halifax described as 'the greatest possible pressure upon Dr. Beneš in person.' The Foreign Secretary was in frequent contact with Henlein through 'our intermediary'; it is clear from the documents that Halifax proved a ready listener, and that he distrusted Beneš.[1] The latter might eventually have to accept a plebiscite internally and neutrality in international politics, though he would still receive no guarantee from Britain. War would serve the purposes only of those whom Henderson described as 'Jews, communists and doctrinaires ... for whom Nazism is anathema. ...'

As the summer dragged on, Chamberlain and Halifax decided that a British mediator might break the deadlock. The latter had in mind 'an ex-Governor of an Indian Province'; tactfully, the Minister in Prague suggested to his Lordship that 'however foolishly', this might be regarded as derogatory by the Czech Government. Eventually Lord Runciman was decided upon,[2] and the proposal was forced upon Beneš. The moment had come, as Henderson wrote, 'for Prague to get a real twist of the screw.' When the President was first told of the idea, 'he seemed greatly taken aback and much upset, flushing slightly and hardly recovering his full equanimity ... for over two hours'; it appeared that the sovereignty of his State was being undermined. By July 23rd, however, Beneš had given in. A request for a mediator was sent to London, ostensibly on the initiative of the Czechs themselves. In reply, it was asserted that Runciman would be acting in a capacity independent of the British Government; no one believed it, and the comments of Berlin were reserved to the point of coolness. During the weeks that followed, the Runciman mission was swallowed up in the hopeless turbulence of what their leader was soon wearily describing as 'this accursed country.'

[1] It would appear that those who suspected Beneš of delaying may well have been correct. The latter assumed that France and Britain would stand by him in a crisis.

[2] According to the Soviet Ambassador in London, Runciman was not certain of the whereabouts of Czechoslovakia.

Warnings of Hitler's intentions reached London through Rumania, Yugoslavia, Switzerland, and the Military Attaché in Berlin. On September 8th, the British Minister in Belgrade wrote:

SHONE: 'German Military Attaché... said Nazi leaders in reality cared little about the Sudeten question though they required a satisfactory solution of it for window dressing. What they did want and what they would sooner or later seek to get, for economic reasons, was Czechoslovakia itself, as other means of improving economic conditions in Germany had failed.'

Warnings were also conveyed by messenger on behalf of those members of the German Foreign Office and Army Staff who felt that ruin must attend Hitler's plans. General Beck had resigned, and a *putsch* was being prepared in the event of an attack on Czechoslovakia. 'Germany,' commented Schacht to Henderson, 'is at the mercy of pathological individuals.' It was announced that there would be additional troop movements and partial mobilisation exercises during September; arms were being smuggled into the Sudetenland. The Nazi Party rally at Nuremberg and Hitler's speech on that occasion were awaited with growing apprehension. 'I do wish it might be possible,' wrote Henderson, 'to get at any rate *The Times*, Camrose, Beaverbrook Press etc. to write up Hitler as the apostle of Peace.'

The French Government suggested to the British that renewed warnings should be given to Germany. In a speech on August 27th, Sir John Simon declared that local wars would spread, and on September 2nd Bonnet reminded the German Ambassador of French obligations. Neither statement was a true reflection of the situation, however. Bonnet had one eye on posterity: he had placed his statement 'among the records of the Quai d'Orsay as an historical document.' For Britain, Newton warned a shaken Beneš that his country would support Henlein's Karlsbad demands rather than risk war. Four days later, on September 7th, Beneš invited the Sudeten German leaders to write out their proposals in full—they would all be met. Henlein, horrified, gave orders that an incident should be staged which would provide an escape from this embarrassing situation, and by the 8th it was done.

Chamberlain remained convinced that no guarantee could be given to Czechoslovakia. On the 11th September, he wrote in his diary:

CHAMBERLAIN: 'I fully realise that if, eventually, things go wrong and the aggression takes place, there will be many, including Winston, who will say that the British government must bear the responsibility, and that if only they had had the courage to tell Hitler now that, if he used force, we should at once declare war, that would have stopped him. By that time it will be impossible to prove the contrary, but I am satisfied that we should be wrong to allow . . . the decision as to peace or war to pass out of our hands into those of the ruler of another country, and a lunatic at that. . . . You should never menace until you are in a position to carry out your threats, and . . . we are certainly not in a position in which our military advisers would feel happy in undertaking to begin hostilities if we were not forced to do so.'

One dramatic move remained possible, however. On the 3rd, he had written to a member of his family:

CHAMBERLAIN: 'Is it not positively horrible to think that the fate of hundreds of millions depends on one man, and he is half mad? I keep racking my brains to try and devise some means of averting a catastrophe, if it should seem to be upon us. I thought of one so unconventional and daring that it rather took Halifax's breath away. But since Henderson thought it might save the situation at the eleventh hour, I haven't abandoned it, though I hope all the time that it won't be necessary to try it.'

If all else failed, he would see Hitler in person. He had reminded Halifax a month before that the dictators were men of moods: catch them at the right time, and they would come to terms with Britain, otherwise they might 'shut up like an oyster.'

Chamberlain had not yet decided on surrender, however, and on the 11th repeated the warning that Britain might well fight over Czechoslovakia. But any possible stand was already being undermined. On September 7th, *The Times* produced a suggestion which was inevitably regarded as being officially inspired:

THE TIMES: 'It might be worthwhile for the Czechoslovak Government to consider whether they should exclude altogether the project which has found favour in some quarters, of making Czechoslovakia a more homogeneous state by the secession of that fringe of alien populations who are contiguous to the nation with which they are united by race. In any case the wishes of the people would seem to be a vitally important element in any solution that can hope to be regarded as permanent. . . .'

Neither Hitler, nor Henlein, nor Runciman had, at the time, openly gone as far as this, though in France *La République* had anticipated it by a day. In addition, a warning that Britain might have to fight which Halifax, on the 9th, ordered Henderson to transmit to Hitler 'without delay' was witheld. The Ambassador urged that it would be fatal to 'repeat May

21st,' and his submission was accepted on the understanding that all other prominent Nazis gathered for the Party Rally were warned in the Fuehrer's place. Henderson obeyed. The German report on his stay at Nuremberg added, however, that he 'expressed his aversion to the Czechs in very strong terms'; when Goering suggested that Britain might disclaim all interest in Czechoslovakia if the four best stags in the Reich were put at Halifax's disposal, he was told: 'Gladly for my part; but unfortunately the decision does not rest with me.'

Bonnet, for his part, was privately remarking that France had no intention of 'jumping from the Eiffel Tower', playing down assurances given by Russia, and making the most of Colonel Lindbergh's report of German air superiority. He now gathered further ammunition to use against Daladier:[1]

BONNET: 'What answer would His Majesty's Government give to the question from the French Government, in the event of a German attack on Czechoslovakia: "We are going to march, will you march with us?" '

HALIFAX: 'The question itself, though plain in form, cannot be dissociated from the circumstances in which it might be posed, which are necessarily at this stage completely hypothetical.'

Phipps reported that Bonnet 'seemed genuinely pleased at the negative nature of your reply,' appearing 'completely to have lost his nerve.' Hitler's speech to the baying crowds at Nuremberg on the 12th was calculated to further the process:

HITLER: 'You will understand, my comrades, that a Great Power cannot for a second time suffer such infamous encroachments on its rights.... I am in no way willing that here in the heart of Germany, a second Palestine should be permitted to arise. The poor Arabs are defenceless and deserted. The Germans in Czechoslovakia are neither defenceless nor ... deserted, and people should take notice of that fact.'

The speech provoked riots in the Sudetenland, huge crowds assembling at Eger and Karlsbad. Scores of Jewish shop windows were broken and tanks and armoured cars were called in under martial law. Henlein fled across the border, where he organised a Sudeten Freikorps:

HENLEIN: 'I hereby declare before the whole world that by the employment of machine guns, armoured cars, and tanks against the defenceless Sudeten Germans, the Czech people's system of oppression has reached a climax.... All attempts to persuade the Czech people ...

[1]'Historic documents' were no longer in mind: Bonnet pressed Phipps to transmit his question without recording it officially.

to accept an honourable and just settlement have been wrecked by their implacable determination to destroy us. . . . We wish to live as free Germans! . . . We want to return to the Reich!'

Clearly, it was time for Chamberlain's personal attempt. On the 13th, he telegraphed Hitler:

CHAMBERLAIN: 'In view of increasingly critical situation I propose to come over at once to see you with a view to trying to find peaceful solution. I propose to come by air, and am ready to start tomorrow. Please indicate earliest time at which you can see me and suggest place of meeting. Should be grateful for very early reply.'

It was agreed that the two men should meet at Berchtesgaden on the 15th. The widespread acclaim which greeted the announcement of the fact may be epitomised by one newspaper:

LE MATIN: 'A man of sixty nine, making his first aeroplane flight, goes by air to another man to see if he can banish the frightful nightmare which hangs over us and save humanity. All honour to him! If he succeeds, Mr. Chamberlain will go down in history as one of the greatest conquerors of all time; the conqueror of peace.'

The Prime Minister later recorded his own impressions of the event:

CHAMBERLAIN: 'I felt quite fresh and was delighted with the enthusiastic welcome of the crowds who were waiting in the rain, and who gave me the Nazi salute and shouted "heil" at the tops of their voices all the way to the station. There we entered Hitler's special train for the three hours journey to Berchtesgaden. . . . All the way up there were people at the crossings, the stations, and at the windows of the houses, all heiling and saluting. . . . We entered the Brown House . . . (and) sat down, I next to Hitler, with the interpreter on his other side. He seemed very shy, and his features did not relax while I endeavoured to find small talk. . . .

"I have often heard of this room, but it's much larger than I expected".'

HITLER: 'It is you who have the big rooms in England.'

CHAMBERLAIN: 'You must come and see them sometime.'

HITLER: 'I should be received with demonstrations of disapproval.'

CHAMBERLAIN: 'Well, perhaps, it would be wise to choose the moment.'

At this Hitler permitted himself the shadow of a smile. . . .
For the most part Hitler spoke quietly and in low tones. I did not see

any trace of insanity, but occasionally he became very excited and poured out his indignation against the Czechs in a torrent of words.'

HITLER: 'I would, of course, be sorry if a world war should result from this problem. This danger is, however, incapable of making me falter in my determination. . . . I do not wish that any doubts should arise as to my absolute determination not to tolerate any longer that a small, second-rate country should treat the mighty thousand-year-old German Reich as something inferior. . . . Whole villages in the Sudeten German region have been evacuated by their inhabitants, 10,000 refugees are already on German soil, places have been attacked with gas, the number of dead already amount to 300 . . . I am firmly resolved to act quickly.'

CHAMBERLAIN: 'If you are determined to settle the matter by force without waiting even for a discussion between ourselves to take place, what did you let me come here for? I have wasted my time . . . I can state personally that I recognise the principle of the detachment of the Sudeten areas. The difficulty seems to me to lie in the implementation of this principle in . . . practice.'

Hitler's 'facts' were without foundation. He agreed, however, to hold his hand whilst Chamberlain consulted his colleagues. He was convinced that the Czechs would refuse any proposals for the cession of territory, and this would then isolate them from Britain and France; his own deadline of October 1st remained, and military preparations continued. Chamberlain wrote privately:

CHAMBERLAIN: '(By the end of the talk) I had established a certain confidence, which was my aim, and on my side, in spite of the hardness and ruthlessness I thought I saw in his face, I got the impression that here was a man who could be relied upon when he had given his word.'

He had now to coerce Daladier, and on the 18th, Anglo-French talks were held in London. Neither side wished to be the first to state the unpleasant necessity, and there was much polite passing of the initiative to and fro. Conveniently, Chamberlain was able to report that Runciman blamed Beneš for the present, acute state of affairs, and that he advocated complete self-determination. This did not remove Daladier's anxiety:

DALADIER: 'I fear that Germany's real aim is the disintegration of Czechoslovakia and the realisation of pan-German ideals through a march to the East. . . . In a very short time, Germany will be master of Europe. . . .'

CHAMBERLAIN: 'I am convinced that it would not be the slightest use to suggest any alternative proposals. The time for that has passed. Negotiations cannot be resumed except on the basis of considering ways and means to put the principle of self-determination into effect. If we will not accept this basis, it means war. . . .'

Reluctantly, Daladier gave way; equally reluctantly, Chamberlain promised that Britain would join France in guaranteeing the rump of the Czech State. It remained only to suggest, in delicate fashion, the threat which France must use in the last resort:

> 'Mr. Chamberlain had one last question to ask. What would be the position if Dr. Beneš said "No" in reply to our representations? M. Daladier did not think such a reply would be possible . . . (but) in that event . . . the Franco-Czechoslovak Treaty of Assistance would come into force.
>
> Mr. Chamberlain asked M. Daladier whether he contemplated that it might be left to M. Beneš to take a decision which would certainly involve France and might perhaps also involve this country in war. . . . M. Daladier replied that the strongest pressure would have to be brought to bear on Dr. Beneš. . . . Mr. Chamberlain had thought it necessary to raise this point, but he did not wish to press it further, and he hoped that it would not in fact arise.'

Beneš was now aware that he must look elsewhere for help. Although always suspicious of Stalin, he addressed two questions to the Soviet Union on the 19th: Would the U.S.S.R. immediately and effectively help if France acted first? Would the U.S.S.R. help as a member of the League of Nations? To the first, it was answered: 'Yes, instantly and effectively'; to the second: 'Yes, in every respect.' Litvinov had also assured Bonnet that Russia would act, though he advised that the dispute should first be put before the League. These things were easily said, but in view of the refusal of Rumania and Poland to allow Russia access to Czechoslovakia they could have been meaningless. As France never acted, the matter can only remain one for speculation.

On the 19th, the Anglo-French proposals were delivered to the Czech Government: the Sudetenland—probably those areas containing 50 per cent or more German inhabitants—should be ceded to Germany. Beneš was 'greatly moved and agitated,' and spoke with bitterness of being abandoned; already Bonnet, having assured his Cabinet to the contrary, was putting the strongest pressure on the Czech Minister in Paris. The plan would involve the surrender of strategic frontiers and the creation of a minority of 800,000 Czechs in Germany. On the 20th, the Czech Government rejected the proffered advice, and appealed to the arbitration treaty signed between themselves and Germany in 1925.[1] The British Minister in Prague warned that Britain would leave the Czechs to their fate and his French counterpart, in tears, did likewise. The former also reported:

NEWTON: 'I have very good reason . . . to believe that reply . . . should not be regarded as final. . . . If I can deliver a kind of ultimatum to President Beneš . . . he and his Government will feel able to bow to *"force majeure".'

A request for a clarification of the French attitude was also interpreted in this sense by Bonnet in order to overcome the fears of less pliant colleagues. At 2.15 a.m. on the 21st, Beneš was told he should 'withdraw (his) reply and urgently consider an alternative that takes account of realities'; if not, he stood alone. At 5 p.m., the Anglo-French proposals were accepted. Next day, Hodža's Government resigned and was succeeded by a Government of National Concentration under General Syrový. The Minister of Propaganda voiced his country's feelings:

VAVRECKA: 'Our Nation has experienced many a catastrophe in the course of history. . . . Such a catastrophe is threatening . . . today. Our allies and friends have dictated to us sacrifices without parallel in history. But we are not defeated. If our government had to accept such cruel conditions, it was because they wished to spare the whole population useless bloodshed. . . . We shall not reproach those who have left us in the lurch. History will judge these. We face the future with our heads high.'

Hitler would be disappointed. On the 20th he had reproached the Hungarians for pressing their claims too feebly, adding:

HITLER: 'I will present the German demands to Chamberlain with brutal frankness. . . . Action by the Army will provide the only satisfactory solution. There is, however, a danger of the Czechs submitting to every demand.'

Chamberlain flew to meet him at Godesberg on the 22nd, and announced that he had obtained a Czech agreement to cede the Sudetenland:

HITLER: 'I am exceedingly sorry, but after the events of the last few days this solution is no longer any use.'

Polish and Hungarian claims and the brutal extermination of many Germans made delay and a boundary commission impossible.

[1]When the British and French Governments published documents relevant to the crisis, neither included the Czech reply.

Chamberlain was stunned; he had 'been obliged to take his political life into his hands,' and now was met with unreasoning stubbornness. Incidents, after all, had been inevitable, and he had just learned that Freikorps and troops had crossed the frontier at Eger. Next morning he emphasised his position in a letter:

CHAMBERLAIN: 'I do not think you have realised the impossibility of my agreeing to put forward any plan unless I have reason to suppose that it will be considered by public opinion in my country, in France, and indeed in the world generally, as carrying out the principles agreed upon in an orderly fashion and free from threat of force. . . . In the event of German troops moving into areas as you propose, there is no doubt that Czechoslovak Government would have no option but to order their forces to resist.'

On the evening of the 23rd, a further meeting was held. Hitler thanked Chamberlain for his efforts to secure peace, but the memorandum he now produced demanded occupation up to a line drawn by the German General Staff, to begin on the 26th and to be completed by the 28th. Additional areas were to be included in a plebiscite. When Chamberlain described this as an ultimatum, Hitler pointed out that the word 'Memorandum' stood at the head of the document. News arrived of Czech mobilisation, and the atmosphere worsened. The most Chamberlain could secure was the substitution of October 1st for the earlier dates, and a few minor alterations in the text. 'You are the only man to whom I have ever made a concession,' remarked Hitler 'somewhat bitterly.'

The British party left for London, faced with a terrible choice:

L'ÉPOQUE: 'Neither France nor Britain, who have gone a long way beyond simple conciliation . . . can capitulate without disappearing from the ranks of the great nations.'

This was underlined by the Czech observations on Hitler's terms, transmitted by their Minister in London:

MASARYK: 'It is a *de facto* ultimatum of the sort usually presented to a vanquished nation and not a proposition to a sovereign State which has shown the greatest possible readiness to make sacrifices for the appeasement of Europe. . . . The proposals . . . deprive us of every safeguard for our national existence. We are to yield up large proportions of our carefully prepared defences and admit the German armies deep into our country before we have been able to organise it on the new basis or make any preparations for its defence. Our national and economic independence would automatically disappear. . . . The whole process of moving the population is to be reduced to panic flight on the part of those who will not accept the German Nazi régime. They have to leave their homes without even the right to take their personal belongings or even, in the case of peasants, their cow. . . . Against these new and cruel demands my Government feel bound to make their utmost resistance. . . . The nation of St. Wenceslas, John Hus and Thomas Masaryk will not be a nation of slaves. . . .'

The Poles increased their demands for Teschen, though warned by Russia; Slovak and Hungarian claims mingled with German vituperation. Roosevelt[1] and others addressed appeals to Hitler. The French manned the Maginot line, though Phipps reported that 'All that is best in France is against war almost at any price.' On the 25th, Daladier and Bonnet again flew to London:

CHAMBERLAIN: 'We must . . . consider the probability that, on receipt of a reply from His Majesty's Government . . . on the lines now under consideration, Herr Hitler . . . will interpret it as a rejection of his proposals and say he will march into Czechoslovakia. . . . Would France declare war on Germany?'

DALADIER: 'The matter is very clear. The French Government has always said . . . that in the event of unprovoked aggression against Czechoslovakia, France would fulfil her obligations.'

Sir John Simon was thereupon asked to cross-examine Daladier as to what active steps France envisaged taking. He received little in the way of a direct reply, but the defendant repeated that 'he would not return to France having agreed to the strangulation of a people.' 'What would happen,' asked Chamberlain, 'if war had been declared and a rain of bombs descended upon Paris, upon French industrial districts, military centres and aerodromes? Could France defend herself, and was she in a position to make an effective reply?' He regretted to have to observe that all did not appear well with the French air-force. M. Daladier replied that he 'thought we were all too modest, and Great Britain as much as anyone.' Eventually, it was agreed that Sir Horace Wilson should take one more message to Hitler, appealing for peace.

At 5 p.m. on Monday, the 26th, Wilson had a stormy interview with the German Chancellor. At one point the latter shouted 'It is no use talking any more,' and made as if to leave the room; Czech acceptance of his timetable must arrive by 2 p.m. on Wednesday, or he would act. This ultimatum was repeated before a vast assembly in the Sportpalast that evening, and a tirade of personal abuse was directed at President Beneš.

[1]American liberals were scornful of appeasement. The possibility of action by America was, however, as Roosevelt made clear to the press, quite out of the question.

That night, an American correspondent who had been watching the scene noted in his diary[1]:

SHIRER: 'For the first time in all the years I've observed him, he seemed tonight to have completely lost control of himself. When he sat down, Goebbels sprang up and shouted ...: "One thing is sure: 1918 will never be repeated!" ... Hitler ... leapt to his feet and, with a fanatical fire in his eyes that I shall never forget, brought his right hand, after a grand sweep, pounding down on the table, and yelled with all the power in his lungs: "Ja!" Then he slumped into his chair exhausted.'

The following morning, Wilson again sought an interview. Having congratulated Hitler on his ovation at the Sportpalast ('it must be a wonderful experience for any man to receive such a reception') he conveyed an assurance from Chamberlain that the Czechs would be made to carry out their promises. Hitler was not interested, several times shouting: 'I will smash the Czechs.' The second part of the message was therefore delivered:

WILSON: 'If the Germans attack Czechoslovakia, the French ... would feel obliged to fulfil their treaty obligations. If that meant that the forces of France became actively engaged in hostilities against Germany, the British Government would feel obliged to support her.'

HITLER: 'If France and England strike, let them do so. It is a matter of complete indifference to me. ... It is Tuesday today, and by next Monday we shall all be at war.'

On the initiative of Duff Cooper, First Lord of the Admiralty, the Fleet was mobilised. 'Keep calm and dig': slit trenches and sandbags began to appear, gas-masks were fitted, and with silent fear the unknown horror of aerial bombardment was awaited. In Paris, a third of the population jammed the roads out of the city in a terror-stricken rush. Phipps reported French opinion to be hardening, but two days later again reversed his judgement. Chamberlain and Halifax now had ears only for what they wished to hear. The latter quoted General Gamelin as saying that Czech resistance would be brief; there was no record of such a statement, and Gamelin's most trusted Staff Officer contradicted it on the 28th. Halifax quoted the British Military Attaché in Berlin to the effect that Czech military morale was low; it was later revealed that the latter was referring to the non-military frontier-guard alone. It was not the time for such hair-splitting. It was time to join Hitler in putting pressure on Beneš:

CHAMBERLAIN: 'I feel bound to tell you ... that the information His

[1]Quoted in his *Rise and Fall of the Third Reich*, Pan edition p. 486.

Majesty's Government now have from Berlin makes it clear that German forces will have orders to cross Czechoslovak frontier almost immediately, unless by 2 p.m. tomorrow Czechoslovak Government have accepted German terms. That must result in Bohemia being overrun and nothing that any other Power can do will prevent this fate for your own country and people, and this remains true whatever may be the ultimate issue of a possible world war. His Majesty's Government cannot take responsibility of advising you what you should do but they consider that this information should be in your hands at once.'

In contradiction to the last sentence, a new British plan was submitted to Beneš shortly afterwards, proposing the occupation of Egerland and Asch on October 1st, with later stages supervised by an international commission. A reminder was included to the effect that even if the West defeated Hitler, Czechoslovakia would still have to be dismembered; it was not worth fighting. At 8.30 p.m., Chamberlain broadcast to the nation:

CHAMBERLAIN: 'How horrible, fantastic, incredible it is that we should be digging trenches and trying on gas-masks here because of a quarrel in a far away country between people of whom we know nothing. . . . I would not hesitate to pay even a third visit to Germany if I thought it would do any good. . . . I am myself a man of peace to the depths of my soul. Armed conflict between nations is a nightmare to me; but if I were convinced that any nation had made up its mind to dominate the rest of the world by fear of its force, I should feel that it must be resisted. Under such a domination, life for people who believe in liberty would not be worth living; but war is a fearful thing, and we must be very clear, before we embark on it, that it is really the great issues that are at stake. . . .'

Immediately afterwards, a new, faint hope appeared in the form of a letter from Hitler: after accusing the Czechs of trying to provoke a 'general warlike conflagration,'[1] it concluded:

HITLER: 'I must leave it to your judgement whether . . . you consider that you should continue your effort, for which I should like to take this opportunity of once more sincerely thanking you, to spoil such manoeuvres and bring the Government in Prague to reason at the very last hour.'

CHAMBERLAIN: 'After reading your letter I feel certain you can get all essentials without war, and without delay. I am ready to come to

[1]Hitler was not alone in making this accusation. Henderson, in a private letter to Halifax, had described Beneš as 'still clinging to the hope of dragging us all down in his own ruin.'

Berlin . . . at once to discuss arrangements for transfer with you and representatives of Czech Government, together with representatives of France and Italy if you desire. I feel convinced we could reach agreement in a week. However much you distrust Prague Government's intentions, you cannot doubt power of British and French Governments to see that promises are carried out fairly and fully and forthwith. As you know, I have stated publicly that we are prepared to undertake that they shall be so carried out. I cannot believe that you will take responsibility of starting a world war which may end civilisation for the sake of a few days' delay in settling this long standing problem.'

A second message was sent to Mussolini, urging him to agree to a meeting and to prevail upon Hitler to do likewise. Mussolini complied:

MUSSOLINI: 'It is far better to pose as a peace-maker than risk being dragged into a war I am not ready to fight; besides, the eyes of the world are on me. . . . There will be no war, but this is the annihilation of English prestige.'

Mussolini's attitude helped decide Hitler. In addition, his own generals and admirals, including Goering, wished to avoid war, and on the 27th an armoured division passed through Berlin before silent, sullen crowds. Mussolini would sponsor the conference, so no face need be lost, and new French proposals[1] went even further than the British to indicate complete surrender. It was only the form of the Fuehrer's proposals that needed altering; Sir Horace Wilson was saying as much to a member of the German Embassy on this very morning, the 28th, a morning which many expected to be their last.

At 1 p.m., it was known in London that Mussolini had advised a conference and that Hitler had postponed mobilisation for 24 hours. When Chamberlain arrived that afternoon to address a packed and tense House of Commons, he must have realised that salvation was probable. Almost discarding his notes, he recalled the stages by which the crisis had developed, though he chose not to mention the Anglo-French pressures of the previous seven days, or the Czech replies. At 4.15 p.m., a note was passed to him. Dramatically, he announced that it was an invitation to meet Hitler at Munich:

CHAMBERLAIN: 'Signor Mussolini has accepted and I have no doubt Monsieur Daladier will accept. I need not say what my answer will be . . . Mr. Speaker, I cannot say any more. I am sure that the House will be ready to release me now to go and see what I can make of this last effort.'

[1]They were the private work of Bonnet.

The House went wild with relief, tears in many eyes, Order Papers flung in the air, and one cry of 'Thank God for the Prime Minister.' When Mr. Harold Nicolson remained seated, he was threatened by those around him. The Czech Minister left for the Foreign Office, where he demanded an explanation from Chamberlain and Halifax:

MASARYK: 'If you have sacrificed my nation to preserve the peace of the world, I will be the first to applaud you. . . . But if not, gentlemen, God help your souls.'

Chamberlain telegraphed to Prague that he would 'have the interests of Czechoslovakia fully in mind.' Next morning, in buoyant mood, he departed for Munich. During the flight, Wilson read out a selection of the letters and telegrams of praise which had arrived at 10 Downing Street.

The meeting which followed in the Fuehrerhaus at Munich was not a turning-point. Hitler's victory and the dismemberment of Czechoslovakia were already assured, and those who might protest—the Czechs and the Russians—were not involved. The memorandum which Mussolini presented as a basis for discussion had been drafted for him by the German Foreign Office and Goering. The conference was conducted without agenda or minutes, to the accompaniment of a confused coming and going of delegates and minor officials. When the climactic moment of signing arrived, the ink-well was found to be empty.

During the meeting, Daladier attempted to get the Czech delegates included and Chamberlain raised detailed points concerning property and compensation. They were brushed aside. At 2.30 a.m. on the 30th the Agreement was signed: the Sudetenland was to be occupied in stages between October 1st and 10th up to a line determined by an international commission; Britain and France would guarantee the remainder of Czechoslovakia, to be joined by Germany and Italy once the claims of the Polish and Hungarian minorities had been satisfied.

The waiting Czech delegates were informed of the outline of the settlement by Wilson whilst the meeting was in progress; the latter refused to discuss matters with them, and another official warned that they would be abandoned by Britain and France if they rejected what was coming. Finally, they were summoned before Chamberlain and Daladier, and 'sentence was passed.' Chamberlain yawned continuously; he was tired, though, as he wrote later, 'pleasantly tired.' Daladier looked a broken man.

The following morning, Chamberlain requested a private talk with the Chancellor. Various topics were discussed, and the Prime Minister particularly asked that, in the event of a Czech refusal, there should be no bombing of Prague. Hitler reassured him: he would try to spare civilians, and 'hated the thought of little babies being killed by gas bombs.' Finally, Chamberlain produced and read a document which Hitler immediately agreed to sign:

CHAMBERLAIN: 'We . . . are agreed in recognising that the question of Anglo-German relations is of the first importance. . . . We regard the agreement signed last night and the Anglo-German Naval Agreement as symbolic of the desire of our two peoples never to go to war with one another again. We are resolved that the method of consultation shall be the method adopted to deal with any other questions that may concern our two countries, and we are determined to continue our efforts to remove possible sources of difference and thus to contribute to assure the peace of Europe.'

Whilst Beneš, in despair, accepted the Agreement, Chamberlain returned to a tumultuous welcome, waving the above document and crying: 'I've got it.'

CHAMBERLAIN: 'Even the descriptions of the papers give no idea of the scenes in the streets as I drove from Heston to the Palace. They were lined from one end to the other with people of every class, shouting themselves hoarse, leaping on the running-board, banging on the windows, and thrusting their hands into the car to be shaken.'

The scene culminated in Downing Street, where he spoke to the crowd from the same window as had Disraeli after the Congress of Berlin:

CHAMBERLAIN: 'My good friends, this is the second time in our history that there has come back from Germany to Downing Street peace with honour. I believe it is peace in our time.'

Later, he warned the Commons not to read too much into these words, 'uttered in a moment of some emotion, after a long and exhausting day.'

Hitler was moody rather than elated, remarking that 'That fellow Chamberlain has spoiled my entry into Prague.' He also declared himself irritated at having 'to deal with nonentities,' later describing his enemies as 'little worms' whom he had seen at Munich.

The Munich Agreement produced the fiercest differences of opinion, reflected in the press of many nations:

MANCHESTER GUARDIAN: 'The pacificators of Munich . . . have done something that has never been done before in history. The snatching of the world at the eleventh hour from a universal calamity. . . . The instinct of people today to praise the peace-makers is sound. None of us can disguise from himself that even if a war had been fought on deeper issues the boundaries of Czechoslovakia could not have remained intact. Great as are the injustices suffered by Czechoslovakia under the Munich agreement . . . they cannot be measured against the horrors that might have extinguished . . . the whole of Western civilisation.'

DAILY HERALD: 'Heavy has been the price of peace. . . . The voice of Czechoslovakia . . . is a voice that must ring in the ears and hearts of all men and women who hold that the obligations of honour and justice are not lightly to be set aside. Czechoslovakia has been sacrificed to the ambitions of German Fascism.'

NEW YORK TIMES: 'Let no man say too high a price has been paid for peace in Europe until he has searched his soul and found himself willing to risk in war the lives . . . of those nearest and dearest to him.'

CHICAGO TRIBUNE: 'It becomes difficult to understand what Chamberlain and Daladier were contending for if they were willing to concede so much. There is little now to prevent Hitler from dominating and organising Middle and Eastern Europe.'

TIDENS TEGN (NORWAY): 'The Nobel Prize should be awarded to Mr. Chamberlain. The whole world agrees that nobody ever did more for peace. The prize was created for men like him.'

LIDOVÉ NOVINY (CZECH): 'If the world is not to be ruled by justice but by force, then our place is on the side of those who possess the greater force and the greater energy of decision. There is nothing else left for us. Let us seek unity with Germany.'

40,000 letters, including many from Germany, thanked Chamberlain for what he had done. In the debate in the Commons from the 3rd to the 6th October, he stated his position:

CHAMBERLAIN: 'I would like to remind the House of two things which it is essential not to forget. . . . We did not go to Munich to decide whether the predominantly German areas in the Sudetenland should be passed over to the German Reich. That had been decided already. . . . What we had to consider was the method. . . . The second point to remember is that time was one of the essential factors. . . . We had populations inflamed to a high degree; we had extremists on both sides ready to . . . provoke incidents . . . it was essential that we should quickly reach a conclusion. . . . What is the difference between the unacceptable terms (of Godesberg) and those (of Munich? The former was) an ultimatum with a time limit of six days. On the other hand the Munich Agreement reverts to the Anglo-French plan . . . (with) international supervision. . . . Again, under Munich . . . occupation of the territory is to be carried out in five clearly defined stages between October 1st and 10th instead of ... in one operation by October 1st. Thirdly, the line up to which German troops will enter ... will now be a line to be fixed by an International Commission. On that Commission, both Germany and Czechoslovakia are represented. ... All plebiscite areas are to be delimited by the Commission. ... I have nothing to be ashamed of. Let those who have, hang their heads. We must feel profound sympathy for a small and gallant nation in the hour of their national grief and loss.'

Men differed with passionate intensity on these issues. The British Government had presented the Czech with an advance of £10 million to assist them in raising a loan of £30 million. In the Smoke Room of the House of Commons, an opponent of appeasement remarked on the new cost of betrayal: what had once been done for thirty pieces of silver now had to be atoned for by £30 million. He was struck to the ground by a supporter of Chamberlain.[1] During the debate, critics who spoke included the First Lord of the Admiralty, who had resigned:

DUFF COOPER: 'The Prime Minister may be right. I can assure you, Mr. Speaker, with the deepest sincerity, that I hope and pray that he is right, but I cannot believe what he believes. I wish I could. Therefore, I can be of no assistance to him in his Government. I should be only a hindrance, and it is much better that I should go. I remember when we were discussing the Godesberg ultimatum that I said if I were a party to persuading, or even to suggesting to the Czechoslovak Government that they should accept that ultimatum, I should never be able to hold up my head again. I have forfeited a great deal. I have given up an office that I loved, work in which I was deeply interested, and a staff of which any man might be proud. ...

I have given up the privilege of serving as lieutenant to a leader whom I still regard with the deepest admiration and affection. I have ruined, perhaps, my political career. But that is a little matter; I have retained something which is to me of greater value—I can still walk about the world with my head erect.'[2]

ATTLEE: 'The Prime Minister, in effect, had really surrendered Czechoslovakia long before. ... All his efforts to save peace—and we all recognise the efforts he has made—do not alter the fact that on the main question, he had already completely given way to the force of Herr Hitler's demands and, therefore, although we have a war averted,

[1]Related in Cato: *Guilty Men* pp. 55-6.
[2]When *The Times* correspondent reported that this speech was well received, Dawson, editor and arch-appeaser, altered the description to 'a damp squib.'

we have the recognition that the will of an armed dictator is supreme in the world.'

CHURCHILL: 'It is the most grievous consequence which we have yet experienced of what we have done and of what we have left undone in the last five years—five years of futile good intention, five years of eager search for the line of least resistance, five years of uninterrupted defeat of British power. . . . We are in the presence of a disaster of the first magnitude. . . .'

But many spoke on Chamberlain's behalf. One argument (though it tended to undermine Chamberlain's insistence on Hitler's good faith) was that of Britain's unpreparedness to go to war, of the need to speed rearmament in the time gained. General Ironside, C.I.G.S. at the outbreak of war, wrote in his diary on September 22nd, 1938: 'Chamberlain is, of course, right. We have not the means of defending ourselves and he knows it. . . . We cannot expose ourselves now to a German attack. We simply commit suicide if we do.' Henderson later argued:

HENDERSON: 'History will be the final judge of the Prime Minister's action in flying to Berchtesgaden, Godesberg and Munich. It may be argued in future that, since war between the Western democracies and Nazi Germany was inevitable, it would have been wise to accept the challenge, unprepared though we were in September 1938, rather than wait till Germany had established her predominance in Central Europe. (I say that) with so little material force behind us, and on such uncertain moral grounds as the refusal of self-determination to the Sudetens, (we could not challenge Hitler).'

One thing seemed clear at the time: Britain, like France, was totally committed to preserve what remained of the Czech State. During the debate in the Commons, Sir Thomas Inskip had declared:

INSKIP: 'His Majesty's Government feel under a moral obligation to Czechoslovakia to treat the guarantee as being now in force. In the event, therefore, of an act of unprovoked aggression against Czechoslovakia, His Majesty's Government would certainly feel bound to take all steps in their power to see that the integrity of Czechoslovakia is preserved.'

The actions of the Government were approved by 366 votes to 144; in the French Chamber of Deputies, the voting was 543 to 75 in favour. On October 5th, Beneš resigned:

BENES: 'I was elected to my present post in very different times. . . . As a convinced democrat I believe that I am doing right to resign.'

His country had lost 11,000 square miles of territory, 800,000 citizens of Czech origin, 70 per cent of its iron and steel capacity, 80 per cent of its textiles, 90 per cent of its porcelain, 86 per cent of its glass, 86 per cent of its chemicals, and 70 per cent of its electric power; its railway system was disrupted. By insisting on the use of 1910 census figures, Germany got the last of the Czech fortifications included in the booty; the International Commission acquiesced. Ribbentrop and Ciano dictated a new Czech-Hungarian frontier and the Poles obtained Teschen, site of coal mines and iron works, and an important railway junction. Germany and Italy ignored their promise to join the guarantors of Czechoslovakia. Thousands of Czechs, Jews, and German Social Democrats from the occupied areas fled across the new Czech frontier; they were forcibly returned at the insistence of the German Government.

On October 21st, Hitler ordered his army to be ready to 'liquidate' the remainder of Czechoslovakia. In January, he told the latter that if she wished to be guaranteed by Germany, she must leave the League, align her foreign policy with that of Germany, reduce her army, surrender part of her gold reserves, dismiss all officials not approved by Germany, obtain permission before developing new industries, pass anti-Semitic laws, and allow German citizens to use the swastika emblem. On February 18th, Britain and France became aware of these demands.

Appeasement continued. Bonnet increased his influence in France and secured the signing of a Franco-German Declaration of Friendship in December. Chamberlain did his best, through Wilson, to secure a docile press in Britain, though anti-Jewish measures in Germany made this difficult for a while. The Anglo-Italian Agreement was brought into force in November, and in January 1939, Prime Minister and Foreign Secretary journeyed to Rome to converse with the Duce and Ciano; appeasement of Italy lacked some of the grim tragedy which was present north of the Brenner, and in the photographs it appeared as if the two tall, gaunt men had inadvertently strayed onto the stage of an *opéra bouffe*.

On March 10th, Chamberlain declared that 'The outlook in international affairs is tranquil.' Four days later, at the instigation of Germany, Ruthenia and Slovakia proclaimed their independence from Prague. The elderly President Hácha, having been subjected to a physical and mental ordeal in Berlin, signed an agreement which granted Germany a 'protectorate' over Bohemia and Moravia. They were occupied on the 15th March. Chamberlain announced that changed conditions had invalidated Britain's pledge, though the anger of his country and the growing disquietude of Halifax brought him to issue a public protest on the 17th. He did so in terms of personal aggrievement.

There followed Hitler's seizure of Memel and his demand for Danzig and a corridor. Chamberlain reversed his previous policy, and the Anglo-French guarantee left it to Poland to decide what constituted a threat to her independence. In July and August, secret attempts were made through Sir Horace Wilson to agree on a formula with Germany that would enable the guarantee to be revoked as being 'superfluous.' With the Nazi-Soviet Pact signed, however, Hitler felt safe to invade Poland on September 1st. After final hesitations, Britain and France declared war two days later. Appeasement, whether right or wrong, had failed.

FURTHER DISCUSSION

1. Does the word 'appeasement' have a pejorative sense only? Can the policies of appeasement be condemned out of hand? It must be understood that they did not originate with Chamberlain and Bonnet; it must also be remembered that Baldwin and Chamberlain expressed, in the main, the mood and will of Britain at the time, and that Blum and Daldier could not escape the conditions imposed by a sick and divided France. Nor is it a simple matter to separate those who had the 'right' approach from those generally condemned: was that reviewer justified, for instance, who remarked that whilst Eden was 'facing the dictators' his Memoirs show that he was in no way facing up to them? The Japanese had to be appeased long after September 1939, as the closure of the Burma to China road made painfully clear. And is it surprising that many people at the time could see no reason why the Germans in Austria and Czechoslovakia should not join the Reich? If many then were not prepared to 'die for Danzig,' would we happily die for South Vietnam or West Berlin?

2. Could Hitler's aggression have been prevented, as is frequently argued, by a firm stand on the part of Britain and France over the reoccupation of the Rhineland? It has been wisely remarked that 'while a more detailed study of the German evidence . . . lends added support to this view, it remains difficult on principle to draw a clear line across any given point of time and to claim that errors of human judgement lie on one side and not the other.'[1] In 1935, for instance, Germany had contravened the Versailles settlement by announcing conscription and the existence of a military air-force; Britain first accepted this, then condemned it at Stresa, then condoned it by signing the Anglo-German Naval Agreement.

Despite warnings from the British Chiefs of Staff, from Sir Horace Rumbold and Sir Eric Phipps in Berlin, from Churchill and from Eden to

[1]Robertson: *Hitler's Pre-War Policy and Military Plans* p. 81.

his colleagues, the pace of rearmament remained slow. Was this inevitable in the face of public opinion? Should those with knowledge and responsibility have run greater risks, politically, in order to awaken that opinion to the danger? Were the Labour Party demanding the impossible in urging strong action through the League, whilst opposing rearmament? Was the failure of the League, and particularly of France and Britain, to check Mussolini in Abyssinia the turning point for all hope of collective security?

3. How much responsibility lies with Chamberlain himself for the state of British armaments in 1938? With MacDonald failing and Baldwin averse to giving a lead, it is clear that the Chancellor of the Exchequer was in many ways the strong figure in the National Government. Three extracts from his letters and diary might be pondered:

> 28th July 1934: 'I was glad to hear of Mussolini's movement of troops. It's the only thing Germans understand.'
> 12th May 1934: 'And so I have practically taken charge of the defence requirements of the country.'
> 6th June 1934: (re proposals by a defence-requirements committee): 'I have now just completed a paper making revised proposals, which bring the 5 years expenditure down from 76 to 50 million, excluding shipbuilding.'

Or does Chamberlain's wish to fight the 1935 election on the defence issue, and his support for a strong line over Abyssinia, point to Baldwin's responsibility above all? In May 1937, Churchill stated to a Conservative Party meeting that 'when the late government were at length convinced of the urgent need to rearm . . . no one was more active than Mr. Chamberlain.'

4. Following the shock of Munich, were armaments increased and improved with sufficient urgency? One should examine the resistance in France of bodies such as the C.G.T. to attempts to increase productivity; the tardy reorganisation of industry and the system of supply to the Services in Britain; the effects of uncertainty on strategy and co-ordination. (The Ironside diaries show the frustrations in such matters experienced by a thinking soldier.) Chamberlain's own insistence that Hitler's word could be trusted helped prevent British rearmament becoming really vigorous, and he was one of those most responsible for the refusal to create a Ministry of Supply and for the low priority accorded the Army. Was it wise to announce in 1939 that 'we are not now contemplating the equipment of an army on a Continental scale'?

The Labour Party did not help, and bitterly opposed conscription in the same year. 'Until the last months before the outbreak of war, it (the British Labour Movement) was prone to regard the threat from the

Government to its own independence as greater than any outside threats from Hitler.'[1] In France, internal strife proved an impossible burden, but Daladier had been Minister of National Defence and Minister of War since 1936; the unpreparedness of the armed forces in 1939 were partly due to the fact that he had 'shirked taking the preliminary steps without which the quantitative and qualitative requirements of the programme could never be met.'[2]

The fact that Britain and France needed a year's 'breathing space' was one of the reasons advanced in support of the Munich Agreement—though it is important to note that this argument was developed later, rather than at the time. Were they, in fact, in a better position to fight in 1939 than a year earlier? From a morale point of view, France was as enfeebled in the first year as in the second. British public opinion displayed a new resolve after March 1939, and the Commonwealth was more ready to fight when the time came than it had been at Munich. It is difficult to weigh such factors, however.

The armaments situation is a little clearer.[3] First, air power. At the time of the Munich crisis it was generally assumed that Britain could have put into the first line about 1,500 aircraft, only a small number of which were up to date. Out of 30 operational squadrons, only 1 was equipped with Spitfires; 5 were in the process of being equipped with Hurricanes; many of the bombers were obsolescent. There was no radar chain.

Even by September 1939 the last named, developed by Watson-Watt, had not been completed, but vital progress had been made, and it was ready in 1940. On the other hand, in spite of government assurances that the plan for 1,750 first-line aircraft had been fulfilled, it seems that the actual strength was still about 1,500. Production had grown rapidly, but resulted in the replacement of obsolete units rather than an increased total. By July 1939 there were 26 Squadrons of modern, 8-gun fighters; about 130 fighters a month were being produced as against about 30 a year earlier, and corresponding bomber figures were 320 as against 120. The total monthly production of military aircraft was 780 in September 1939, as against 250 in August 1938.

France in 1938 had about 1,100 front-line aircraft, mainly obsolescent types. Figures given for production in the ensuing year seem to have been exaggerated; the disruptive effect of strikes was considerable. In the Battle of France in the summer of 1940, barely 500 French fighters were

[1]Viscount Chilston; a chapter in Toynbee (ed.): *The Coming of War.*
[2]Ibid.
[3]This section is based mainly on the work of Chilston already cited.

in action; none of the 390 bombers available at the outbreak of war was up to date, and their production seems actually to have declined since 1938. The Czechs had well over 1,000 aircraft in 1938 though only about half were front-line; they had, of course, disappeared a year later.

The Germans had 2,928 first-line aircraft in September 1938; they were well ahead in the development of modern fighters, especially the Me 109. In September 1939 the total had risen to 3,750, including a formidable bomber strength—Heinkel III's, Dornier 17's, Junkers 87 dive-bombers, and the new Junkers 88. The German rate of productivity, however, increased only from 450 to 700 a month during the year. In other words, they were reaching the limits of their air expansion in numbers and types, whilst that of Britain was getting into its stride, making up the leeway in modern planes as it did so.

On land, the 35 Czech divisions were eventually lost to the Allies, and the mountain fortress line which, at the time of Munich, had required the deployment of 30 German divisions. German generals were greatly impressed with the Czech defences when they inspected them at their leisure; even Hitler later admitted: 'We had run a serious danger. The plan prepared by the Czech generals was formidable. I now understand why my generals urged restraint.'[1] The withdrawal of October 1938 left the rump of Czechoslovakia almost defenceless; the way to Rumania was open, that to Poland greatly simplified. In March 1939, Germany collected from the Czechs 469 tanks, 43,000 machine guns, 500 A.A. guns, and a million rifles, in addition to the great Skoda arsenal; the production of the last-named between August 1938 and September 1939 was, according to Churchill, nearly equal to the total British arms output in the same period.

The British Army at the time of Munich was in a state of extreme unreadiness. General Ironside (as he was then) had written in his diary on March 29th, 1938:

> 'The paper on our rearmament has come in. It is truly the most appalling reading. How we can have come to this state is beyond believing: Present situation:
> (i) We can put into the field 2 divisions only, with an incomplete quota of Corps troops, and deficient of many types of equipment essential for warfare under modern conditions.
> (ii) The main deficiencies are:
> *Cavalry*
> *Mechanized Division:* Cavalry regiments are not yet equipped or trained.

[1] An estimate of the strength of Czech defences in March 1938 by the British Military Attaché is produced in *Documents on British Foreign Policy*, 3rd Series vol. I, No. 120.

Artillery

Field Artillery: We have 18-pdrs. and 4.5 howitzers only, with maximum ranges of 9,000 and 6,000 yards respectively; the German 33-pdr. field artillery is reported to have a maximum range of 17,000 yards.

Medium Artillery: We have 60-pdrs. and 6-inch hows. with maximum ranges of 15,000 and 10,000 yards respectively; the corresponding German weapons have ranges of 21,700 and 16,700 yards.

Anti-tank Artillery: The delivery of 2-pdr. guns is only just beginning.

A.A. Artillery: One A.A. brigade only available. All 3-inch guns.

Infantry

No Bren guns.

No armoured carriers.

75 % deficiency of anti-tank rifles.

No 2-inch mortars.

75 % deficiency in 3-inch mortars.

A.F.V.s

Obsolete medium tanks.

No cruiser tanks.

No "I" (Infantry) tanks.

Obsolete armoured cars.

No light tanks (we have one unit now in Egypt).

Miscellaneous

Considerable deficiencies in up-to-date engineer and signal equipment.

And this is the state of our Army after two years warning. No foreign nation would believe it if they were told it.'

Between 1938 and 1939 there was an increase on paper of sixteen times the existing Field Force and double the Territorial Army; in April a programme of 32 divisions was approved by the Cabinet and in May military conscription was introduced. Yet by the outbreak of war, there were ready, in fact, only one armoured division and one Army tank brigade, both only partially equipped with the right tanks, and five Infantry Divisions. Four Divisions went to France at the outbreak of war. The fact that there was no Ministry of Supply in Britain till April and none in France till war had begun was a retarding factor. And whilst, in 1938-9, British military expenditure of all kinds reached £304 millions, Churchill estimates that of Germany as at least £1,500 millions.

In France, little increase of the army was possible. Long-standing compulsory service enabled over 5 million men to be called up in a short time, and the 2-year compulsory service was prolonged. But the year's delay inevitably put France in a worse position vis-à-vis Germany, who had instituted conscription only in 1935, and by 1938 had scarcely begun to reap the advantage of a population twice that of France. By the war,

France had about 2,200 modern tanks available, and though the Germans had more, they were of about equal quality, since the German heavy tanks that were so effective in 1940 had not yet appeared in large numbers. The French dispersed their armour throughout the army, however, in contrast to the German Panzer formations.

In 1939, as in 1938, Germany could mobilise over 5 million men immediately. In 1938, however, only a small proportion of these were trained reservists, and many staff officers greatly feared a conflict in the light of their unreadiness, as they had in 1936 when Hitler reoccupied the Rhineland. We have already seen that these fears had driven some generals, notably Colonel-General Beck and Colonel-General Halder, into active conspiracy. It should also be remembered that 1938 had witnessed a clash between the professional leaders of the German Army, and Himmler and Goering, with the fall of the War Minister, Field Marshall von Blomberg, and the Commander in Chief of the Army, Colonel-General von Fritsch.

Between 1938 and the war, conscription greatly increased the number of trained German reservists, and industrial mobilisation was already in action. The number of Panzer divisions rose from five to seven, and in the Battle of France 3,000 German tanks, of which 1,000 were heavy, outnumbered the French by several hundred. The 600 British tanks were too inferior to redress the balance.

At sea, the Allies could feel happier. Churchill remarked soon after Munich that 'it is the only one of our defence services which is in a high state of efficiency and which is far stronger relatively to Europe than it was in 1914.' In the financial year 1938-39, 53 warships were added, and during 1939, 60 more. In January 1939, British tonnage was more than that of Germany, France and Italy together. The same was true of tonnage building, with a larger aircraft-carrier programme than anyone else and the first of the five *King George V* battleships laid down in 1937 nearly ready. At the outbreak of war, Britain had 12 battleships and three battle-cruisers to Germany's three 'Pocket' battleships and two battle-cruisers (*Scharnhorst* and *Gneisenau*), though the massive *Bismarck* and *Tirpitz* (in contravention of the 35,000 ton limit agreed in 1937) were nearing completion. The French had eight battleships of sorts, and the modern battle-cruisers *Dunkerque* and *Strasbourg*.

In cruisers and destroyers the allies had a clear superiority, though the new German 10,000 ton 8″-cruisers were formidable. The main menace lay in the submarine field. The Anglo-German Naval Agreement of 1935 gave the latter the right to build submarines, and at the end of 1938 she had more submarines built and building than Britain, though the total tonnage, in accordance with the Agreement, was within 45% of the

British total, nearly half of the vessels being small coastal ones. In December 1938 Germany invoked that clause of the Agreement whereby 'in special circumstances' she could build up to 100% of British submarine tonnage, thus enabling ocean-going vessels of 1,000 tons and over to be built. At the outbreak of war Germany had 56 submarines (Churchill gives 57) with 40 building. France, having had the largest European submarine tonnage in 1938, was dropping behind, taking 18 months to Germany's eight to build a new vessel. Ominously, Italy possessed 105 submarines in September 1939.

The final aspect to be considered is Civil Defence. At the time of Munich, Air Raid Precautions were totally inadequate, and there were only about 100 anti-aircraft guns for London and about 200 for the rest of the country, only a few being the new 3.7″. In February 1939 a programme aimed at 1,264 heavy A.A. guns and 4,728 searchlights, but only about a half of these existed at the outbreak of war, since much of the best material went to France to protect the Expeditionary Force. Long before Munich, on the other hand, Germany had had up-to-date A.A. defences; in May 1938 these included between 1,200 and 1,300 mobile and over 3,000 fixed guns, all modern. At least great strides were made in Britain by Sir John Anderson, appointed Minister of Civilian Defence in November 1938. By August 1939 he had secured 1,900,000 volunteer workers and 1,000,000 steel shelters had been delivered out of the $2\frac{1}{2}$ million ordered.

From this mass of information, only tentative conclusions may be drawn. Allied rearming was only slowly gathering pace in the Autumn of 1939; on the other hand, German strength was less than many thought at the time, and she took risks that only success could justify, such as entering the war with only three months' supply of aviation spirit. Of the German situation at the time of Munich, Field Marshall von Manstein (who was not on trial for his life) said at Nuremberg:

> 'If war had broken out, neither our western border nor our Polish frontier could really have been effectively defended by us, and there is no doubt whatsoever that had Czechoslovakia defended herself, we would have been held up by her fortifications, for we did not have the means to break through.'[1]

Such evidence is not conclusive; it cannot easily be dismissed.

5. In any such conjecturing, Russia, as at Munich, looms like a great shadow in the wings. Would Stalin have complied with the 1935 treaty if France had fought for Czechoslovakia, or was he relying on the refusal of Poland and Rumania to permit the passage of Russian troops? Was

[1]Quoted in Shirer, op cit p. 518.

it a mistake for the British and French governments to look with coolness and distrust on the idea of a defensive alliance with Russia? The latter's attitude to Germany had changed considerably since Rapallo, and a Franco-Russian treaty had followed the Non-Aggression Pact of Germany and Poland in 1934. On March 17th 1938 Litvinov suggested 'the consideration of practical measures . . . (aimed at) stopping the further developments of aggression and the elimination of the increased danger of a new world slaughter.' Was the offer a sincere one? Chamberlain returned a negative reply on the grounds of wishing to avoid the development of power-blocs. Was he right? Would Stalin have maintained such an alliance if better prospects had offered elsewhere? Did the attitude of Poland, Rumania and the Baltic States make such an alliance impossible? It should be remembered that Russia's great fighting capacity had not yet been demonstrated; many felt that the widespread purges Stalin had carried out in the ranks of the Red Army officers would prove fatal in time of war.[1] On the other hand, the British refusal to consult Russia throughout the Munich crisis is startling, and can only be understood if Chamberlain's personal antipathy, made clear in his private letters and diary, is borne in mind.

The Soviet view of these matters, and of their later offers (e.g. in March 1939) will be found in Maisky: *Who Helped Hitler?* It is a work which becomes highly tendentious when dealing with the 1939 negotiations; the subsequent fate of Eastern Poland, Finland, the Baltic States and Northern Rumania is omitted.

6. Daladier did little more than Chamberlain to consult and involve Russia. Caught between a fiercely independent trade union movement and an extreme Right who would rather see Hitler in Paris than the Popular Front, Daladier had to work with a Foreign Minister who was eager for appeasement and totally unscrupulous in his methods. The atmosphere was one which Benda has brilliantly described in *La trahison des clercs*.

To these problems Furnia, in his book, *The Diplomacy of Appeasement* would add the duplicity of Chamberlain. In the words of the preface 'The evidence now reveals Chamberlain as a man of appalling ignorance in dealing with the forces with which he was involved. It shows him stooping to petty parochial politics, shabbily pursuing a goal whose complexity he did not understand. . . . However, Daladier emerges . . . as a man of honour and integrity, valiantly trying to save the faithful Czechoslovakian nation, and crudely betrayed by his bungling British counterpart, and cruelly sabotaged by his own foreign minister.'

[1] See, for instance, a report of April 1938 from the British Military Attaché in Moscow; *British Documents*, *3rd Series* Vol. I, No. 148.

The style and some of the adjectives are open to question, but Furnia's case deserves consideration. It is that the choice between war and dishonour could have been prevented by an extension of the *Entente Cordiale* to include French ties with Czechoslovakia. (It may be remarked in passing that this would involve the reversal of a steady British refusal—at Locarno, for instance—to undertake definite commitments in Eastern as opposed to Western Europe.) It is suggested that Chamberlain utilised divisions between Left and Right in France to avoid such a move, and to continue his own role of arbiter and appeaser. Evidence is produced, not only from Chamberlain's handling of the Anglo-French talks of April 1938, but from secret communications from the Foreign Office between May 12th and September 17th, telling Daladier and Bonnet that they should disregard any public statements by the British Government which suggested that Britain would support France in a war over Czechoslovakia. By this duplicity, it is concluded, Chamberlain gave Bonnet the ammunition to undermine Daladier's will to resist Germany when the matter brought conflict within the French cabinet.

Does this reveal a policy of pure egocentricity and duplicity on the part of Chamberlain, or was he facing the realities of the situation and attempting to make the best of it by the use of legitimate diplomatic manoeuvres? It should be remembered that Daladier himself was no supporter of the Versailles treaty; had Germany accepted a limited revision of the Czech frontiers, leaving her defences (and therefore her value to France) intact, he was ready to consider a détente. He chose the slippery Bonnet instead of Paul-Boncour as Foreign Minister. He knew of the activities of the former and of the feebleness of Gamelin, yet he tolerated them. He sensed disaster and raised objections, but never stood firm. After Munich he was plunged into gloom, but on September 14th it was he who had personally confirmed a message of the day before imploring Chamberlain to appease at any price. Furnia's hero had only the outward appearance, none of the real stature for the part.

7. How much emphasis should be placed on the *putsch* planned against Hitler's aggressive foreign policy, if not against the régime itself, by Colonel-General Halder and others in the autumn of 1938? Is there any truth in the assertion by those involved that it was frustrated only by the decision of Chamberlain to fly to Munich?[1]

8. Did Hitler have a strict time-table for war and expansion, or did he merely wait for others to present him with the opportunities for success? The dispute caused by Taylor's *Origins of the Second World War* is well known, and some useful revision is likely to come of it. It is difficult, for

---

[1]Note, for instance, the differing interpretations of Wheeler-Bennett, *The Nemesis of Power* pp. 404-424, and Rothfels, *The German Opposition to Hitler* pp. 56-63.

instance, to interpret the Hossbach Memorandum as a careful plan, and on a larger scale Robertson has recently concluded that 'the view that (Hitler) had tried to put into operation a programme carefully formulated is quite untenable.'[1] It is also clear that others—Schuschnigg, Chamberlain and Bonnet, for instance—made things easier for him.

On the other hand, it is tendentious to play down Hitler's constant intention to secure 'lebensraum' in the East, or to ignore the fact that in essence, the Third Reich was a military machine, and one that was intended to be used. To be more specific: Mr. Taylor quotes a German draft directive of May 20th as 'striking proof of Hitler's restraint':

> 'It is not my intention to smash Czechoslovakia by military action in the immediate future without provocation. . . .'

The remainder of the sentence is not quoted:

> 'unless an unavoidable development of the political conditions within Czechoslovakia forces the issue, or *political events in Europe create a particularly favourable opportunity* which may perhaps never recur.' (My italics.)

The nature of the restraint is hardly the same. It is similarly difficult to believe that Hitler was 'playing for time' at Godesberg. His subsequent remarks and behaviour indicate that he expected the Czechs to refuse his demands; Britain and France would then stand aside and he could safely enjoy his 'entry into Prague'—an entry obtained by force, in spite of his timid generals. That such an aim remained after Munich would seem apparent from Hitler's order of 21st October, that the Army must be ready for the 'liquidation of the remainder of the Czech state.' Mr. Taylor will not have it so: 'These were measures of precaution, not plans for aggression. The continuation of the directive makes this clear: "It must be possible to smash the remainder of the Czech state, should it pursue an anti-German policy".'[2] Such a formidable menace were the remains of Czechoslovakia after Munich and the Polish and Hungarian seizures.[3]

Hitler's later policies do not fall within the scope of this study. One may merely note that it seems ironic that the man who was capable of bluffing his generals and 'playing for time' over Czechoslovakia should, according to Mr. Taylor, accidentally slip into war over Poland at the end of August 1939 because he was the 'prisoner of his own time-table.'

9. What, finally, may one conclude from the events of September and October 1938? The humiliation for Britain and France shines through any thin screen which attempts to distinguish between the Munich

---

[1]Op cit p. 1.   [2]Op cit pp. 192-3.
[3]An appendix to the directive issued on 17th December, makes Hitler's aggressive intentions even clearer.

Agreement and the Godesberg Memorandum. Was this humiliation inescapable? Did the Czechs save the West, rather than vice-versa, by accepting the final terms without fighting? If there is blame for these events, does it lie with the historical development of Bohemia, with the Versailles settlement, with the mood and spokesmen of Britain and France, or with Hitler alone?

FURTHER READING

I have used the following documents:

Documents on German Foreign Policy, 1918-45: Series D, Vols. I and II (H.M.S.O.)

Woodward and Butler (eds.): *Documents on British Foreign Policy*, 1919-39: 3rd Series, Vols. I, II and III (H.M.S.O.)

For speeches and press comments of the time I have used

Hansard

Keesings Contemporary Archives

Memoirs and similar sources include:

Ciano: *Diaries*, 1937-8

Henderson: *Failure of a Mission*

Templewood: *Nine Troubled Years*

The Ironside Diaries, 1937-40 (Constable & Co. Ltd., and David McKay Company, Inc.)

Churchill: *The Second World War, Vol. I: The Gathering Storm*

Avon: *The Eden Memoirs: Facing the Dictators*

Duff Cooper: *Old Men Forget*

Maisky: *Who Helped Hitler?*

There are many extracts from the letters and diaries of the subject in

Feiling: *Life of Neville Chamberlain*

and further light is thrown on the supporters of appeasement in

The History of 'The Times', Vol. IV

The arguments of Beneš for including the Sudeten areas in Czechoslovakia will be found in

Lloyd George: *The Truth About The Peace Treaties*, Chap. XX

and subsequent events within the new State in

Wiskemann: *Czechs and Germans*

The most valuable historical survey of the subject remains

Wheeler-Bennett: *Munich: Prologue to Tragedy*

Other works on the international situation include

Carr: *International Relations Between the Two World Wars*

Namier: *Diplomatic Prelude*

Brook-Shepherd: *The Anschluss*

For the view that Hitler was a gifted extemporisor rather than a man with a strict time-table leading to war, read

Taylor: *The Origins of the Second World War*

*Acknowledgement is made to the publisher for permission to quote from this book.

A somewhat tendentious view of Anglo-French relations will be found in
  Furnia: *The Diplomacy of Appeasement*
whilst
  Gilbert and Gott: *The Appeasers*
throws some light on those who supported Chamberlain. The German background is depicted in
  Shirer: *The Rise and Fall of the Third Reich*
  Bullock: *Hitler, A Study in Tyranny*
  Robertson: *Hitler's Pre-War Policy and Military Plans*
The role of the German Army, and opposition to Hitler is surveyed by
  Wheeler-Bennett: *The Nemesis of Power*
A post-war German work on the same subject is
  Rothfels: *The German Opposition to Hitler*
The question of armaments during and after 'Munich' is dealt with in
  Toynbee (ed.): **The Coming of War* (One of the volumes in the series, Survey of International Affairs, 1939-46) (Oxford University Press, under the auspices of The Royal Institute of International Affairs)

*Acknowledgement is made to the publisher for permission to quote from this book.

the development of modern nationalism

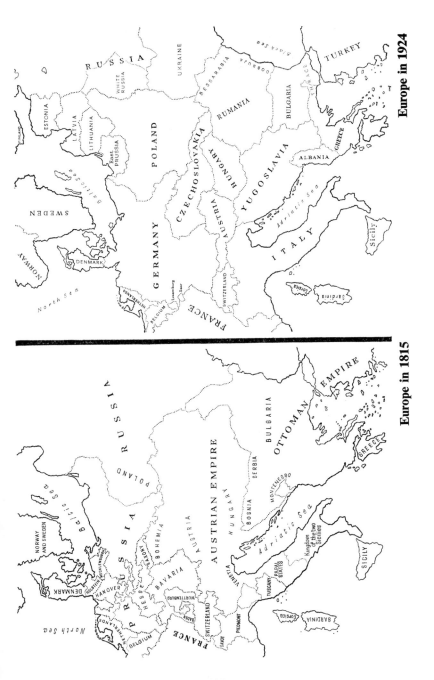

Europe in 1924

Europe in 1815

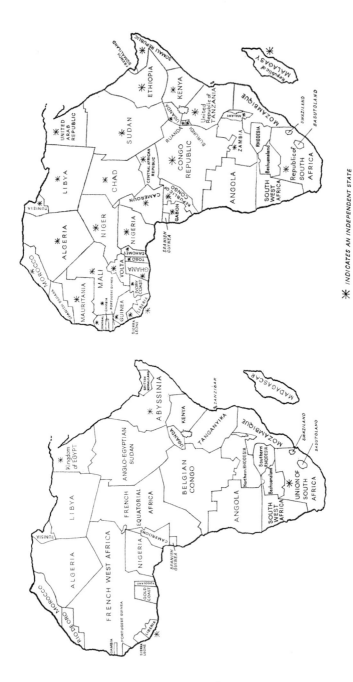

Independent states in 1964

Independent states in 1945

✳ *INDICATES AN INDEPENDENT STATE*

AFRICA

146

THE DEVELOPMENT OF MODERN
NATIONALISM[1]

If we are to examine further the meaning of nationalism, so often referred to in 1938, our first task must be one of definition. The words nation and nationalism are used loosely and in a variety of ways, and additional complications arise when rendering from other languages those words— *volk*, for instance—which must play an important part in a study of the subject.

A distinction may be made at the outset between the nation and the State. The latter is a political unit, the recognised machinery of government within a given area. A nation, on the other hand, is much harder to define; some would describe it as a cultural unit, and its members may or may not be united in a single State. There is a Welsh nation but not a Welsh State. One might argue that the League of Nations should have been termed the League of States.

But here difficulties begin, as they have for those (at Versailles for instance) faced with the task of distinguishing one nationality from another. It soon becomes apparent that there is no single, objective criterion of a nation. A common language and culture will help promote national feeling, but in Switzerland, Canada and Belgium, for instance, a sense of nationhood can exist in spite of this fact. You will reply that Walloon disturbances or Francophil sentiment in Quebec point to the contrary; the most one may say, however, is that in the making of a nation, language may well be the most important single contributory factor.

In the same way the role of religion may be significant, as in the separation of Pakistan and India, and a church like that of Spain in the sixteenth century may assist in the development of national self-consciousness. Yet many nation-states—Germany, for instance—transcend religious differences, and the notion that Holland owed its independent existence to a concerted religious revolt has long since been dispelled.

The doctrine of 'natural frontiers' may suggest another apparently essential element: a well-defined geographical area. The insularity of

[1]This essay has been written with two speakers in mind, but more could be used. Change of speaker is indicated by an additional space and by setting the beginning of the section full out to the left.

Britain is frequently cited to support this view. Certainly, from a negative angle, geographic divisions were a major factor in the centrifugal movement of the South American Republics. Not only did Bolivar's Great Columbian Republic split into Ecuador, Colombia and Venezuela, the United Provinces of La Plata into Uruguay, Argentina and Paraguay, but geography helped perpetuate separatism within states themselves, as in the case of Argentina and Brazil. German unification was delayed by the absence of clear frontiers. Much of China's history can be understood only in terms of the struggle for supremacy between geographically defined economic regions. 'Unity and centralisation of State power simply meant . . . the control of an economic area where agricultural productivity and facilities of transport permitted a supply of grain-tribute so superior to that of any other areas, that the group which controlled the key area controlled China. . . . Eventually the overwhelming Mongol might brings about a final unification, and by the end of the fourteenth century transport facilities have so much improved that whether under the Chinese dynasty of the Ming, or the foreign Manchu dynasty of Chhing, the country does not splinter again.'[1]

Yet there are many examples to be set against these. Ireland, a clear geographical unit, remains, in a very real sense, two nations; American nationalism crossed the Appalachians; a great river like the Rhine may appear divisive in some places, yet in others is an artery linking the people of both banks. Perhaps the most remarkable case is that of the Jews who retained self-awareness as a distinctive people without any existing territorial basis—only an exclusive religion, a memory of the past and a hope for the future.

Another notion, suggested by Hitler, for instance, that race is the basis of a nation must also be rejected. To quote Dr. David Stafford-Clark: '. . . there is no such thing as a pure race. Groups of human beings are constantly mingling and separating; new groups are constantly being formed, all racial origins are mixed. The concept of a pure race is not simply a myth, for a myth can be valuable; it is rather a dangerous and often hideous illusion: and the cruel and evil things which have been perpetrated in its name have in fact been based upon an assumption which is entirely fallacious.'[2]

A stronger and more genuine basis of a nation is a common history, a sense of common achievement in the arts, in politics, in war, of common hardship and agression resisted, of common heroes like Tell or Hus. It

[1]Needham, *Science and Civilisation in China* Vol. I, pp. 115-6.
[2]*The Psychology of Persecution and Prejudice* p. 7.

must be said that this, too, may be based on myth rather than fact: the legend of the brutal extermination of all Czech liberties at the Battle of the White Mountain, though not entirely false, comes within this category. The 'sleeping Barbarossa' who will see Germany reunited is a more obvious example. But the strength of such sentiments is undoubted, and one example will serve to underline the impossibility of a simple, objective definition of a nation. The people of Tessin (Ticino) had been absorbed by the Swiss Confederation in the fifteenth century, though separated from the latter by mountains and language. By geographic, linguistic, racial, and economic standards, in fact, the area belonged naturally to Lombardy, a Lombardy that in 1798 was being fostered by Napoleon whilst the Confederation was on the verge of collapse. Yet existing political attachments and common ideals moved the Tessin to adhere to the latter, and reject by force of arms the advances of the Cisalpine Republic; the same attitude was adopted towards Mussolini's Italy over a century later. 'A nation,' writes Halle, 'is essentially nothing more than a myth that men enact.'

We find ourselves left, in fact, with a purely subjective definition of the nation. It is difficult to improve upon what John Stuart Mill wrote in 1861:

> 'A portion of mankind may be said to constitute a Nationality if they are united among themselves by common sympathies which do not exist between them and any others—which make them co-operate with each other more willingly than with other people, desire to be under the same government, and desire that it should be government by themselves or a portion of themselves exclusively. This feeling of nationality may have been generated by various causes. . . . None of these circumstances, however, are (sic) either indispensable, or necessarily sufficient by themselves.'

Yes, even size cannot form, on its own, a clear criterion. One thinks of a nation as something bigger than a city-state, though retaining a certain closeness of contact. Yet what this size must be is difficult to say; it has been pointed out that in 1939 there were many more Yorkshiremen than Estonians but it was the latter who formed a nation. Nor can the nation be envisaged in entirely static terms. Emigration alone would prevent this, and you have the instance of Macedonians who, in the early part of this century, were ready to describe themselves as Greek, Bulgar or Serb according to who brought pressure to bear on them.

And so we may echo Renan who, in 1882, described a nation as 'a soul, a spiritual principle.' Though 'nations are nothing eternal' and 'the

European confederation will probably replace them,' they are, says Renan, the law of the century in which he lives; the existence of one of them is, for him, a 'plébiscite de tous les jours.' Nationalism itself usually involves political aspirations concerning State as well as nation; it may be defined as an awareness of belonging to a national group, a conscious desire to contribute to its freedom and strength as distinct from those of other groups.

This, clearly, is on a different scale from the love of family, friends and familiar surroundings; it involves the identification of oneself with countless strangers, with areas unknown. Before this can happen, certain conditions have to be fulfilled. 'The growth of nationalism is the process of integration of the masses of the people into a common political form. Nationalism therefore presupposes the existence, in fact or as an ideal, of a centralised form of government over a large and distinct territory. This form was created by the absolute monarchs, who were the pacemakers of modern nationalism; the French Revolution inherited and continued the centralising tendencies of the kings, but at the same time it filled the central organisation with a new spirit and gave it a power of cohesion unknown before. Nationalism is unthinkable before the emergence of the modern state in the period from the sixteenth to the eighteenth century. Nationalism accepted this form, but changed it by animating it with a new feeling of life and with a new religious fervour.'[1]

But don't forget that not only the framework for nationalism—the centralised State—but also the idea itself did appear before modern times. In their sense of history, their belief in the Covenant and in their spiritual and cultural mission, the Jews of ancient Israel possessed self-consciousness as a group which anticipated later nationalism. In ancient Greece, too, there existed a strong sense of superiority vis-à-vis the Barbarian; limited, city-state patriotism found its complete expression in Plato and Aristotle, in the funeral oration of Pericles:

'What I would prefer is that you should fix your eyes every day on the greatness of Athens as she really is, and should fall in love with her.'

One must recall, however, that Thucydides was writing of internecine war. The heritage of the West from both Greek and Hebrew civilisations was to lie in wider and richer fields than that of nationalism alone.

And the idea then ceased to exist. The Middle Ages, like the Roman Empire, rested upon universal premises: one church, one education, one

[1]Kohn: *The Idea of Nationalism* p. 4.

community, one social order; it combined with these, minute sub-divisions in everyday life that ensured the absence of wide political consciousness. The rivalries of the time were concerned with universal supremacy, or dynastic ambition. The Hundred Years War might seem to stir 'national' sentiment, but Burgundians allied with English, and the German 'nation' which formed one of the four groups of voters at the Council of Constance embraced the delegates from all Northern and Eastern Europe.

Yet in Western Europe significant developments were soon to take shape. The revival of papal absolutism which was heralded at Constance was followed by the slow growth of centralised royal power in England, Spain and France. By the end of the fifteenth century the foundations of Tudor government were laid, Castile and Aragon were at least united by marriage, Burgundy, Brittany and Anjou had been subjected to the King of France. This is grossly simplifying the process, of course. One may note in passing the previous importance of geographical factors such as the focal attributes of the Ile de France, of legal reform, of personalities such as that of Henry II, of struggles against 'outsiders'. More important still is the fact that political consolidation tended to precede and foster national feeling, and not (as was later to be the case in Central and Eastern Europe) the reverse.

The process found its clearest advocate in Machiavelli,[1] lone fore-runner of Italian nationalism, prophet of the sovereign, secular and amoral nation-state. It was assisted by the questioning spirit of the Renaissance, the rise of the vernacular and of new commercial and property-owning classes. The Reformation gave it strength by ending the fiction of a united Christendom. From Luther the Prince received fresh acquiescence, and although 'cuius regio eius religio' helped prolong the division of Germany, it assisted the unity and self-consciousness of England, and was matched, within the Roman fold, by Gallicanism and the independence of the Spanish Inquisition. Between the new States, striving for power, the principle of balance was to be hopefully enshrined in the Treaty of Westphalia; the economic counterpart of étatism was to emerge in the doctrines of mercantilism.

The nature of these European States varied a great deal and in England the Puritan and Glorious revolutions helped create something approach-ing modern nationalism, a climate of opinion in which the word 'patriot' took on a broader meaning. This did not pass unnoticed elsewhere, and in France its contribution blended with the powerful rationalism and

[1]See in particular the final chapter of *The Prince*.

aspirations of the Enlightenment. Here, too, 'patriotism' was extending its meaning before 1789; in Scandinavia, Greece, Bohemia and the Low Countries there were new quests to discover the true value of the community. 'All Europe at the end of the eighteenth century passed through a deep crisis, a search for regeneration, for better foundations of social life, for new concepts of public and private morality.'[1]

Yet nationalism still had no meaning for the masses and did not guide the policies of monarchs. Local dialects and loyalties persisted at the lower levels of society, cosmopolitan culture at the higher. Frederick the Great might describe himself as the 'first servant' of the Prussian State, but it was 'slaves' he was 'tired of ruling' on his deathbed, and it was a 'barbaric' German dialect he despised. Nowhere in Italy was there encouragement for the nationalist and in Poland and the Dutch Republic foreign invasion only emphasised the apathy of the majority. Even where there existed the most heterogeneous populations—in Hungary, for instance—there was little or no resentment on the basis of nationality; even the ghetto walls of Central Europe, artificial aids to natural group awareness, enclosed communities on the verge of bitter class war. The decisive change that was to affect the whole of modern history was still awaited. In other words, 'European nationalism in its modern sense, of the desire ... of a community to assert its unity and independence vis-à-vis other communities or groups, is mainly a product of the nineteenth century.' This point cannot be made too strongly. 'The self-consciousness of nations is a product of the nineteenth century.'

A major reason for this change was, of course, the impact of the American and French Revolutions. Though neither the Declaration of Independence nor the American Constitution use the term 'nation', the implications of the following for the creation of new, national States, are obvious:

'We hold these truths to be self-evident, that all men are created equal, that they are endowed by their Creator with certain unalienable Rights, that among these are Life, Liberty and the pursuit of Happiness.—That to secure these rights, Governments are instituted among Men, deriving their just powers from the consent of the governed,—That whenever any Form of Government becomes destructive of these ends, it is the Right of the People to alter or abolish it, and to institute new Government, laying its foundation on such principles and organising its powers in such form, as to them shall seem most likely to effect their Safety and Happiness.'

Article III of the Declaration of the Rights of Man and of Citizens reinforced this idea:

[1]Kohn, op cit p. 572.

'The Nation is essentially the source of all sovereignty; nor can any individual, or any body of men, be entitled to any authority which is not expressly derived from it.'

The government of a country should express the 'general will' of all its subjects who have a fundamental interest in the management of that country, whose fortunes are inextricably bound up with its own. This was so, even though universal suffrage, anathema to the property-owners who dominated the National Assembly, remained a distant achievement. It was of the greatest significance when the title of the sovereign was changed from 'Louis, by the Grace of God, King of France and Navarre,' to 'Louis, by the Grace of God and the constitutional law of the state, King of the French.' Loyalty is owed to the State, the nation-state, not to the man.

The repercussions were to be widespread. The French Revolution has, for instance, been described as 'the most significant single factor which changed the intellectual relationship of Europe and Asia. . . . Not only did the . . . revolutionary doctrines become in due course an influence on European thought in relation to the East, but they provided the Asian peoples with their first political ideology.'[1]

In both America and France, of course, the effect of these ideas was enhanced by the fact that the nation, new in its entirety or in its form, had to fight for existence. The levée-en-masse, the response to the cry of 'la patrie en danger' heightened the sense of the personal involvement of all. For some, inspired later by Jefferson, for instance, there was also the belief in the Providential mission of their nation.

But nationalism in Europe was also fostered when the French themselves turned to a career of conquest under Napoleon. On the one hand, Napoleon recreated a Polish State, reduced the German States from over three hundred to under forty, abolished the Holy Roman Empire, created the Confederation of the Rhine, the Helvetic Republic and the State of Illyria, and welded the fragments of Italy into three units. The ensuing simplification and standardisation of laws and administration was significant for the future. Even in a federal state like Switzerland, 'the foundations of modern nationhood were laid . . . by Napoleon in the constitution which his mediation imposed in 1803; it was to its principles that the Swiss returned in 1848 when they built their own nation out of their own strength and resources.'[2] Even earlier, the Helvetic Republic had given French and Italian equal rank with the German language.

[1]Panikkar: *Asia and Western Dominance* pp. 315-6.
[2]Kohn: *Nationalism and Liberty* p. 33.

On the other hand, although French rule did not always create resentment, there arose in places national resistance to France and French rational, cosmopolitan culture. Fichte's 'Addresses to the German Nation' called upon the latter to avenge the humiliation of Jena. The literature of the time tended to be romantic and particularist, and writers like Schlegel based their nationalism on the conviction of the decadent inferiority of other cultures. The Prussian victory at Leipzig in 1813, the resistance of Russia to the Great Army in 1812, the Spanish revolt and Constitution of 1812, such events became legends to stimulate later patriotism. This mattered more than the fact that the depiction of concerted national sentiment and effort was frequently untrue. The work of Scharnhorst and Gneisenau to create a 'people in arms', the poetic and gymnastic effusions of Arndt and Jahn, even the appeals of Stein, affected the minds of only a small proportion of German society; but the myth now existed, and with it the gathering effect of universal military service and state-centred education.

Many of those intellectuals who were attempting to further the cause of nationalism had been inspired by the work of Johann Herder. 'To him nationality was not a political or biological but a spiritual and moral concept.' Only as a member of a truly national community, the *volk*, only through his native tongue and culture could a man realise his creative potential; only then would peace come to the world. Moreover, no one nation possessed innate cultural superiority; all tongues, all folk-groups and their spiritual essence, or *volksgeist*, were owed equal respect:

> '. . . the historian of mankind should beware lest he exclusively favours one nationality and thereby slights others who were deprived by circumstances of chance and glory. From the Slavs too the German learned; the Welsh and the Latvians could perhaps have become Greeks, if their situation had been geographically different. . . . It would . . . betray the ignoble pride of a barbarian, to . . . regard the Germans as God's chosen people in Europe, destined by its innate nobility to rule the world and to enslave other peoples. The barbarian rules and dominates; the educated conqueror educates.'

It was in the spirit of Herder that German priests in the nineteenth century revived Lettish and Estonian literary traditions, that Palacký explored the history of the Czechs in Bohemia, that Rumanians sought before independence to replace Greek text books with their own, that the brothers Grimm produced their German folk-tales. The effect in Bohemia and Moravia has been described by Wiskemann: 'In the Historic Provinces, now all but entirely German in outward aspect, a tremendous transformation took place. Slav consciousness was stirred afresh by the

Russian defeat of Napoleon, but it was also matured by the German romantic writers, by the Bohemian Germans and even by the German-speaking aristocracy. The attitude of Germans like Herder to the Slavs was something like that of Rousseau to the noble savage . . . (and) the local aristocracy . . . in their resistance to the absolutism of the dynasty, took up the Czech language . . . and encouraged all provincialisms.'[1]

Yet this is only one strand in the intellectual background to modern nationalism. Herder's kinship to Rousseau leads us to a second, and to a fuller consideration of the latter's importance for our subject. So great was his influence on not only the French Revolution and Napoleon but also German nineteenth century philosophers that he must be regarded as one of the founders of modern nationalism.

His work on the constitutions of Poland and Corsica led him to accept the nation, and not merely the city-state, as a valid political unit, but his legacy has been a divided one. He stresses that the laws which govern a community must come from the will of the people themselves, that this will is the sovereign force within a State; liberty and justice precede Corsica itself in the oath he drafted for that nation. Yet it is easily forgotten that Hobbes' *Leviathan* was the work of a utilitarian individualist, and in providing the modern nation with its foundation—the participation of every citizen—Rousseau unwittingly contributed to trends he would have abhorred. He scorned representative institutions, insisting that the individual can be virtuous and free only by obeying the 'general will':

> 'Whoever refuses to obey the general will shall be compelled to do so by the whole body. This means nothing less than that he will be forced to be free.'

But the general will is not necessarily the will of the majority or even the overt will of all:

> 'Left to themselves, the People always desire the good, but, left to themselves, they do not always know where that good lies. The general will is always right, but the judgement guiding it is not always well informed. It must be made to see things as they are, sometimes as they ought to appear to them.'

By implication, there is an invitation to 'enlightened' interpreters of the general will to step forward.

Moreover, Rousseau announced that man is incapable of loyalty to any unit larger than the *patrie*; to place humanity higher in one's priorities is a disguise for selfishness. Within the State all associations are

[1]*Czechs and Germans* pp. 14-15.

to be discouraged as creating lesser 'general wills', and loyalty to the State should be fostered by a civil religion:

'There is therefore a purely civil profession of faith of which the Sovereign should fix the articles, not exactly as religious dogmas, but as social senti-ments without which a man cannot be a good citizen or a faithful subject. While it can compel no one to believe them, it can banish from the State whoever does not believe them . . . as an anti-social being, incapable . . . of sacrificing, at need, his life to his duty. . . . The dogmas of civil religion ought to be few. . . . The existence of a mighty, intelligent and beneficent Divinity, possessed of foresight and providence, the life to come, the happiness of the just, the punishment of the wicked, the sanctity of the social contract and the laws: these are its positive dogmas. Its negative dogmas I confine to one, intolerance. . . .'

It is hardly surprising, then, that Rousseau found a disciple in Robespierre as well as Jefferson. And in the same way Burke was hailed by German Romantics as a prophet of the true nation-state. His respect for individual liberty, his efforts against the encroachment of the executive in parliamen-tary life, his attitude towards gradual reform meant little to them. What did appeal to them was the mysticism and reverence with which he surrounded the nation-state, its history a continuous creative process, its roots in the past, its strength in God's purpose:

'Society is indeed a contract . . . but the state ought not to be considered nothing better than a partnership agreement in a trade of pepper and coffee, calico or tobacco, or some other such low concern, to be taken up for a little temporary interest, and to be dissolved by the fancy of the parties. It is to be looked upon with reverence. . . . It is a partnership in all science; a partnership in all art; a partnership in every virtue, and in all perfection. As the ends of such a partnership cannot be obtained in many generations, it becomes a partnership not only between those who are living, but between those who are living, those who are dead, and those who are to be born. Each contract of each particular state is but a clause in the great primeval contract of eternal society. . . .'

But the glorification of the nation-state reached new heights with the German Idealist school of philosophy. Fichte moved from a youthful belief in liberalism and a joyful acceptance of the French Revolution to an authoritarian and étatist position. The State, based on the *volk*, should control the economic activity of its citizens, should strive for economic self-sufficiency, and should be the supreme object of devotion. Each nation must develop its own character in this way, but some, notably the German, are by nature superior. The warnings of Herder are forgotten.

With Hegel, the final stage is reached and the State becomes more than a means to virtue; it is an end in itself. His work has been described as 'the most complete and uncompromising philosophy of nationalism that has yet been conceived,' directly influencing Treitschke and Ranke in Germany, Gentile, Rocco and other forerunners of Fascism in Italy. For him, as for Rousseau, true freedom lies in complete subservience to the State. In the rise and fall of States may be seen the unfolding of the Universal Mind, and the State that triumphs through force and in disregard of the idea of international morality is the true agent of progress. In patriotism, a man may lose his selfishness, and in war his patriotism and morality will be strengthened the more:

> 'The State is the Divine Idea as it exists on Earth. We have in it, therefore, the object of History in a more definite shape than before; that in which Freedom obtains objectivity. . . . When the State or our country constitutes a community of existence; when the subjective will of man submits to laws—the contradiction between Liberty and Necessity vanishes. . . . For the History of the World occupies a higher ground than . . . the conscience of individuals. What the absolute aim of Spirit requires and accomplishes . . . transcends the obligation . . . of good or bad motives. . . .'

Hegel came to glorify the existing Prussian State and to urge the unification of Germany; his theories must be seen in part as 'the painful search for a national vocation.' Nothing could be further from the concurrent stream of German culture represented by Schiller and, above all, Goethe. 'The German nation is nothing,' wrote the latter, 'but the individual German is something, and yet they imagine the opposite to be true. The Germans should be dispersed throughout the world, like the Jews, in order fully to develop all the good that is in them for the benefit of mankind.'

Clearly, the forces of nationalism were likely to manifest themselves differently in States where Hegelian ideas were largely accepted than in those dominated by the belief that the rights of the State over the individual must be limited, that his freedom and consent are essential. The assertions of John Locke, that the individual possesses certain natural rights, that the body politic exists on a contractual basis only to preserve and foster those rights, and that the legislature may be removed or altered by the sovereign people, found deep roots in his own country. In the American colonies it blended with the spirit of Milton and the Puritan revolution. The same emphasis—however inadequate for the social needs of the time—is to be found in the following century in the work of John Stuart Mill:

> 'The object of this Essay (i.e. "On Liberty") is to assert one very simple

principle, as entitled to govern absolutely the dealings of society with the individual in the way of compulsion and control, whether the means used be physical force in the form of legal penalties, or the moral coercion of public opinion. That principle is, that the sole end for which mankind are warranted, individually or collectively, in interfering with the liberty of action of any of their number, is self-protection. That the only purpose for which power can be rightfully exercised over any member of a civilised community, against his will, is to prevent harm to others. His own good, either physical or moral, is not a sufficient warrant. He cannot rightfully be compelled to do or forbear because it will be better for him to do so, because it will make him happier, because, in the opinion of others, to do so would be wise, or even right. These are good reasons for remonstrating with him, or reasoning with him, or persuading him, or entreating him, but not for compelling him, or visiting him with any evil in case he do otherwise. . . . Over himself, over his own body and mind, the individual is Sovereign.'

And lest it should be thought that such a view was an Anglo-Saxon prerogative, one might mention that in Switzerland, Pestalozzi urged it side by side with the need for a genuine, Swiss nation-state. It was commonly assumed at the time, of course, as it was by President Wilson later, that nationalism and liberalism were natural and inevitable allies. Both were opposed by the reactionary powers (not least the Roman Catholic Church); both, it was hoped, would lead to universal harmony. Even thinkers at the opposite ends of the political spectrum, messianic nationalists like Michelet and class-conscious socialists like Saint-Simon did not consider their views to be diametrically opposed; they felt, rather, a sense of kinship, in opposition to the easy-going pragmatism of the centre.

But the note sounded by Pestalozzi made less impact on the divided nationalities of Europe in the first half of the nineteenth century than did the fervent appeals of other prophets: Mickiewicz, the Polish poet who saw his country as the Christ among nations, leading the world to freedom through its sufferings; Mazzini, founder of Young Italy, calling upon his countrymen to remember duties before rights, to inspire Europe by the heights of their unselfish patriotism:

'The individual is too weak, and Humanity too vast. . . . But God gave you (the) means when he gave you a Country, when . . . he divided Humanity into distinct groups upon the face of our globe, and thus planted the seeds of nations. Bad governments have disfigured the design of God, which you may see clearly marked out, as far, at least, as regards Europe, by the courses of the great rivers, by the lines of the lofty mountains, and by other geographical conditions; they have disfigured it by conquest, by greed, by jealousy of the just sovereignty of others. . . . But the divine design will infallibly be fulfilled. Natural divisions, the innate spontaneous tendencies of the peoples will replace the arbitrary divisions. . . . The Countries of the People will rise, defined by the voice of the free. . . . Between these Countries there will be harmony and brotherhood. . . . Without Country you have neither name, token, voice, nor rights, no admission as brothers into the fellowship of the Peoples. You are the bastards of Humanity. Soldiers without a banner, Israelites among the nations, you will find neither faith nor protection; none will be sureties for you. Do not beguile yourselves with the hope of emancipation from unjust social conditions if you do not first conquer a Country for yourselves.'

We may summarise the ideological background in the early nineteenth century, then, by saying that for some the nation-state had become an overriding goal, whilst for others it needed balancing against the rights of the individual. The former view was more likely to be held by those whose national unity and independence had yet to be won, though the division of opinion was not strictly conditioned by this factor. The situation was surveyed by Acton in 1862, in an essay in which he attacked the dangerous and utopian principles of Mazzini:

'These two views of nationality, corresponding to the French and to the English systems, are connected in name only, and are in reality the opposite extremes of political thought. In one case, nationality is founded on the perpetual supremacy of the collective will, of which the unity of the nation is the necessary condition, to which every other influence must defer, and against which no obligation enjoys authority, and all resistance is tyrannical. The nation is here an ideal unit founded on the race, in defiance of the modifying action of external causes, of tradition, and of existing rights. It overrules the rights and wishes of the inhabitants, absorbing their divergent interests in a fictitious unity; sacrifices their several inclinations and duties to the higher claim of nationality, and crushes all natural rights and all established liberties for the purpose of vindicating itself. Connected with this theory in nothing except the common enmity of the absolute state is the theory which represents nationality as an essential, but not a supreme element in determining the forms of the State. It is distinguished from the other, because it tends to diversity and not to uniformity, to harmony and not to unity; because it aims not at an arbitrary change, but at careful respect for the existing conditions of political life, and because it obeys the laws and results of history, not the aspirations of an ideal future.'

In a way, it is surprising that men like Mazzini and Mickiewicz were able to keep their ideals alive, for the situation in Europe after the Congress of Vienna might well have led to despair. The Habsburg, Ottoman and Romanov empires denied their principles from the Baltic to the Balkans;

the German Confederation represented nothing but Austrian and Prussian supremacy; Poland remained partitioned and Italy a 'geographical expression'. The greater part of Central and Eastern Europe was a patchwork of languages and religions, further complicated by economic and social divisions—in the Balkans, for instance, by the commercial position of the Greeks and the status of the Greek Patriarch in Constantinople.

Yet there were moments of encouragement. An Irish revolt had soon followed that of the American colonies. Secret societies like the Carbonari developed in Italy and elsewhere. Some Serbs were able to defy the Turks in the mountains of Montenegro, and the Obrenović and Karagjorgjević dynasties gradually forced a greater degree of autonomy for Serbia itself, the Turks finally departing in 1867. And just as Serbs looked back to the battle of Kossovo in 1389, when a Great Serbian Empire had come to an end, so in Rumania a national hero was found from the late sixteenth century in the person of Michael the Brave; as Vuk Karadžić elevated vernacular Serb to the level of a literary language and Agram became the centre of a literary 'Illyrian Movement', so the revival of Greek learning spread from the island of Chios, the first Bulgarian school not to use Greek opened in 1835, and a chair for Ukrainian language and literature was created at the University of Lemberg.

There were even more tangible victories. The Greek uprising of 1821 produced, after the intervention of Navarino, an independent Kingdom, and a proclamation of the Greek National Assembly in 1822 epitomised a cry that was to become familiar in the next hundred years:

'The war which we are carrying on against the Turk is not that of a faction or the result of sedition. It is not aimed at the advantage of any single part of the Greek people; it is a national war, a holy war, a war the object of which is to reconquer the rights of individual liberty, of property and honour—rights which the civilized people of Europe, our neighbours, enjoy today; rights of which the cruel and unheard of tyranny of the Ottomans would deprive us—us alone—and the very memory of which they would stifle in our hearts.'

Belgium, partly inspired by the 1830 French Revolution, succeeded in severing her ties with Holland shortly afterwards. In Spanish America, the leadership of men like Bolivar and San Martin created independent republics, guaranteed by the words of Monroe, the interests of British commerce and the guns of the Royal Navy. In Hungary, Kossuth led a movement for complete Magyarization and freedom from Vienna, and in the North, Norway successfully resisted the effects of union with

Sweden. Even at Westminster, O'Connell—soon to be outdone by Young Ireland—bedevilled the Whigs and frightened the Tories.

We've been concentrating on various intellectual stimuli to national self consciousness. Remember that the swift growth of populations, together with industrialisation, urbanisation, and the uprooting of people on a large scale were to be equally great factors. The cohesive effect of railways as they began to link the Swiss valleys can epitomise for us the results of swiftly developing communications of all kinds, including the press. In some areas there was, in addition, national service in the armed forces and state-directed education; everywhere, social and economic problems would eventually create an increased political awareness, a growing 'interdependence of government and the governed'. The growing amplitude of trade-cycles and the fact that they were European and even wider in extent would mean that workers and industrialists alike would seek protection within the strong nation-state. Within the Zollverein, for instance, economic cooperation between small States helped prepare the ground for unification.

You are making the whole process sound far too swift and widespread, you know. As late as 1846, your happy Swiss railways had neither a common gauge, nor the power to prevent the imminence of civil war. If the Zollverein did assist in some way in creating the sense of one German nation it was certainly not the intention of its creators that this should be so, and those members who were in a position to do so fought for Austria and not Prussia in 1866. The nationalist outcries in Germany that ended with the Karlsbad decrees have been fittingly described as 'undergraduate follies', and German and Italian unifications looked no nearer in 1847 than they had in 1815. You must realise that the Romantic nationalists, the poets and political philosophers, reached a minute audience. In 1827 the South Slavs had only $\frac{1}{2}\%$ literate, in 1840 Russia only 2%. Only in Western Europe was industrialisation at all advanced by the middle of the century; even in Prussia 72% of the population were classed as rural in 1846, and the difference in political and economic circumstances east and west of the Rhine had been emphasised by the results of the 1830 revolutions. Systems of land ownership and social stratification were a great barrier to genuine national feeling: 'it was said of a Croat landowner of the nineteenth century that he would sooner have regarded his horse than his peasant as a member of the Croat nation.' Even in some places where independence was obtained, notably South America, economic, political and educational development was not sufficiently advanced to bear the new circumstances, and disintegration of all kinds ensued. There is a strong parallel here with the situation in many of the swiftly emerging States of our own day which often possess, like South America, artificial, bequeathed frontiers.

The limited influence and strength of nationalism was clearly demonstrated during the 1848 revolutions. Catholic and conservative peasants cheered on Radetzky as he rode to crush what to them was a rising of lords and freethinking entrepreneurs. The regenerated man of Mazzini's dreams was little in evidence. Separatist feelings remained decisive in Tuscany, and the disturbances in Naples and Sicily had nothing to do with Italian unification. 'There was . . . no singleness of purpose, no clearness or largeness of aim, to justify our considering the (Italian) uprisings of 1848-49 truly nationalist.'[1]

It was the same elsewhere: the liberal-nationalist had no programme to attract peasant or proletarian. Frederick William rode in national colours and the Frankfurt Assembly sounded its phrases; Archduke John's 'government' was still a mockery, the problem of Austria within Germany remained unsolved, and the Prussian army waited, unmoved. Nor was a clear national solution emerging further East. Palacký's refusal to go to Frankfurt was a major stage on the road that led to Munich, but the Slav Congress offered assurances of loyalty to the Habsburgs; there was further reassurance whenever it touched on the bitter relations between Poles, Ruthenes, and the Russian Empire. Magyar chauvinism was repaid in the person of Jellačić, and Russian Poland, already crushed in 1831, remained passive.

But you have yourself indicated the growing significance of nationalism in these years; how else should one interpret Magyar intolerance and the reactions against it, for instance? Again, it was clear that in Germany the force of nationalism would take precedence over liberalism if ever the two were in conflict. The Frankfurt Assembly rejoiced at the destruction of the Prague revolt and at the war against Denmark over Schleswig and Holstein; the creed by which it called for the absorption of the Grand Duchy of Posen was that of 'healthy national egoism'. National legend, too, was created in the revolutionary years and the republics of Rome and Venice received more widespread devotion in the memory than they had in the event. Remember also that from the Swiss civil war of 1847 (when the Sonderbund posed the same question over the Federal Pact of 1815 that the Southern States were to raise in 1861) came the Federal Constitution of 1848, foundation of perhaps the most remarkable nation of modern Europe, triumph over linguistic division, over economic, religious and constitutional antagonism.

[1]Ramm: *The Risorgimento*: Historical Association pamphlet, p. 13.

Moreover we are now entering the period in which nationalism achieved its greatest triumphs in Europe in the shape of German and Italian unifications. In Germany, especially, cultural nationalism had long preceded the attainment of a nation-state. Now, under leaders whose own aims were not truly nationalist and through the instrument of unscrupulous wars, the desires of the national-liberals were realised. But they were realised, especially in Germany, at the expense of liberal principles; to those who had turned in despair from politics to business after 1848, means mattered less than the end. The indemnity granted Bismarck for his non-parliamentary rule, the hollow constitutions of 1867 and 1871, the high-handedness of Turin over plebiscites and administration in the South, suggested that neither State would fall within the second of Acton's categories. Germany in particular was culturally and politically rejecting the traditions of Western Europe; the new centre of the nation, in the disciplined and military eastern marches, symbolised the fact. 'Blood and iron' seemed to guarantee success. 'The Prussian victories of the 1860's, the transformation which they wrought in the mind of most Germans, laid the foundations for the defeats of 1918 and 1945.'[1]

Although Germans had to conquer divisions between themselves and not an alien oppressor, both unifications represented a defeat for the Habsburgs, of course. The problem presented by the Empire's Czechs, Poles, Ruthenes, Croats, Rumans, Serbs and others remained unsolved. It would be an oversimplification to divide Austria into rulers and oppressed, for by 1914 the nationalities had found their place in 'an intricate hieratic system'; yet the situation was marked by increasing bitterness, and since our starting-point was Bohemia, events there will best illustrate the fact.

The Czech national movement was assisted by the emancipations of 1848 which increased the political importance of Slav peasant proprietors, and by the growing number of Czech bourgeoisie in the second half of the century. At the same time the concession of Dualism to the Magyars—despite bitter warnings by Palacký—made a deep impression. Already the dynasty had rejected the Kremsier Constitution, which would have granted separate Czech and German 'circles' for local government, and enforced that of 1861, which rested upon German centralism and Slav political inferiority. There were, indeed, periods of concession and improvement, particularly under Taafe: the Czechs agreed to return to the Reichsrat in 1879, obtained the Language Decrees of 1880, opened

[1]Kohn: *The Mind of Germany* p. 161.

the first national theatre in Prague in 1881, and were granted a separate part of Prague University in 1882.

Yet there was no lasting settlement. Concessions in 1871 had been withdrawn in the face of strong German opposition, and the same happened to the Badeni decrees two years after their promulgation. The Compromise of 1905, fixing the proportion of Czech and German representatives in the Moravian Diet, offered some hope, as did the granting of universal suffrage for Reichsrat elections in 1907. But in Bohemia and Silesia bitter contests continued in local government elections. Czech children were taught that it was their duty to settle in German areas and thus win back provinces that were once entirely theirs; trade boycotts were pursued on national lines; the German minority obstructed the work of the Bohemian Diet, whilst the Czech minority in the Reichsrat did the same. Before 1914, government had increasingly to be carried on by emergency decree. With Serbia adopting a policy of creating discontent among the Habsburg South Slavs, with Polish restlessness and Magyar insolence, the future for the Dual Monarchy seemed an anxious one.

This was particularly so because, as you have indicated, the Balkans were now in turmoil. Moldavia and Wallachia had been granted autonomy by the Turks after the Crimean War, and had united under Cuza in 1858; after the liberal revolt of 1866, Rumania settled down to the long reign of King Charles, apprehensive of Russia but a reproach to Turkey. In Bulgaria, discontent was increasing, fostered by exiles like the poet Rakovsky, hardened by Levski's death as a national martyr in 1873. Soon the peninsula was aflame, with Bosnia and Herzegovina in revolt in 1875 and Bulgaria in the following year. Serbia and Montenegro declared war on the Turk, and there ensued Russian intervention, San Stefano, and the Berlin Congress. Though Bulgarian aspirations were partly satisfied in 1885, Pan-Slav and Pan-German tensions, the presence of Austria-Hungary in Bosnia, Herzegovina and the Sanjak, and continued Turkish misrule ensured future trouble. The Young Turk revolution of 1908 hastened the process. In response to the policy of turkification which followed, risings occurred in Albania, and an Albanian Congress adopted the Latin alphabet in place of Turkish characters. The First Balkan War seemed to preface the end of the Turk in Europe; salvation appeared only when the force of nationalism which had created such a situation escaped into internecine channels among the victors.

But one musn't give the impression that nationalism was striking only at the empires of Central and Eastern Europe. Catalan and Basque separatist movements existed in Spain, and Norway won its independence from Sweden in 1905. More turbulent was Irish nationalism in the form of Fenianism, and although its literary counterpart in Hyde, the Gaelic League and the Abbey Theatre was less violent, Ireland, having broken Gladstone's Liberal Party, had brought England close to civil war by 1914. The failure of the latter to appreciate the full nature and force of Irish nationalism—a failure repeated in the case of Arab nationalism, for instance, before and after Suez—is reflected in what Mill wrote in 1861:

> 'No Irishman is now less free than an Anglo-Saxon, nor has a less share of every benefit either to his country or to his individual fortunes than if he were sprung from any other portion of the British dominions. The only remaining real grievance of Ireland, that of the State Church, is one which half, or nearly half, the people of the larger island have in common with them. There is now next to nothing, except the memory of the past, and the difference in the predominant religion, to keep apart two races, perhaps the most fitted of any two in the world to be the completing counterpart of one another. The consciousness of being at last treated not only with equal justice but with equal consideration is making such rapid way in the Irish nation as to be wearing off all feelings that could make them insensible to the benefits which the less numerous and less wealthy people must necessarily derive from being fellow-citizens instead of foreigners to those who are not only their nearest neighbours, but the wealthiest, and one of the freest, as well as most civilised and powerful, nations of the earth.

Alas for the hopes of liberal England. But the Irish question serves to underline some common characteristics of many of the national movements thrusting forward before 1914. Colonisation and conquest had frequently failed to obliterate loyalties to the memory or myth of past independence, especially when the ruling nation kept itself apart socially as well as politically. The work of small numbers of intellectuals and a literary revival often paved the way for wider movements, and though retarded economic development often proved a formidable barrier to this latter aspect, the question of land could be an important element in its own right. Ireland, Bulgaria, Serbia, Latvia, Estonia and Bohemia furnish examples of this. In the last-named, the Czech nobility dwindled with the upheavals of the seventeenth century; the higher ranks of society, the owners of estates, were now almost exclusively German; Czech became the language of workmen and peasants alone. Religious separatism, too, could help promote national movements, as it did for the Poles; it could also, of course, as with Catholic and Protestant Irish, and Catholic Croat and Orthodox Serb, contain complications for the future.

Religion, language and strong individual national sentiment rendered insubstantial a supranational movement like Panslavism. The abortive Slav Congress of 1848 had indicated as much; continued hopes of 'Austro-Slavism' and bitter Russo-Polish relations—political and religious—were only two of the ensuing complications. Despite the appeals of Danilevsky and the Slavophil sentiments of Ignatiev, Russian Panslavism barely concealed expansionist Russian nationalism, failed to conceal it, in fact, in a case like Dostoevsky's. Slavophil and Westerner had shared a belief in Russia's special mission; the drives towards Constantinople and the East and the policy of russification within the Empire showed the forms this mission might take. On the other hand, the particularism of the new Slav States was emphasised by the Russian failure to enforce mediation in the Second Balkan War, and the alliance of Bulgaria with the Central Powers. Subsequent trends such as Polish-Czech hostility between 1919 and 1939 merely confirmed the weakness of an ideal like Panslavism when faced with the realities of nationalism.

The expansion of Russia should remind us of another important national development in the nineteenth century. As Alexis de Tocqueville observed in 1835:

> 'There are, at the present time, two great nations in the world which seem to tend towards the same end, although they started from different points: I allude to the Russians and the Americans. Both of them have grown up unnoticed. . . . All other nations seem to have nearly reached their natural limits, and only to be charged with the maintenance of their power . . . these are proceeding with ease and with celerity along a path to which the human eye can assign no term.'

The same writer observed of the United States that 'although the citizens are divided into twenty-four distinct sovereignties, they nevertheless constitute a single people'; but a new nation, or the hopes of one, had yet to be born at Appomattox. Similarly, de Tocqueville distinguished between the conquests of America 'by the ploughshare' and those of Russia 'by the sword'; but the Alamo and its consequences were only a year away, and American imperialism was to be as real as Russian. Professor Van Alstyne has commented: 'The Monroe doctrine, so-called, has the qualities of a powerful negative . . . and in time it turned into a potent psychological weapon in the stimulation of American nationalism. But it is not the negatives of the Monroe doctrine that really count: it is the hidden positives to the effect that the United States shall be the only colonising power in North America and that it shall be the directing power in both North and South America. This is imperialism preached in the grand manner. . . . The Monroe doctrine would be better described as "the Monroe manifesto".'[1]

The expansionist spirit of American nationalism found perhaps its most celebrated nineteenth century expression, remember, in an article by John O'Sullivan in 1845:

> 'Texas is now ours. . . . She is no longer to us a mere country on the map. She comes within the dear and sacred designation of Our Country; no longer a *pays*, she is part of *la patrie*; and that which is at once a sentiment and a virtue, Patriotism, already begins to thrill for her too within the national heart. . . . Why, were other reasoning wanting, in favour of now elevating this question . . . up to its proper level of a high and broad nationality, it is surely to be found . . . in the manner in which other nations have undertaken to intrude themselves . . . in a spirit of hostile interference against us, for the avowed object of thwarting our policy and hampering our power, limiting our greatness and checking the fulfilment of our manifest destiny to overspread the continent alloted by Providence for the free development of our yearly multiplying millions.'

But remember also that those 'yearly multiplying millions' must recall another remarkable aspect of the growth of the United States: the assimilation into one nation of peoples from a host of different nationalities. Among the 30 million immigrants between 1860 and 1930, the four and a half million Irish were equalled by Germans and by Italians, the four million English, Scots and Welsh by Balkan and Austrian peoples, not to speak of two and a quarter million Scandinavians and three and three-quarter million Poles and Russians. That they could come to feel themselves Americans was a great and significant achievement.

Among these new Americans were a considerable number of Jews. Though in Western Europe loyalty to existing nation-states had triumphed over Jewish separatism, in the East, and particularly in Russia and Rumania, officially-inspired pogroms fostered traditionalism and mass emigration. Encouraged by scholars of Judaism and by fears of assimilation, by episodes like the Dreyfus affair and by men like Moses Hess and Leon Pinsker, the movement for a Jewish national home in Palestine resulted in the formation of a World Zionist Organisation under Herzl in 1897. Yet another manifestation of nationalism was ready to add to the confusion of the First World War.

Clearly the pressure of nationalism in Europe was increasing in the

[1] *The American Empire:* Historical Association Pamphlet, p. 15.

second half of the century, forced on by the demands for security of peoples faced with rapidly changing economic and social conditions. In this sense, socialism and nationalism may be said to have a common root; their strength when combined, as they frequently have been in the twentieth century, is hardly surprising.

Nor is it surprising that, as the nineteenth century progressed, the British liberal dream of free trade and peace, the dream of Cobden and of *Locksley Hall*, faded away in the face of international economic rivalry, the Bismarck and McKinley tariffs, the nationalist economic theories of Friedrich List, the boycotting of foreign goods by nationalists in Ireland and India.

In the political sphere, too, ideas and events marched hand in hand. Treitschke, for whom the essence of the state was *macht*, for whom war was 'the one remedy for an ailing nation,' justified the taking by Germany of Alsace and Lorraine in the following fashion:

> 'These provinces are ours by the right of the sword, and we shall dispose of them by a higher right—the right of the German nation, which cannot allow its lost children to remain forever alien to the German Empire. We Germans . . . know better what is for the good of the Alsatians than do those unhappy people themselves. . . . We desire, even against their will, to restore them to themselves.'

Ranke, too, saw in the Prussian victory of 1870-71 the hand of God, the triumph of an established social order that would inaugurate the reign of peace and stability in Europe.

You're in danger of creating a stereotyped picture, you know; there were still some German intellectuals ready to protest against the direction which events were taking. The historian Gervinus, though desirous of national unity, wrote in 1870:

> 'The German Confederation has been created for the very purpose of forming in the centre of Europe a neutral state which would by its federal organisation guarantee peace. By the disruption of the Confederation in 1866, two-thirds of the German territory have been transformed into a warrior-state ever ready for aggression, in which one can see, without being an enemy of Prussia and Germany, a permanent threat to the peace of the continent and to the security of the neighbouring states. Prussia has been reproached with having by its war and its methods transformed the whole of Europe into one armed camp; it would be impossible to regard as a malevolent phrase in the mouth of an enemy what can be simply proved by facts.'[1]

Remember, too, that Germany was not alone in her chauvinism.

[1]Quoted in Kohn: *The Mind of Germany* p. 170.

'The good repute which nationalism commonly enjoyed in the nineteenth century should not blind us to its constant association with aggression and incitement to war. In this respect, Britain, France and Russia set the pace; Germany and Italy . . . proved apt pupils; and towards the end of the century, Japan and the United States join belatedly in the game.'[1] Consider, for instance, what Charles Kingsley, author of *The Water Babies*, wrote in a letter about the conquest of Sarawak by Rajah Brooke:

'I say at once that I think he was utterly right and righteous—"sacrifice of human life"? Prove that it is human life. It is beast-life. These Dyaks have put on the image of a beast, and they must take the consequences. . . . Physical death is no evil. It may be a blessing to the survivors. Else, why pestilence, famine, (and) Cromwell . . . in Ireland, Charlemagne hanging 4,000 Saxons over the Weser bridge: did not God bless those terrible righteous judgements? Do you believe in the Old Testament? Surely then, say, what does that destruction of the Canaanites mean? If it was right, Rajah Brooke was right. If he be wrong, then Moses, Joshua, David were wrong. . . . You Malays, and Dyaks of Sarawak, you . . . are the enemies of Christ, the Prince of Peace: you are beasts, all the more dangerous, because you have a semi-human cunning. I will, like David, "hate you with a perfect hatred, even as though you were my enemies". I will blast you with grape and rockets, "I will beat you as small as the dust before the wind".'

For Kingsley, of course, as for Carlyle, Macaulay and others, particular pride was to be taken in England's apparently limitless material progress:

'Remember that . . . England is . . . the nation which above all others conquered nature by obeying her; that as it pleased God that the author of that proverb, the father of inductive science, Bacon Lord Verulam, should have been an Englishman, so it has pleased Him that we, Lord Bacon's countrymen, should improve that precious heirloom of science, inventing, producing, exporting, importing, till it seems as if the whole human race, and every land from the equator to the pole, must henceforth bear the indelible impress and sign manual of English science. . . . Do you not see, then, that by following these studies . . . you are training yourselves in that habit of mind which God has approved as the one which He has ordained for Englishmen, and are doing what in you lies toward carrying out, in after life, the glorious work which God seems to have laid on the English race to replenish the earth and subdue it?'

Again, however, we must beware of producing a false stereotype. It is true, for instance, that Kingsley's outlook may be found reflected in much of the history of British India in the nineteenth century; yet con-

[1]*Nationalism*, R.I.I.A. pp. 186-7.

sider also the advice given by Sir Thomas Munro, Governor of Madras, to other imperial administrators:

'Your rule is alien, and it can never be popular. You have much to bring to your subjects, but you cannot look for more than passive gratitude. You are not here to turn India into England or Scotland. Work through, not in spite of, native systems and native ways, with a prejudice in their favour rather than against them; and when in the fulness of time your subjects can frame and maintain a worthy Government for themselves, get out and take the glory of the achievement and the sense of having done your duty as the chief reward for your exertions.'

In England itself, we must mention the significance of the Oxford Idealist philosophers, T. H. Green, Bosanquet, and Bradley. Instead of Spencer's *Man versus the State* the State becomes an instrument for virtue, removing obstacles from the individual's path to this goal, legislating to abolish ignorance, drunkenness and pauperism. This was Green's position; Bradley and Bosanquet moved closer still to Hegel in the subordination of the individual will to the 'common mind' of the community, to the ethical principle enshrined in the State.

But there were more ominous doctrines than these becoming entangled with those of nationalism. Anti-Semitism was no stranger to Europe, but now, in the writings of Wagner, for instance, it built upon the work of Fichte and Hegel to reach new extremes as it glorified Germanic superiority:

'If emancipation from the yoke of Judaism appears to us the greatest of necessities, we must above all prove our forces for this war of liberation. Now we shall . . . win these forces . . . only from an accurate acquaintance with the nature of our involuntary feeling of an instinctive repugnance against the Jew's essential character. Through it . . . must there become plain to us what we hate in that essence; what we then know clearly, we can oppose; nay, through his very laying bare, may we even hope to rout the demon from the field, whereon he has only been able to maintain his stand beneath the shelter of a twilight darkness—a darkness we good-natured humanitarians ourselves have cast upon him, to make his look less loathsome.'

Add to such sentiments the cloudy identification of Barbarossa with Siegfried, the Nibelungen Hoard with the destiny of the German Reich, and their potential becomes obvious. Bismarck's Germany after 1871 was quite inadequate for their fulfilment so far as Wagner was concerned; the genuine folk-prince was still awaited.

Wagner was not alone, of course, in his racialist doctrines. The Frenchman Gobineau was emphasising the distinctive emotional, mental and physical attributes of races, the inherent superiority of white over yellow, of yellow over black, of Aryan over Semite and Slav. His ideas, transmitted through Wagner and the 'Gobineau Club' received more attention in Germany than in his own country. The same was true of Houston Stewart Chamberlain, married to Wagner's daughter, striving to prove himself more German than the Germans, glorifying not only the Aryans but the Teutonic 'sub-race' above other Aryans. Deriving from the Jews his Christianity, from the Greeks his art, literature and science, from the Romans his legal and political organisation, the Teuton rejected the weaknesses of these peoples to become the predestined cultural and political leader of the world. In Chamberlain, Hitler and Rosenberg found a kindred spirit.

Irrationalism, too, was a growing force at this time, and the work of men like William James and Bergson was later taken and twisted to justify political doctrines far removed from the intentions of the authors concerned. This was particularly the case with Nietzsche. His condemnation of the existing, effete Western civilisation, his later call to live dangerously and to conquer in a harsh world, obscured his opposition to racial, national and totalitarian beliefs. His superman was hailed, not as a conqueror who rises above his own weakness, but as a ruler of lesser beings. Similarly Georges Sorel, though a revolutionary socialist, urged heroic action in terms that were to be entirely acceptable to Fascists and Nazis; his emphasis upon the value of 'social myths' finds a direct echo in Rosenberg's *Myth of the Twentieth Century*, in the pronouncements of Mussolini:

> 'We have created our myth. The myth is a faith, it is a passion. It is not necessary that it shall be a reality. . . . Our myth is the nation, our myth is the greatness of the nation.'

One should also mention Pareto, whose influence on Mussolini earned him the description of 'the Karl Marx of Fascism', and those students of eugenics and politics who were advocating at this time State encouragement of superior stock and the limiting of inferior by sterilisation and other means. Often unwittingly, a vicious metaphysical brew was being prepared, awaiting only its appropriate political, social and economic environment, and the men to use it.

Meanwhile, remember, for reasons of prestige, economics and power, nationalism was being projected beyond Europe in the shape of late-nineteenth century imperialism. This might take the form of direct or indirect rule, of 'spheres of influence', or special trading rights. The work of men like Rhodes and Karl Peters was fostered by bodies like the

Pan-German League and King Leopold's African Association; it was championed by 'liberals' like Max Weber ('We alone made out of the Poles human beings') and 'radicals' like Joseph Chamberlain ('The Anglo Saxon race is infallibly destined to be the predominant race in the history and civilization of the world.') The fact that whereas one-tenth of Africa was colonised in 1875 only the same amount remained untaken in 1895 illustrates a process that was taking place from Central America to the Yangtze, from the Persian Gulf to the Pacific. At the same time as Germans, Turks, Magyars and Russians engaged in attempts to impose their cultural or political superiority on others, and as Home Rule ran into new obstacles, the United States was reaching out to take the Philippines and Hawaii, to dominate Cuba and Panama, the Dominican Republic, Haiti and Nicaragua.

Imperialism, of course, involved the reverse of national self-determination, and the result bears some resemblance to the Napoleonic era. The doctrine of nationalism was fostered in Asia and Africa by the European development and administration of territories, and by the ensuing reaction against alien rule and exploitation.

Yes; in a sense imperialism, whether in this period or during Hitler's drive for *lebensraum*, was the negation of nationalism, but it was also its offspring. Meanwhile, in Europe itself, the strength of nationalism was also being demonstrated by its triumph over international socialism. Despite the 'age of the masses', the Marxist condemnation of the existing State and the fears aroused by the Internationals, revolutionary socialism in the West found itself being revised in the direction of achieving reform through national, parliamentary institutions. The career of Lassalle and the Gotha Programme had foreshadowed the support given by German socialists to national military expenditure in 1907; the appeals of the Stuttgart Congress went largely unheeded. In 1914, there were few socialists not ready to vote war credits; even in discontented Russia, the outbreak of war produced widespread patriotic fervour. For the crowds in the capitals of Europe, it was enough that their nation was in danger. In German, in English, in French, the diaries on the bodies of young patriots soon recorded the same sentiments on the Western Front.

But what of the position beyond Europe? One could produce Asian examples of national self-awareness long before the nineteenth century—in the Celestial Empire, for instance—and the Indian rebellion of 1857-8 and the Boxer rising suggest national reaction against the foreigner.

This is true; but, as in much of Eastern Europe, fully conscious nationalism in the modern sense was far from complete by the turn of the century. There were, however, significant developments in this direction. In India, the very fact of a single ruling power; the promotion by Macaulay of a uniform English education and the ensuing influence of, for instance, Benthamism; the flowering of vernacular languages under the hand of Tagore and others; and a Hindu Reformation that would permit fundamental social reform were as great in their import as the well-known founding of the Indian National Congress in 1885. For some, a new vision was arising:

'Freedom from fear is the freedom I claim for you, my Motherland!—fear, the phantom demon, shaped by your own distorted dreams;
Freedom from the burden of ages, bending your head, breaking your back, blinding your eyes to the beckoning call of the future;
Freedom from shackles of slumber wherewith you fasten yourself to night's stillness, mistrusting the star that speaks of truth's adventurous path;
Freedom from the anarchy of a destiny, whose sails are weakly yielded to blind uncertain winds, and the helm to a hand ever rigid and cold as Death;
Freedom from the insult of dwelling in a puppet's world, where movements are started through brainless wires, repeated through mindless habits; where figures wait with patient obedience for a master of show to be stirred into a moment's mimicry of life.'

('Freedom'; from the collected poems and plays of Rabindranath Tagore[1])

One should remember, however, that the same poet fiercely rejected intolerant, Western nationalism,

'the vast flesh—the self-love of the Nation—dead under its own excess',

though he was powerless to prevent its coming.

In Japan, particularly after the Meiji Restoration, Western military and cultural examples were studied with a view to producing the strength that would remove the legacy of Perry's Black Ships; at the same time, a Shinto revival underlined the religious duties of emperor-worship, education, and the expulsion of the foreigner. The defeat of Russia in 1905 had repercussions throughout Asia; indeed it may be said that the prestige of the European never recovered, a situation again furthered by the Japanese between Pearl Harbour and the Coral Sea. In Indo-China, resistance to the French was encouraged by Japanese-educated students, and the removal of the Manchu dynasty in 1912 suggested that in China, too, new outlets would be found for an increasingly aggressive nationalism.

But in Asia, as in Europe, it was the 1914-18 war that opened a decisive

[1]Quoted by permission of the publisher, Macmillan & Co. Ltd.

new stage in the development of that nationalism. It was not at first obvious that this would be so. The emergence after the war of new States like Czechoslovakia and Yugoslavia must not produce the idea that their independence was long-awaited or their composition inevitable. The possibility of further autonomy under the Habsburgs satisfied many Southern Slavs before 1914—to the alarm of Serbia. Many Croats regarded the Serbs as barbarians, unfit for a civilised State, and after Sarajevo there were anti-Serb riots in Bosnia, Herzegovina and Croatia. As late as January 1917, the Czech National Committee in Prague was assuring the dynasty of its loyalty, and even at the end of the war the idea of a Czechoslovak State commanded in Slovakia the allegiance of only a small intelligentsia.

Moreover Germany, the strongest product of nineteenth-century nationalism, was the protector of two of the great non-national empires, and although Asquith declared that Britain would fight 'until the rights of the smaller nationalities of Europe are placed on an unassailable foundation' he referred to Belgium and Serbia, not to Czechs and Ruthenes. Britain was more concerned to destroy the German fleet than to espouse a principle of self-determination that would not accord with her own position in Ireland and India. This principle was not present when Britain informed her allies that she intended to annex Egypt, and agreed with France over the division of Syria and Mesopotamia; nor was it present when Russia was secretly promised Constantinople, Eastern Thrace, and Gallipoli in 1915; nor when Italy, at the same time, and in return for a guarantee that she would enter the war within a month, was promised the South Tyrol and Istria (Italians were not in a majority in either), the Croat part of Dalmatia, and a protectorate over Albania; nor when a treaty with Rumania envisaged assigning to her hundreds of thousands of aliens.

Nevertheless, the existence of discontented minorities on both sides of the battle-lines was a factor the belligerents could not afford to ignore. The Grand Duke Michael's declaration to the Habsburg nationalities in September 1914 was soon answered by a similar German appeal to those within the Russian Empire. In November 1916, the Austrian and German Emperors promised independence to Poland (though with reservations where their own Polish subjects were concerned); Ukrainian hopes were exploited, encouragement given to Flemish and Irish separatism. The realities of imperialism were contrasted with the sanctimonious principles of official Allied war-aims, and at Brest-Litovsk the Russian Empire was dismembered with abandon.

The Allied approach was far more cautious, but self-determination, originally called in to vindicate policy, then used as an aid to victory, became an uncomfortable but formidable principle by which world opinion expected the Allies to abide when peace was made. Three things hastened this process. The first was the Russian Revolution. To the ending of an autocratic and imperialist dynasty was added the stirring example of a people creating their own State anew. The Bolshevik Declaration on Nationalities was followed by the embarrassing publication of the Allied secret treaties. Finland, Latvia, Estonia and Lithuania were breaking away; so too (to the Soviet annoyance) was the Ukraine. When the Russian plenipotentiaries arrived at Brest-Litovsk on 22nd December, 1917, their proposal stirred millions:

> 'Complete political independence to be given to those nationalities which had been deprived of it before the beginning of the war. . . . Nationalities not hitherto in the enjoyment of political independence to be allowed the right to decide by means of a referendum whether they elect to be united to other nations or to aquire independence.'

The second impetus came from Woodrow Wilson. It would be quite wrong, of course, to regard the Fourteen Points as simply the manifestation of idealism; they were, in part, a response to the Bolshevik publication of secret treaties, and to the failure of an inter-allied conference to agree on peace terms. The Points dealing with international diplomacy, trade and armaments may seem, in the light of later events, far-removed from reality; but Points 6 to 14 were concerned with concrete proposals which included only 'the freest opportunity for autonomous development' for the subject nationalities of Austria and Turkey. Only in the case of Poland was the creation of a new State declared imperative, and here, as with Serbia, an outlet to the sea was promised, regardless of the wishes of the territory involved. Moreover it was Lloyd George who had announced on January 5th, 1918—three days before the promulgation of the Fourteen Points—that 'a territorial settlement must be securely based on the right of self-determination or the consent of the governed'; as long before as January 1917 an Allied note to Wilson had talked of 'the liberation of Italians, of Slavs, of Rumanians and Czecho-Slovaks from foreign domination.'

However, Wilson's Four Principles went further:

> '1. Each part of the final settlement must be based upon the essential justice of that particular case.
>
> 2. Peoples and provinces must not be bartered about from sovereignty to sovereignty as if they were chattels or pawns in a game.
>
> 3. Every territorial settlement must be in the interests of the populations concerned. . . .

4. All well-defined national elements shall be accorded the utmost satisfaction that can be accorded them without introducing new, or perpetuating old, elements of discord and antagonism.'

To Congress, Wilson affirmed: 'There shall be no annexations, no contributions, no punitive damages. . . . Self-determination is not a mere phrase. It is an imperative principle of action. . . .'

The events of 1917 and Wilson's statements 'added a new dimension to the struggle in Europe'; it was now looked upon as a conflict between despotism and democracy, and the repressed nationalities increased their demands accordingly. They had, in fact, been anticipated by their exiles, by the South Slav Committee of 1915, the Czechoslovak National Council of 1916. Paderewski was active at the highest levels in America on behalf of an independent Poland; in London Beneš and Masaryk found ready allies in Wickham Steed and Dr. Seton-Watson. Polish units were fighting for the Allies in France, and Czech units in Italy; the exiled Czech Legion had not yet disappeared into the whirlpool of civil war in Russia.

The exiles' vision of independent States had at first produced friction with the politicians at home; the latter now moved in the same direction, for food shortages and widespread social unrest were speeding the corrosion of the Habsburg dominions. The third impetus towards self-determination—the actions of the nationalities themselves—came swiftly to the fore as the war neared its end.

A declaration in January 1918 by the Czech and South Slav Reichsrat deputies anticipated Allied approval of the dissolution of the Empire, and the Poles turned away from the Central Powers after the separate peace accorded the Ukraine in February. The harsh terms of Brest-Litovsk and the failure of the German Spring offensive encouraged the process.

The dangers of this same Spring offensive further committed the Allies to self-determination. Northcliffe, as Director of Propaganda in Enemy Territories, was assisted by Wickham Steed and Seton-Watson. Leaflets proclaiming independence for the nationalities were dropped on the Italian front, and a Congress of Oppressed Nationalities was allowed to meet in April. 'The Allies . . . sanctioned the break-up of the Habsburg monarchy before the actual event took place; they did so at a time when military necessity outweighed all other considerations.'[1] In June, for instance, the French Government recognised the right of Czechoslovakia to independence: on August 14th Britain acknowledged her to be an Allied nation and the U.S.A. followed suit in September. Beneš formed a Czech Provisional Government in Paris on October 14th. Apprehensive

[1]Zeman: *The Break-up of the Habsburg Empire* p. 216.

approval had already come from the German Social Democrats in Austria:

> '(We) recognise the right of the Slavs to form their own national states; we resist, however, resolutely and for good, the subjection to these national states of German territories. We demand that all German territories in Austria should be unified in one state. . . .'[1]

Their fears were well-grounded. In October armed Czechs occupied German areas in Bohemia, Moravia and Moravian Silesia. Munich was another step nearer.

The war had brought national complications beyond Europe as well, remember. The McMahon-Hussein note of October 1915 had recognised the independence of the Arabs. The areas it exempted are still not agreed upon, however, and it appeared to be contradicted by the Sykes-Picot agreement of 1916 (which reserved Iraq for the French[2] and the area that was to be Trans-Jordan for the British) and by the Balfour Declaration of November 1917 (which announced British support for 'the establishment in Palestine of a national home for the Jews.')

But one must look further still. The Revolution of 1917, Lenin's analysis of imperialism and the Bolshevik emphasis on self-determination had a profound effect upon Asia. Already the 'European civil war' was weakening the power and prestige of the West. Japan helped eradicate German influence in China; the French and British had to appeal to their subjects for every form of support; Indians, Chinese and Indo-Chinese came to Europe and saw democratic societies, heard Wilsonian principles. Tanks, ships and shells were devouring Europe's economic supremacy; the confidence and vision of imperialism could scarcely survive Verdun and the Somme. The Russian Revolution hastened Asian nationalism and thrust upon it a new sense of the urgency of economic planning and social reform. Communism itself made less progress in an area like India, where a reasonably firm framework of government and administration existed, than in the vacuum of China. But by 1919 the era of Western dominance, begun with da Gama, was drawing to a close.

Few in Europe saw this however. Most eyes were fixed upon Versailles in the hope that the seeds of war—national grievances prominent among them—would be removed for ever. New States and a new world would be born together: 'The concepts "Germany", "Austria", "Hungary", "Bulgaria" or "Turkey" were not in the forefront of our minds. It was the thought of the new Serbia, the new Greece, the new Bohemia, the new

[1]Quoted in ibid p. 232.
[2]Subsequently changed to Syria.

Poland which made our hearts sing hymns at heaven's gate.'[1] The expected architect of this regeneration, the man whose gleaming principles would cut through the tired entanglements of the old world, was Wilson.

Yet the principles were already somewhat tarnished. The 'commentary' on the Fourteen Points drawn up by Colonel House in October 1918 had envisaged a Brenner frontier for Italy (despite the Germans involved), Palestine, Arabia and Iraq for Britain, and the Dobrudja for Rumania. Later, Japanese rights in Shantung would be recognised, racial equality refused a place in the League Covenant, and the fact made clear that that document would not override the Monroe Doctrine. Other leading States behaved similarly: the Italians renounced any adherence to Point Nine and pursued a policy of 'sacred egoism'; Clemenceau ignored Points and Principles whenever possible; the Empire and 'strategic necessity' were obvious reservations where Britain was concerned. The American delegation was itself divided. Lansing, the Secretary of State, bemoaned the fact that the phrase 'self-determination' had ever been pronounced and foresaw the false hopes it would create; the United States, after all, had survived in 1861 only by denying the principle. Even the President, 'alone with God and the People', wearily regretted his confident utterances as he summarily dismissed the awkward Irish. As Lloyd George raised the problem of Germans in Silesia and demanded more plebiscites, Wilson felt only 'very sick . . . very tired.'

The entanglements were indeed far stronger than he expected. Bohemia was only one area where claims had already been staked out by emergent nation-states; self-determination had been at work and at Versailles was adopting a defensive, not offensive, posture. Moreover, the ceaseless process of migration and settlement had created in much of Europe problems of impossible complexity when it came to frontier demarcation. The chairman of the committee considering the boundaries of Yugoslavia reported that

> 'the linguistic frontiers do not only fail to coincide, in any place, with the natural or administrative frontiers, but they are uncertain among mixed populations. The ethnographic statistics cannot then be sufficient to lead to the solution of the problem.'

Matters were made worse by the fact that different committees found themselves dealing with the frontiers of one nation without mutual reference, and without receiving any guidance as to the priorities to be followed when linguistic, economic, and strategic considerations failed to coincide. The fact that self-determination would have to be qualified by other circumstances was not made clear. 'Too often . . . instead of

[1]Nicolson: *Peacemaking,* 1919 p. 33.

frankly admitting the difficulties, the Allied delegates glossed them over, and presented a settlement determined on many other considerations as in conformity with the strict principle of self-determination. . . . In this procedure there was a fundamental intellectual dishonesty which, both at the time and subsequently, did much to undermine general respect for the peace treaties.'[1]

We must be careful, of course, not to depict the treaties as a complete betrayal of principles and promises. The Fourteen Points (modified regarding reparations and freedom of the seas) were the formal basis of negotiations with Germany alone, and not with Austria-Hungary, Bulgaria or Turkey. And although Nicolson, for instance, considered that 'of President Wilson's twenty-three conditions (i.e. Fourteen Points, 4 Principles and 5 Particulars) only four can with any accuracy be said to have been incorporated in the Treaties of Peace,' Lloyd George could not find 'a single particular in which it (the Versailles Treaty) departed from the terms of peace laid down by the Allies.' Clearly, the conditions in question are capable of various interpretations: what, in the Balkans, are 'historically established lines of allegiance' (Point 11)? How far should 'such adjustments as are most likely to bring a peace that will be permanent' modify settlements 'based upon the essential justice of that particular case' (Principle 1)? What are 'well-defined national elements', and which can be satisfied 'without introducing . . . elements of discord and antagonism' (Principle 4)?

But one must note that the Allies, in their reply to German protests, emphatically claimed to have acted in accordance with the principle of self-determination,[2] even though the decision of the rump of Austria to seek union with Germany was vetoed.

In considering Czech frontier claims, the adhesion of territory to the new State was approved on widely varying grounds—historic, ethnographic, economic and strategic; in justifying the decision to include German areas, the Allies argued that

> 'the populations of German speech inhabiting the borders of these provinces should remain associated with them in the development of the national unity with which history has bound them up.'[3]

Some, however, including Lloyd George, remained unconvinced:

> 'I cannot conceive any greater cause of future war, than that the German people . . . should be surrounded by a number of small States, many of

[1]Cobban: *National Self-determination* p. 33.
[2]See Macartney: *National States and National Minorities* p. 194.
[3]Quoted in ibid p. 201.

them consisting of people who have never previously set up a stable government for themselves, but each of them containing large masses of Germans clamouring for reunion with their native land. . . . What I have said about the Germans is equally true of the Magyars.' (Memorandum of March 25th 1919.)

Proudly, however, the new states that emerged from the collapse of the Austrian, Turkish and Russian Empires declared themselves to be national States:

'We, the Czecho-Slovak nation, wishing to consolidate the complete unity of the nation. . . .'

'The Kingdom of Rumania is a national, unitary and indivisible State.'

The fact that none was, in fact, a single-nation State was glossed over. Yet minorities were frequently considerable, totalling 34.7% of the population in Czechoslovakia, 30.4% in Poland and 25% in Rumania.[1]

Set against such figures were hopes of 'assimilation' and promises for the future, perhaps the most remarkable being that of Beneš in a note to the Czecho-Slovak Committee at Versailles:

'The present State in which the Germans had an overwhelming preponderance will remain; only, the privileges that the Germans enjoyed will be reduced to their just proportion. . . . It will be an extremely liberal regime, which will very much resemble that of Switzerland.'

Yet the same document stated that within this 'Czecho-Slovak State,' that 'language and element' would have 'a certain special position.' The Swiss parallel might seem a poor one, but the architects of the new State remained confident, and as late as 1927 Masaryk could declare in his political memoirs that

'the Peace Treaties have created juster conditions throughout Europe, and we are entitled to expect that the tension between States and races will decrease. . . . The new order . . . has shorn nationalism of its negative character by setting oppressed peoples on their own feet.'

Such hopes were encouraged at first by the promises which these States had to make regarding the rights of their minorities, promises which were in turn guaranteed by the League of Nations. The League system was concerned primarily with world peace; this was held to depend upon the internal stability of the Treaty States, which in turn depended upon contented minorities. Matters concerning the treatment of minorities could be raised by members of the League Council or, more usually, by petition. Petitions were scrutinized by the Secretariat and, if deemed

[1]Full details for these and other States will be found in Macartney, op cit, Appendix III.

'receivable', were then submitted to ad hoc Committees of Three who reported back to the Council; later, a single *rapporteur* superseded the Committees.

The Guarantee was not a success, however. The Treaties would have been more suited to the already assimilated minorities of Western Europe, since the predominance of a single national culture was not questioned. Moreover, the Treaty States regarded the Guarantee with resentment as an encouragement to dissatisfaction and a barrier to assimilation; the appearance of discrimination—Italy, for instance, did not have to sign a Treaty whereas Yugoslavia did—increased the bitterness. The information available to Committees was often inadequate and delays of up to three years were frequent: in 1930-31, 204 petitions were received of which 73 were declared receivable; of these, 18 had been examined by the end of the year. It was also easy to allow considerations of political expediency to override those of justice; fellow-members of the League were close at hand, minorities far away.

Yet the very number of petitions—525 before February 1931—indicated the continuing discontent of these minorities on matters such as land, education, administration and language. 'Almost every state has committed, and every minority suffered under, flagrant violations of the Minority Treaties. And these have been committed, to all intents and purposes, with impunity.'[1] In Southern Dobrudja, for instance, the Rumanian government closed Bulgarian State schools. When the fathers of 14,000 schoolchildren signed a petition against this, they were arrested and forced to declare themselves content with Rumanian schools. The League managed to stop the persecution, but the schools remained closed.

It was hardly surprising, therefore, when minorities like Germans turned to the nation-states of their kinsmen for protection and when, in turn, Poland announced in 1934 that she no longer accepted the League's jurisdiction in minority matters. Most to be pitied, however, were the tens of thousands in Europe who had been declared stateless, for they lacked both citizenship and external protectors.

Again, let us take Czechoslovakia as our one major example of these inter-war years. Despite the assurances of Beneš and the hopes of Masaryk, the history of the previous three hundred years suggested that the problem of the $3\frac{1}{4}$ million Germans would prove intractable. At bottom, it was one of feeling. The Sudeten German regarded the Czech as 'a half-educated . . . creature, to some extent saved by German influence, who is politically intolerable and unreliable, socially never

[1]Macartney, op cit p. 390.

satisfied and always pushing for his nation, while the Czech sees in the Sudeten German the invader, the remorseless conqueror, the apostle of German world hegemony, the economic tyrant who only lives in the land in order to subject the Czech people socially, politically, and in every other way.'[1]

Understandably, therefore, with their political positions now reversed, the Czechs set out to humiliate the Germans in the early days of the Republic 'in a thousand little ways.' The Constitution and Language Law of 1920 increased German bitterness, as did the official pressure put on individuals to register as Czechs in the 1921 census and the fact that Beneš at Geneva was managing to forestall German petitions. The industrial decline of 1922 fell with particular severity on the German areas as did that of 1929-31. In the latter case, the china, glass, textile and lignite mining industries of the Sudetenland came almost to a standstill, with unemployment frequently over 25% of the able-bodied adults. Czech demands that Germans be laid off before themselves were answered by fierce resentment against the Government and the State.

There were other causes of friction. Enforced land redistribution with inadequate compensation particularly affected German owners of large estates and their German employees. German street and shop names in Prague were removed, and whereas only 5,000 Czech children had to attend German elementary schools, 16,000 German were affected in the opposite way. Theatres, libraries, secondary education and universities were the subject of further disputes, and after 1933 a Nazi cultural offensive from across the border forced the Czechs to curb German newspapers and textbooks. Wireless propaganda could not be checked, however, and a situation of psychological warfare accompanied the dissolution of the Sudeten Nazi Party in 1933 and the rising strength of Henlein's Sudeten German Party in its place. Many of those Germans who still cooperated with the Republic were Jews, and accusations were hurled at Czechoslovakia as being a Jewish-run State and a Bolshevik weapon thrusting at the heart of Western culture.

By 1935, when Beneš became President, there was a growing sense of national danger. The army increased in popularity and efficiency. The 1936 State Defence Law put legal procedure and frontier fortifications on a war-footing, and further enraged the German population of these areas. An agreement between the Government and German moderates in February 1937 was too late, as were the efforts of Beneš to render more flexible the attitudes of other Czech politicians. Polish and Hungarian minorities were also becoming restive, and in a speech at Eger in the

[1]Gustav Peters; quoted in Wiskemann, op cit p. 118.

previous June Henlein had indicated his growing allegiance to Nazi doctrines. Though the Czech treatment of minorities compared favourably with that of Poland, Rumania and, indeed, Germany itself, in the context of the time her problems began to appear insoluble.

Despite the League, this context was one of growing international anarchy. The Poles had seized Vilna, the Lithuanians Memel, the Italians Fiume; disarmament negotiations had failed and the Japanese defied the League with impunity. Catalan and Basque separatism blended into the heat of civil war in Spain, and Abyssinia experienced the blessings of a higher civilisation. From Matteotti to Dollfuss, from Amritsar to Guernica, wanton political violence shouldered its way to the fore.

The environment was changing in which nationalism, already strengthened by the Great War, now manifested itself. Universal suffrage had acknowledged the popularisation of the State, war had widened the already-growing power and activity of governments, the legacy of conflict had increased the talk but lessened the reality of international cooperation. Many now believed the notion of international law to have been a convenient fiction; 'modern wars are fought to a finish and the loser has no rights.' Increasing demand had postponed for a while the disintegration of the nineteenth century economic framework, but signs of strain and of economic nationalism had appeared well before 1914. 'The will to defend a privileged position in which all social classes shared had welded together each of the great Western nations into a community of economic interests strong enough to appeal to all emotions of aggressive nationalism.'[1] The absence of favourable economic conditions after the War, and particularly the breakdown of 1929-31, hastened national economic planning, the 'management' of national currencies and the heightening of tariff barriers in a frantic *sauve qui peut*. The Treaty States were no different from the land of Hawley-Smoot and Fordney-McCumber, and World Economic Conferences in 1927 and 1930 were doomed to failure.

States which had been humiliated in the War, disappointed with the settlement, or isolated afterwards, were the breeding-grounds of particularly vocal nationalism. In Italy and Poland, in Weimar Germany and Republican Spain, democratic governments failed and were replaced by dictatorships, by the sacrifice of individual liberties for the sake of national strength, prosperity and prestige. Rumania's 'Legion of the Archangel Michael' and the 'Third Hellenic Civilisation' of Metaxas Greece bore witness to the widening appeal of Fascism.

In Japan, too, there were changes. Against a background of economic

[1] *Nationalism*, R.I.I.A. p. 231.

and social upheaval, of disillusionment with the West after the Washington Treaty, pure Shinto doctrines revived in a new form: a true restoration of imperial power was needed, a rejection of politicians and a recognition of the Army as the real expression of divine national destiny. Assassination had long been a feature of the political scene, and in 1931 it was the Army, not the Cabinet, who decided on action in Manchuria. In 1936, new 'Basic Principles of National Policy' enshrined a programme of expansion, strength, and preparation against Britain and the United States.

Isolation from the West was shared with Japan by Russia, and as the hopes of international proletarian uprising receded, 'Socialism in One Country' gave new expression to national self-awareness. Legendary heroes, poets and princes, were recalled from the past. When Georgians and Armenians rose, they were crushed in defiance of the November Declaration. 'Scratch a Communist and you will find a Great Russian Chauvinist'; Lenin's sarcasm seemed to contain the truth.

Fascism and Nazism provided the best-known doctrines of virulent nationalism, however, even though Hitler's indifference to the fate of the Germans of the South Tyrol reminds us that at times expediency could override true nationalism and racial mysticism alike. In Italy, the pronouncements of Mussolini, Gentile, Rocco and others reflected the mixture of traditionalism and idealism, social-Darwinism and irrationalism which we have seen developing in the late nineteenth century:

> 'Strife is the origin of all things. . . . Peace is hence absurd, or rather it is a pause in war'. . . . 'Before all, I trust my insight. What I call my insight—it is indefinable'. . . . 'The state is not only the present, it is also the past'. . . . 'The Fascist State . . . has curtailed useless or harmful liberties while preserving those which are essential. In such matters the individual cannot be the judge, but the state only'. . . . 'All is in the state and for the state; nothing outside the state, nothing against the state'. . . . 'Fascism is the purest form of democracy if the nation be conceived . . . as the most powerful idea which acts within the nation.'

Italy had been prepared for Fascism by the political chaos which followed and partly sprang from Cavour, by the disappointments of 1919, by economic and social upheaval. The last two factors were present in Germany also; so too was a century and more's preoccupation with *geist* and *macht*. Obsessions clouded the German mind in the first half of the twentieth century: 'a romantic interpretation of the past; a feeling of having been unjustly treated by history and of having suffered at the hands of inferior people; a conviction that Germany's great merits were not recognised by mankind; finally, the expectation of a future in which the myths of the past would turn into realities and thereby German history and destiny find their fulfilment. This point of view . . . made many Germans jubilantly welcome the Third Reich. What was it but a fusion and consecration of the many myths that had defeated the Enlightenment in Germany?'[1]

Unemployment and the hatred of Versailles were not alone in corroding the Weimar Republic. The Germany of Spengler, like France in this period, had her *trahison des clercs*. 'From the beginning (it) was undermined by the bureaucracy, the judiciary, and the universities on which a government has to rely.'[2]

The folk-prince came, and with him a creed which bore some resemblance to Fascism, but which far exceeded it in exalting the race:

'The State is a means to an end. Its end lies in the maintenance and development of a community of physically and spiritually similar beings. . . . We, as Aryans, can thus conceive of the State only as the living organism of a nationality which not only ensures the preservation of that nationality, but which also leads it to the highest freedom through development of its spiritual and ideal abilities'. . . . 'All that is not race in this world is trash'. . . . 'The stronger has to rule . . . only the born weakling can consider this as cruel'. . . . 'It is not accident that the heroic figure of Siegfried is both a creation of German minds and a model for German minds, while the unscrupulous and deceiving Jacob is the ideal character of the Jews. . . . It is no accident that those who hold fast to honour are slender, tall, light-eyed, powerful men, while the descendants of Father Jacob are bent, flat-footed, dark, curly-locked figures'. . . . 'We renounce international science. We renounce research for its own sake. We teach and learn medicine, not to increase the numbers of known microbes, but to keep the German people strong and healthy. We teach and learn history, not to say how things actually happened, but to instruct the German people from the past.'

The methods by which the modern one-party, totalitarian State educates its citizens, the use made of mass-psychology and modern communications, need no rehearsing here.

Whilst Europe carried its confusion through to another war, nationalism advanced its hold on the rest of the world. The impact of the West on law, politics, economics and education was helping to change the face of Asia; so too was anti-European nationalism. 'It was the acceptance of the doctrine of a national personality, of an identification of all the people within the territory with the individuality of the State, of a belief in a kind

[1]Kohn: *The Mind of Germany* pp. 14-15.
[2]Ibid p. 318.

of mystic brotherhood of the people that constituted the nation.... (And) if nationalism developed directly by resistance and indirectly by the recovery of historical sense and pride in cultural achievement as a result of Western contact, the sense of Asianism is exclusively the counterpart of the solidarity of European feeling.'[1]

Many leaders of Asian nationalism had been educated in the West; indeed, when Nehru returned to India in 1912, he 'looked upon the world almost from an Englishman's standpoint.' New educational facilities within colonies produced equal trouble, and when the French founded the University of Hanoi in 1907 an outburst of student nationalism resulted in its closure a year later. The conflict between what was learned and what experienced was bound to prove disruptive outside Europe. It continued to be so after the Second World War, in Egypt, for instance: 'A civilisation whose modern impulse and spirit seemed to young Arabs to be the very antithesis of imperialism, was practising imperialism all around them.'[2] The preservation of the vernacular was equally important. In the words of Lawrence, the Arabs had 'lost their geographical sense, and their racial and political and historical memories; but they clung the more tightly to their language, and erected it almost into a fatherland of its own.' In China, the New Culture movement raised the vernacular to fresh heights; in its call to youth, it was 'the real beginning of the revolution.'

Don't overlook more mundane factors, such as the oil of the Near East and the tin and rubber of South East Asia, attracting the colonialist and adding to the grievances of those under him. The problems of domestic poverty, of the great landowners in Egypt, of disease and ignorance in India, did more than produce protests like the *Swadeshi* movement; together with the Russian Revolution they ensured that nationalism and socialism would become interwoven. Nehru and Nasser, Nkrumah and Sun Yat-sen, the Indian and other Five Year Plans are evidence of this process.

It was a process made difficult by religion, however, whether in the form of the Moslem Brotherhood in the Egypt of 1952, or of the obstacles which Mustafa Kemal had faced when creating modern Turkey. It was only when Gandhi had championed the untouchables that India as a whole might move forward. Similarly, though Nehru remained very obviously a Kashmiri Brahmin, his 'broad secular outlook' was 'one of (his) significant contributions to the nationalist movement;'[3] even so,

[1]Panikkar, op cit pp. 321-2.
[2]Childers: *The Road to Suez* p. 80.
[3]Brecher: *Nehru* p. 41.

Jinnah and the Muslim League, the events of 1947, and his own funeral were to show that even this contribution could not be decisive.

Discontent beyond Europe increased between the wars. There were some successes, represented for Turkey, for instance, by the Treaty of Lausanne and for China by her status at the Washington Conference. Mainly, however, Western dominance, though weakened, remained. Though Egyptian independence arrived in 1922, it was in name only; the broken promises and false hopes of 1914-18 'seared into the Middle-Eastern mind a bitterness that cannot be over-emphasised.'[1] Concessions were too late and too little, and came to be regarded as signs of weakness. The administration of Palestine angered Zionists and Arabs alike and though the League's 'A' mandates spoke of eventual independence for the territory concerned, 'B' and 'C' mandates remained silent on the subject. The Government of India Act of 1919 and the Constitution of 1935 failed to satisfy the growing strength of the Congress Party, a party refashioned in 1920 'from an upper-class urban club into a nation-wide mass organisation capable of penetrating to the grass roots, to the village, the heart of Indian society.'[2] With the leadership of Ghandi, the tactics of civil disobedience and the aim of *Swaraj*, this reform made 1920 'the great divide in the history of Indian nationalism.' The Congress pledge on 'Independence Day' in 1930 echoed the Declaration of 1776:

'We believe that it is the inalienable right of the Indian people, as of any other people, to have freedom and to enjoy the fruits of their toil. . . . We believe also that if any government deprives a people of these rights and oppresses them, the people have a right to alter it or abolish it.'

As Gandhi began his march to the sea to inaugurate the salt-tax revolt, Kipling's words came again with Nehru:

'Who lives if India dies? Who dies if India lives?'

Europe was faced with the implications of her own ideas.

The Second World War, whilst finally terminating Europe's political dominance, renewed the pledges of principle which had hastened nationalism during the First. After the 'Four Freedoms' came the Atlantic Charter, in which President and Prime Minister declared that

'. . . they desire to see no territorial changes that do not accord with the freely expressed wishes of the peoples concerned;
. . . they respect the right of all peoples to choose the form of government

[1]Childers, op cit p. 31.
[2]Brecher, op cit p. 72.

under which they will live; and they wish to see sovereign rights and self-government restored to those who have been forcibly deprived of them. . . .'

To some, this did not accord with Churchill's remark in 1941 that he had 'not become His Majesty's first minister to preside over the liquidation of the British Empire.' Indian nationalism had been angered when, without consultation, she was declared a belligerent in 1939; the offers and negotiations of Cripps in 1942 failed, and, with the Japanese at hand, the 'Quit India' campaign produced a police-state. Yet it would be true to say that the war made independence inevitable in the near future; only the form of the independent State was increasingly uncertain.

The triumphs of the Japanese 'New Order' in the Far East, like the German advance on Suez, increased the non-European ferment. Within the 'East Asian Co-Prosperity Sphere', Burma, Indonesia and the Philippines were given a kind of independence; this did not diminish the 'Freedom Struggles' against the Japanese themselves. A sense of importance was added as a colony found its men and raw materials urgently needed by the governing country. As the pattern of the post-war world came to be discussed, America and Russia united in their hostility to colonialism, and the left-wing governments that emerged in Europe after the war generally added opposition in principle. The climate was reflected in chapter XI of the United Nations Charter, which declared that those responsible for trusteeship recognised that

'the interests of the inhabitants of these territories are paramount, and accept as a sacred trust the obligation to promote to the utmost . . . the well-being of the inhabitants of these territories, and, to this end:

a. to ensure, with due respect for the culture of the peoples concerned, their political, economic, social, and educational advancement, their just treatment, and their protection against abuses;

b. to develop self-government, to take due account of the political aspirations of the peoples, and to assist them in the progressive development of their free political institutions, according to the particular circumstances of each territory and its peoples and their varying stages of advancement. . . .'

Thus, when an Indonesian Republic was proclaimed in the hiatus following the Japanese defeat, it was not likely that the Netherlands could reverse the situation; nor would the French struggle in Indo-China have evoked much sympathy had it not been for the threat of Communism. The nature of the new States was being shaped accordingly. 'The characteristic qualities of the Indonesian struggle originated in the repressive nature of Dutch rule, which prevented the formation of a political movement for independence; the hothouse experience of

Japanese 'co-prosperity' then produced overnight a national leadership and mass following—on a para-military basis; and finally, the violent tussle against the Dutch counter-revolution put a premium on physical force, the mob and the military, and consolidated in power a fanatical, implacable leadership, rooted in hatred.'[1] Philippine independence was recognised by America in 1946, Malayan by Britain in 1957. The greatest change of all, the independence of India and Pakistan, had taken place in 1947, together with that of Burma and Ceylon.

Independence added new problems to old throughout Asia: how to replace the existing framework of administration; how to replace an imperial language with a national one when law and administration were based on the former, when there were thirty distinct languages in Indonesia, when the vernacular in Indian States resisted the imposition of Hindi; how to come to terms with religious complications, with Buddhism in Vietnam and with Muslim settlers and Hindu extremists in India; how to deal with Chinese in the Philippines and Indians in Burma; how to prevent the disintegration of the Congress Party and the Muslim League; how to reconcile government by consent with ignorance, apathy and obstruction; how to find capital for essential reform; how to provide posts of sufficient status and reward to satisfy those with education; how to deal with students for whom violent political demonstrations had become an easy and accepted alternative to work. Threats from outside— China against India, India against Pakistan, Indonesia against Malaysia —often arrived to foster unity; they offered no permanent solution, however.

In the Caribbean and in Africa most colonies moved along the path towards national sovereignty, some, like the Gold Coast, independently, others, in the British West Indies and French West Africa, intended for federation. The independence of Ghana in 1957 gave new vigour to the development of nationalism in Africa, a development which repeats many of the patterns we have seen elsewhere. 'Firstly, the education provided by Christian missionary organisations, combined with the creation of an urbanised wage-labour force, "mobilised" a substantial proportion of the population by freeing them from traditional tribal controls, but subjected them to economic and psychological insecurity. Secondly, an accumulation of conscious economic grievances among the mobilised groups, and consequent hostility towards European governments and commercial enterprises. Finally, the emergence of a Western-educated minority who under the system of indirect rule were excluded from any meaningful role in the government of the country.'[2]

[1]Tinker: *Ballot Box and Bayonet* p. 26.
[2]Richmond: *The Colour Problem* pp. 330-1.

This minority were frequently able to arouse sufficient support to obtain independence. In an area such as East Africa, however, the disruptive effects of de-tribalisation, a money economy, disease and ignorance were still present when the new status was gained. Regionalism in Nigeria, mutiny in Tanganyika and anarchy in the Congo were reminders of some of the difficulties involved in 'instant nationalism'. Furthermore, the Pan-African ideals accepted at the Casablanca conference were regarded with caution at Monrovia; here, as with 'Arab solidarity', particularism threatened to prove the same obstacle that had faced Panslavism.

In the Arab world, Iraq had become independent in 1937; Syria and Lebanon were freed by France in 1944, and the three joined Egypt, Transjordan, Saudi Arabia and the Yemen to form the League of Arab States in 1945. The shock of defeat in the war against Israel (independent in 1948) and the continued presence of foreign bases and influence further inflamed Arab nationalism. The Egyptian revolution of 1952 linked nationalism and socialism, and the Baghdad Pact and the Bandung Conference ensured, in their opposite ways, that neutralism would accompany both. Further West, Morocco, Tunisia and Algeria indicated that the concept of an extended metropolitan France would not be proof against a determination to achieve independence.

It was not only in colonies that nationalism emerged strengthened from the war. 'The fundamental force motivating Communist China's new role in international affairs is her militant nationalism. . . . Just as Japan's invasion was the climax of a century of imperialist oppression, so was her defeat a symbol of the end of an era of humiliation.'[1] For Eire, on the other hand, it was neutrality that marked her fierce sense of independence.

The war also exposed the tensions within some of the Treaty States of 1919, and the weakness of Czechoslovakia and Yugoslavia was symbolised by the Nazi patronage of Slovakia and Croatia. The nations of Eastern Europe disappeared, after German, under Russian imperialism, whilst those of the West struggled towards some form of closer association. For some, the Commonwealth and the Statute of Westminster contained the hope of maturer national cooperation, but the racial nationalism of South Africa and its church raised embarrassing issues of principle. For others, the future lay with the United Nations, but here, too, the feelings of the Great Powers were not easily reconciled with the 'sovereign equality of all its Members.'

The years since 1945, in fact, have witnessed the continuing strength of

[1]Ping-chia Kuo: *China: New Age and New Outlook* pp. 219 and 221.

nationalism. It causes restlessness within Belgium and Canada, in the Tyrol and in the land of the Nagas. In Cyprus it produces bloodshed and renewed suggestions for the large-scale transference of populations, a solution which has been described as 'the most specific exaltation of the nation over the individual as an end in itself, the mass sacrifice of human beings to the idol of nationalism.'[1] Less harmfully, it renews demands for the 'Welshness' of the University of Wales.

Nationalism triumphed over neutralism when China invaded India, and the ideal of self-determination has not been extended to Kashmir. Between Russia and China, nationalism proves stronger than Marxist idealism; between America and Cuba it obscures the principle of 1776. In its milder form, it talks in terms of 'league tables' for production and exports, or blusters when a friend suggests that Britain has yet to find her new role in the world; more ominously, it mentions the Oder-Neisse line, the Jordan waters, and the Sino-Indian border. 'Nationalism', in the words of its greatest historian, 'has become the determining political and cultural force among all the races and civilisations on earth.'[2]

FURTHER DISCUSSION

1. 'Do you hate the Russians, or despise the Americans, or loathe the Germans? Who adores the Italians? Do you find the French charming, repulsive, decadent? And the Laputans—dangerous? And the Yahoos— the last best hope of mankind?'[3] The concept of national character has, of course, frequently produced Buchan-like stereotypes which we may dismiss in discussion, but which seem almost an inherent part of our mental processes. Is there such a thing as national character? If so, what forms it, and can it change?

It is clear that circumstances can change the opinion of the beholder. The early eighteenth-century European view of China had radically altered by the end of the nineteenth, due to far-reaching changes in the West as well as the decay of the Manchu in the East:

'Better fifty years of Europe than a cycle of Cathay';

between Tennyson and the eulogies of Voltaire lay an age of revolution. Change may take an even shorter time, of course. Not many years separated the Russian of Stalingrad from the one of the Hungarian uprising, but to many in the West he was a different being.

Yet at a first glance there seem to be grounds for accepting the notion of permanent natural characteristics. Of the English, G. J. Renier observed in 1932 that

[1] Carr: *Nationalism and After* p. 34.
[2] Kohn: *Nationalism* p. 89.
[3] *Encounter* April 1964.

'The things of the mind must be kept in their proper place: intelligence is a subordinate, character has the place of honour. . . . The English never like to go farther than their own experience. They are the empirical race par excellence. . . . It is (a) conviction of obvious supremacy over non-English people which constitutes their very special brand of patriotism.'[1]

Almost a century before, Emerson and Taine had said the same things in *English Traits* and *Notes sur l'Angleterre* respectively.

'There is a necessity on them to be logical. . . . They are impatient of genius, or of minds addicted to contemplation. . . . When he adds epithets of praise, his climax is "so English"; and when he wishes to pay you the highest compliment, he says, I should not know you from an Englishman.'

'On peut comparer assez exactement l'intérieur d'une tête anglaise à un Guide de Murray: beaucoup de faits et peu d'idées: quantité de renseignements utiles et précis . . . nulle vue d'ensemble. . . .'

One could multiply such instances. Yet one must also recall those which suggest changes in national character. In contrast to later times, Enlightenment Europe would have expected a riotous mob, not in France, but across the Channel among what Horace Walpole termed 'a gaming, robbing, wrangling, railing nation.' Only twelve years after writing a book on *The American Character*, Professor Brogan found himself wondering 'whether the great changes that have come about since 1943-4 have not, among other things, deeply changed the American.'[2]

What factors could create such changes? The international situation, possibly: external pressures and the existence of the atomic bomb; or internal changes: growing wealth and urbanisation, improved communications. One must also consider a nation's image of itself, which may affect and be affected by the image others hold. The pioneering image of America in the early nineteenth century, the challenge of the times, produced, as Professor Brogan reminds us, the need for overstatement in order to attract settlers, a 'passion for dealing in futures, . . . prophetic brooding on material expansion,' fierce civic pride and an optimism justified by experience.

Immigration may also produce change, but in varying ways. The 'admixture' which Mill thought so beneficial to a country and which occurred in South America failed to appear after the thirteenth century German settlements in Bohemia. In America, too, clear distinctions often remained, but education and the passing of generations tended to wear them away, and helped reduce state separatism in the face of new, American consciousness.[3]

[1] *The English: Are They Human?*
[2] An even swifter change was noted by observers as it overcame the normally placid citizens of Vienna on March 14th, 1938.
[3] See on the subject of Texas, however, Steinbeck: *Travels with Charley.*

Religion may have helped mould national character and activity. The theme of 'religion and the rise of capitalism' is familiar enough, as is the effect of religion (including the 'religion of disbelief') on mid-nineteenth century England. Religious zeal undoubtedly contributed to the character of Spain in the sixteenth century; yet it has also been suggested that 'the history of Belgium proves, by its absence, the success of the Catholic government: for to the Catholic there is no history, merely the working of the divinely ordained machinery, varied only by changes in the official personnel.'[1] Is it possible that religion has been less powerful an influence than the structure of society, the distribution of property, and the different attitudes involved in both?

Geography may be counted a more constant factor (though developments in armaments can alter the value of strategic frontiers just as those in transport can shrink distances). 'L'histoire est d'abord toute géographie,' wrote Michelet, and proceeded in his *Tableau de la France* to examine the people of his country's regions on that basis; many Swiss came to feel that 'an invisible idea existing in these mountains has created the distinct Swiss nationality as its embodiment.' How far can the thesis of historians like Michelet and Buckle be accepted? What have been the effects of the insularity of Britain, the North-African, rather than European, character of Spain, the extremes of Russia?

2. The history of the last hundred years has given rise to the question of German attributes above all, and many would agree with Taylor that 'there has been a German "national character" for more than a thousand years, a character not strictly identical, but recognisably the same.'[2] In examining this subject, the effects of the following should be taken into consideration:

1. Geography: in particular the absence of clear and defensible frontiers and the situation between 'civilised' West and 'barbaric' East.

2. The Holy Roman Empire from Charlemagne to the nineteenth century.

3. German trading prosperity in the Middle Ages, and the spread of urban colonists in Eastern Europe.

4. The Reformation: on national self-consciousness, on the political structure, and on attitudes to authority.

5. The 'age of exploration and discovery' in relation to the economic position of Germany, and the subsequent effects of the Thirty Years War.

[1]Trevor-Roper; *Laud* p. 22.
[2]*The Course of German History* University Paperback edition, p. 3.

6. Eighteenth-century Prussia's lack of economic resources, her history as a marcher state, and the work of Frederick the Great.

7. German Romanticism and opposition to the Enlightenment.

8. The lateness of German unification.

9. The methods which brought about that unification and the work of Bismarck.

10. The main stream of German intellectual life in the 19th and 20th centuries.

11. The power of the army to influence politics, from Schlieffen and Ludendorff to Seeckt and Schleicher.

These and other factors produced what, for Lord Vansittart, was a 'black record' from the times of Tacitus to the present day. Yet no subject attracts greater over-simplification than that of 'the German character'. One could, for instance, distinguish between the western Germany of the Roman Empire, the central area absorbed by Charlemagne, and the eastern marches conquered by the Teutonic knights. There are also the examples of Germans like Gervinus who have preserved an independent judgement outside the sphere of national hysteria. The poet Hans Enzensberger provides a more recent example:

> 'My nationality . . . represents something expected of me by others. . . . The idea of the nation state may have ceased to correspond to any concrete reality, but it lives on obstinately in the form of an illusion, and illusions on this scale deserve to be taken seriously. They constitute realities in their own right, psychological realities with explosive potential: and I have often asked myself what binds us so fast to them. Presumably it is too troublesome for us to develop our own individual resentments and complexes, our own idiosyncrasies and neuroses. The phantom of the state provides every man with spiritual lodgings among whose furniture he can make himself at home; what's more it's a ready-made assortment, with no necessity for individual choice, and with the enormous advantage of being shared with many others. This creates the kind of cosy solidarity which can be seen among people who drive the same car; whether the model in question is the fastest or the slowest, the best or the worst, is quite immaterial.'[1]

But do such individual exceptions completely undermine generalisations concerning aggressive German militarism? The 'myth' of the nation is easily exposed, less easily weakened. Should we be grateful for the present division of Germany, or is this a heartless way of ensuring future trouble? One thing may be said with certainty. Russian fears of Germany are very real and are based on equally real evidence; the West all too readily forgets the casualty figures and experiences endured by Russia in two World Wars.

[1]*Encounter* April 1964.

3. Why has nationalism taken on particularly aggressive aspects in the twentieth century? Is it true to say that 'it is from the ideology of the State rather than from that of the nation' that such aspects are derived, or are the two merely 'different phases in the development of the same phenomenon'?[1] Should we agree with Cobban that 'triumphant nationalism almost invariably tends, whenever it has the opportunity, to swell into imperialism'? What part has public opinion played in such processes? 'The assertion of national power, domination, is always in line with popular feeling. And, in crises, popular feeling dictates policy.'[2] Sir Lewis Namier once reflected that:

'The rise of pathological nationalism ten or fifteen years after a national defeat seems a recurrent phenomenon. . . . It comes apparently when the children of the war period attain the age of twenty to thirty; adults may learn the lessons of war and defeat, but those who have experienced the passions of war and the bitterness of defeat while still incapable of critical understanding seem burdened with frantic, almost insane resentments. . . .'[3]

If the post 1945 period furnishes grounds for more hope in this respect, it may be due to the nature of modern, total war.

4. Should one, then, not regard nationalism as 'good' or 'bad' per se, but consider it as conditioned by the situation in which the national group finds itself? Between Germany and the West different concepts of nation and nationalism go back at least as far as the consequences of the Renaissance and Reformation, but might not certain circumstances alter the complexion of Western nationalism? Is this what the careers of, say, Horatio Bottomley and Senator McCarthy suggest?

Does the root of the problem lie, in fact, in man's capacity for evil as well as good? Does the fanaticism which the nation can arouse have something in common with mass-hysteria associated with 'pop' stars and football teams? 'It is not so much that nationalism leads inevitably to conflict as that the nation, in the present phase of history, is the political unit in which men organise themselves for defending and promoting their most important interests in rivalry with other groups. . . . The necessity of conflict resides neither in nationalism nor in the nation, but in the nature of man.'[4]

5. Frequently, the nation-state has been elevated to the position of a moral absolute: 'my country right or wrong'; 'who dies if England live?' Is nationalism, therefore, something of a religious substitute? 'Diversion

[1]*Nationalism*, R.I.I.A. p. 331.
[2]Angell: *The Great Illusion* 1933 edition p. 309.
[3]From a short essay on 'Pathological Nationalisms', to be found in *In the Margin of History*.
[4]*Nationalism* R.I.I.A. p. 335.

to nationalism of emotions and conflicts formerly associated with religion has strengthened nationalist sentiment and at the same time weakened the restraints which the existence of a universalist ethic imposed.'[1] Frequently, of course, the two loyalties have been linked, and in this respect the Bishop of London in the First World War was probably more typical than the Bishop of Chichester in the Second. As General Charteris noted in his diary in 1917 after listening with Haig to a sermon declaring that God was fulfilling His purpose through their Army: 'all very cheering if you are quite certain that the purpose is our victory. But it is difficult to see why a German preacher could not preach just such a sermon to Hindenburg and Ludendorff.'[2]

One step in the elevation of the nation has been its personification. We speak of 'she', of 'Germany thinking' and 'France desiring'. Such personification became, once absolute monarchs disappeared, 'a necessary convenience in international relations and international law. But it was far more than a convenient abstraction. The idea of the personality and character of the nation acquired a profound psychological significance. Writers like Mazzini thought and argued about nations exactly as if they were sublimated individuals.'[3] Is such a process entirely dangerous?

6. Some of the results of nationalist prejudice are well known: the influence on international relations of the heirs of Mr. Podsnap; the tendency to forget a question like Dresden and to remember a certainty like Coventry; the rewriting of history to suit the totalitarian idol. History, of course, will always reflect something of the society of the historian, and it can easily reflect national and doctrinal bias. One East German account of the war of 1939-45 does not mention Britain; few British text-books record the secret agreement with Germany in 1898 which parcelled out beforehand the Portugese Empire ('our oldest ally') in the eventuality of its collapse.

More contentious is the effect of nationalism upon culture. That it is deleterious is often supported by reference to *Henry V* or the First Part of *Henry VI*, to the '1812' Overture or the 'official' work of David. Yet it could be answered that the nation has been, in Cobban's words, 'a forcing ground for art and letters, for religion and social idealism,' and one could cite *War and Peace*, Smetana's portrayal of the Vltava, Sibelius' *Finlandia*, or Turner's *Death of Nelson*. Similarly, it might prove difficult to distinguish between the feelings generated on the last night of the Promenade Concerts and those which made Britain resolute when she stood alone in 1940. A nation may take pride in its social welfare and its overseas

[1]Ibid p. 336.
[2]Quoted in Terraine: *Haig* p. 175.
[3]Carr: *Nationalism and After* pp. 8-9.

volunteers as well as in its navy; it may find an outlet for its wealth in Marshall Aid as well as in the Cuban Telephone Company.

7. How far can the principle of self-determination be applied? If an independent choice for the Thirteen Colonies, why not for the Confederacy; if for Kenya, why not for the Somalis; if for India, why not for Kashmir? It is a sad irony of history that the treatment received by Nehru at the hands of the British should have been received by Shaikh Abdullah at the hands of Nehru. Can such policies be justified on the grounds that fragmentation has proved an invitation to aggression and unrest?

8. Is it a matter for surprise and regret when the structure of Western democracy fails to survive alongside the nationalism of many emergent nations? Why have military leaders so often taken over power? Is the pyramid structure, as found in President Ayub Khan's 'Basic Democracy', for instance, more suited to its environment than representative democracy? Can we look contentedly at the Western examples themselves in the light of the choked machinery of decision in America, the authoritarian chauvinism of de Gaulle, the sham fight between 'ins' and 'outs' which takes place at Westminster before the gaze of a society whose apathy exceeds its affluence? Is genuine participation and consent possible in the age of the expert, the swift decision, and that triumph of bathos foreseen by Matthew Arnold?

9. Will nationalism decline? Neither religion nor international socialism have had this effect; will the insufficiency of a single country in matters of defence and economics? Does the future lie with regionalism; did Palacký's aphorism regarding the Austrian Empire underline its value in the past? We may agree with Professor Carr that 'What has to be challenged and rejected is the claim of nationalism to make the nation the sole rightful sovereign repository of political power and the ultimate constituent unit of world organisation.'[1] The history of the League, the attitude of all major Powers to U.N.O., and the relations of de Gaulle's France with the Common Market and N.A.T.O. may not, however, make one particularly sanguine as to the realisation of this aim.

Will man grow out of national conflict as he grew out of religious war? In the meantime, is there such a thing as a public conscience which may restrain nationalist excesses or devious national policies? Did the mixed reactions to Suez provide an example of this, or the outcry over the Hoare-Laval pact? But here one is back with the problem of interpretation: what is an 'un-American activity'; what is in the British 'national interest' in South Arabia; are criteria which claim to be higher merely utopian? Can Europe move towards a truly supranational framework, or will The Six produce merely a *Europe des patries*? In the age of national-

[1] Op cit p. 39.

ism, will the Universal Declaration of the Rights of Man follow the Kellogg Pact into that limbo reserved for vain idealism?

FURTHER READING

The roots of modern nationalism are brilliantly surveyed in
> Kohn: *The Idea of Nationalism*

and the same author's
> *Prophets and Peoples: Studies in* 19*th Century Nationalism,* and
> *Nationalism: Its Meaning and History*

carry the subject to modern times, with selected readings.
> *Nationalism,* a survey published by the Royal Institute of International Affairs in 1939, is invaluable for the facts it assembles and the questions it poses.

> Carr: *Nationalism and After*

does the same thing on a smaller scale. This is not the place to repeat the general history of nineteenth century developments, but some sources for less familiar aspects may be useful:
> Talmon: *Political Messianism: the Romantic Phase*

enlarges on the beliefs of some early nationalist prophets;
> Kohn: *Nationalism and Liberty*

surveys the Swiss example;
> Seton-Watson: *The Rise of Nationality in the Balkans,* and
> *The Southern Slav Question*

are indispensable, but should be treated, in part, as propaganda.
The same remark should be applied to the later sections of
> Sacher: *The Course of Modern Jewish History,*

which nevertheless contains important and little-known material.
> Brogan: *The American Character*

is unusual and enjoyable.
The subject of Germany and German nationalism may be studied in:
> Taylor: *The Course of German History*
> Hawgood: *The Evolution of Germany*
> Kohn: *The Mind of Germany (Macmillan & Co. Ltd.)
> Wheeler-Bennett: *The Nemesis of Power*
> > *Encounter:* the issue of April 1964 is given over to essays on Germany.

The development of national self-determination in Europe during the First World War and the consequences during the settlements will be found in:
> Zeman: *The Break-up of the Habsburg Empire*
> Cobban: *National Self-determination*

Personal accounts of the peace settlements include:
> Lloyd George: *The Truth About the Peace Treaties* (2 vols.)
> Nicolson: *Peacemaking,* 1919

*Acknowledgement is made to the publisher for permission to quote from this book.

The minorities problem between the wars is dealt with in detail in
> Macartney: *National States and National Minorities*

whilst the Munich crisis is put in perspective in
> Wiskemann: **Czechs and Germans* (Oxford University Press, under the auspices of the Royal Institute of International Affairs)

The political creeds of this period are illustrated in
> Oakeshott: *Social and Political Doctrines of Contemporary Europe*

More detailed reading might begin with *Mein Kampf*, whilst there is an outstanding essay on economic developments by Asa Briggs in the *New Cambridge Modern History*, Vol. XII.

Nationalism beyond Europe, the conditions from which it sprang and the problems which it faces may be studied in:
> Panikkar: **Asia and Western Dominance* (George Allen & Unwin Ltd.)
> Tinker: *Ballot Box and Bayonet*
> Brecher: *Nehru: A Political Biography*
> Erskine Childers: *The Road to Suez*
> Ping-chia Kuo: *China, New Age and New Outlook*
> Fitzgerald: *The Chinese View of their Place in the World*
> Richmond: **The Colour Problem* (Penguin Books Ltd.)

The last-named contains only a brief summary of African nationalism; those who want more detail on the problems faced by new African states might consult
> Hailey: *African Survey*
> *Royal Commission Report on East Africa*, 1955

Other recent events and institutions will be found in
> Crowley: *Background to Current Affairs*

whilst the United Nations is discussed in
> Nicholas: *The United Nations as a Political Institution*, and
> Boyd: *United Nations: Piety, Myth and Truth*

Psychological aspects of the subject may be approached in
> Eysenck: *The Psychology of Politics*, and
> Stafford-Clark: *The Psychology of Persecution and Prejudice*

the latter being the Robert Waley Cohen memorial lecture for 1960.

A particular example of 'pathological nationalism' is studied in
> Rovere: *Senator Joe McCarthy*

The effects of national prejudice upon the writing of history are illustrated in
> Dance: *History the Betrayer*

whilst geographical aspects of the subject will be found in some detail in
> Pearcy & Fifield: *World Political Geography*

Useful Historical Association Pamphlets include those on:
> *Panslavism; English History Through Foreign Eyes; The American Empire; Ranke; The Risorgimento; European Rule in Africa; The Rise of Modern China.*

*Acknowledgement is made to the publisher for permission to quote from this book.